SO-AAC-516

PRAISE FOR *BAND OF GIANTS*

"A highly engaging read."

—Library Journal

"Lively narrative of the Revolutionary War realistically assesses the motley collection of men who led the military struggle against Britain, revealing both their strengths and weaknesses."

—The Wall Street Journal

"Armed with the latest research burnished by a bright, brisk writing style, Jack Kelly has done a masterful job of retelling the story of the Revolutionary War by focusing on the key figures and battles of the long-protracted military struggle that undergirded the political war for independence. His cast of Cincinnatus-like amateurs put aside their plows, lock up their shops, kiss their wives goodbye and strap on their shields and bucklers. Facing the hangman's noose if they fail, they outfight, outmaneuvered and outlast the thousands of professional killers and bungling courtier-generals arrayed against them. This book is highly recommended for anyone seeking to understand the birth of the United States."

—*Willard Sterne Randall, award-winning Founding Fathers biographer-historian*

"Jack Kelly has managed to accomplish something remarkable in *Band of Giants*: to give a concise and accurate overview of the Revolutionary War without losing the intimacy and detail that go into a good yarn. And in doing so, Kelly shows us the essence of the Revolutionary miracle—that America owes its independence to a group of military amateurs . . . talented and tough, but amateurs all the same."

—*Paul Lockhart, author of* The Whites of Their Eyes

"Jack Kelly's *Band of Giants* is a sprightly and illuminating history of the Revolutionary War. It captures the terror of battle, the ecstasy of victory, the character of the leading generals, and the travail of the ordinary soldiers. Readers will take from this engaging book a better understanding of the true nature of America's struggle to win independence."

—*John Ferling, author of* Jefferson and Hamilton: The Rivalry that Forged a Nation

"Jack Kelly's superb writing enhances this fast-paced account of the Revolutionary War. Kelly doesn't just narrate a series of events. Instead, he reveals the war's most compelling dramas and personalities, giving the reader a sense of what it was like to experience the Revolution firsthand. Band of Giants is both entertaining and informative."

—*Edward G. Lengel, author of*
General George Washington:
A Military Life

"Jack Kelly's shrewd novelist's eye and the narrative velocity that propels his writing should make any student of history delighted that he is turning his formidable gifts to telling the great founding tale of the American republic."

—*Richard Snow, former editor-in-chief,* American Heritage,
author of I Invented the Modern Age: The Rise of Henry Ford

BAND *of* GIANTS

BAND of GIANTS

GIANTS

THE AMATEUR SOLDIERS WHO
WON AMERICA'S INDEPENDENCE

JACK KELLY

St. Martin's Griffin ✱ New York

BAND OF GIANTS. Copyright © 2014, 2016 by Jack Kelly. All rights reserved.
Printed in the United States of America. For information, address St. Martin's
Press, 175 Fifth Avenue, New York, N.Y. 10010.

www.stmartins.com

Frontispiece: *Title* by H. Charles McBarron. Courtesy of the U.S. Army Center
of Military History.

Design by Letra Libre, Inc.

The Library of Congress has catalogued the hardcover edition as follows:
Kelly, Jack.
Band of giants : the amateur soldiers who won America's independence / Jack
Kelly.
    pages   cm
Includes bibliographical references and index.
ISBN 978-1-137-27877-7 (alk. paper)
1. United States—History—Revolution, 1775–1783—Campaigns.
2. United States—History—Revolution, 1775–1783—Biography.
3. Generals—United States—Biography. I. Title.
    E230.K45   2014
    973.3'3—dc23

2014002004

ISBN 978-1-4668-9328-3 (trade paperback)
ISBN 978-1-137-47456-8 (e-book)

Our books may be purchased for educational, business, or promotional use. For
information on bulk purchases, please contact the Macmillan Corporate and
Premium Sales Department at 1-800-221-7945, extension 5442, or write to
specialmarkets@macmillan.com.

First St. Martin's Griffin Edition: January 2016

10 9 8 7 6 5 4 3 2 1

In Memory of

Edmund Kelly,
Continental Army 1782–83

and his descendant

William H. Kelly, my father,
United States Army 1941–45

. . . behold an inspired yeomanry, all sinew and soul.

—Thomas Dawes, March 1781

Contents

ONE

KNOWLEDGE OF THE MILITARY ART

1754

Silence. Rain spat cold on the napes of forty armed Virginians groping through "a Night as dark as Pitch." They found the camp of their Indian ally Tanaghrisson and his braves. The two groups of men could smell each other: the rancid odor of the greased natives, the fetor of the unwashed white men. Tanaghrisson told their leader that the French raiding party was camped in a nearby hollow. He would take them there. Would show them.

They padded on through the soggy forest "one after another, in the Indian Manner." The rain ceased, the mist brightened. A summer day was percolating into the Ohio Country, then a vast wilderness, now western Pennsylvania. On that breathless late-May morning in 1754, each man listened to his own anxious heartbeat.

Their commander, a twenty-one-year-old lieutenant colonel named George Washington, crept with Tanaghrisson to the edge of a low cliff and peered into the hollow where about thirty-five French soldiers and Canadian militiamen were waking. Washington listened to the murmur of foreign tongues, breathed the incense of smoky fires. The enemy had posted no sentries and had chosen a poor defensive position. Washington lacked formal military training, but he recognized that high ground and surprise afforded him a masterful advantage.

The Virginian had orders to enforce the sovereignty of His Britannic Majesty, King George II. In that endless western forest, Washington relied on the guidance of Tanaghrisson, known as the Half King. It was Tanaghrisson, a man in his fifties, who had alerted him to the danger, who waited silently beside him, watching.

At six foot three, Washington stood eight inches taller than the average man of his day. Gilbert Stuart, the portrait artist who would become most intimate with Washington's face, would see in his features "the strongest and most ungovernable passions." If let loose from his exacting will, Stuart speculated, those passions would make Washington "the fiercest man among the savage tribes."[1]

Born to a prosperous tidewater planter family, Washington had lost his father to fever when he was eleven. The death meant that George, unlike his older brothers, had missed the chance for a classical European education. Instead, he had learned the craft of surveying. Long trips to delineate claims on behalf of the powerful Fairfax family had hardened his already vigorous constitution and solidified valuable social connections. He had come to know the backcountry and had developed an eye for the lay of the land, a boon to a military mind.

Now, cotton-mouthed with excitement, the young officer directed his men with hand signals and whispers. The Indians circled to the downhill side, ready to block the Frenchmen's escape. Washington's lieutenant Adam Stephen shifted half of the Virginians into positions along the top of the fifteen-foot-high ridge. Washington led the others down the slope to the right. He was about to plunge into his first battle.

Each soldier became acutely aware of the heft of his loaded musket and of the vulnerability of his own precious flesh. Fear and excitement crowded the men's minds. A Frenchman, suddenly alert to the danger, grabbed his musket and fired. Washington rose to his full height. Fire! The crash of his men's volley shattered the quiet. Time galloped. The startled Frenchmen scrambled. Some fell. Some lifted their firelocks to shoot back. No man could reload quickly enough.

The milky gunpowder smoke smeared the air with a sulfurous haze and the taste of burnt metal. Washington stood exposed on the right, sword in hand, shouting orders to his men. An officer must post himself in the thickest of the fighting—throughout his military career, Washington would never shirk the danger of combat. He heard the thud of a bullet tear into the torso of the man beside him. A leaden musket ball three-quarters of an inch across could penetrate six inches of pine. Its effect on flesh from short range was murderous. The Virginian fell heavily to the ground, blood gushing.

The enemy were running, intent on escape. Faces painted with yellow, black, and red stripes suddenly leered through the leaves in front of them. The Frenchmen came sprinting back, throwing down their weapons, begging for mercy.

Washington's initial taste of combat, lasting less than fifteen minutes, had ended in the savor of victory. Still sizzling with adrenaline, he would write to his eighteen-year-old brother Jack, "I can with truth assure you, I heard Bulletts whistle and believe me there was something charming in the sound."[2] What happened next was not charming, and Washington would write of it to no one.

As the Indians pushed forward, Washington ordered his men, giddy with the thrill of their first fight, to close ranks around the French prisoners. The frightened captives cringed at the Indian war whoops. Their ten wounded comrades sobbed as pain lit their flesh. In the confusion, Washington's interpreter was conveying the words of a man who said he was Ensign Joseph Coulon de Villiers, sieur de Jumonville, the commander of this small battalion. The British officer, Jumonville insisted, had made a mistake. The French soldiers were not a war party, merely an escort. He was an envoy sent to deliver a message from His Most Christian Majesty Louis XV, *le roi*. He produced a document that established his authority and contained a proclamation.

His words clouded Washington's mind. Violating the customs of diplomacy could stain a man's honor. Worse, his blunder could spark a war. Britain and France had managed six years of uneasy peace since the Treaty of Aix-la-Chapelle. This incident might threaten the delicate equilibrium.

One of Jumonville's aides began to read the proclamation in French. The decree claimed the Ohio region for France based on the explorations of La Salle in the 1680s. Washington was chagrined by his own ignorance of French, the language of European culture and diplomacy. Tanaghrisson, an overseer of the interests of the Iroquois federation in the region, knew French well and keenly understood the situation. Discord between his British allies and the encroaching French was what he wanted, was why he had brought the Virginians to this glen. He approached Jumonville and said in French, "You are not yet dead, my father."

Mon père. He jerked his tomahawk high and brought it down on Jumonville's skull. Another blow struck off the nobleman's cranium. The Half King returned his bloody weapon to his belt and plunged his hand into the pulp of Jumonville's head. He tore out the man's brain and mashed it between his palms.

A minute earlier, Washington had been concerned about diplomatic protocol. Now he faced responsibility for the murder of a royal envoy.

Savagery was staring him in the face. Tanaghrisson's braves leapt onto the wounded Frenchmen, slit their scalps, and peeled their hair away. They decapitated one of the enemy soldiers and raised his head on a pole. They danced, sang. Licks of blood splashed onto the green shoots of the spring-time forest.

Red is a startling color in a world of greens and browns. Before marching, Washington had hoped to outfit himself and his company with scarlet uniforms. To Indians, Washington wrote, the color red is "compared to Blood and is look'd upon as the distinguishing marks of Warriours and great Men." He added, "It is the nature of Indians to be struck with, and taken by show."[3]

Now it was the young commander who was being struck by show, who was getting an eyeful of the bloody hue. The intimacy of the violence hurled him across the gap that separates the fighting man from the farmer, the surveyor, or the drawing-room gentleman. The rush of uncontrollable events, the impinging chaos, and the shame at witnessing the butchering of one's own species were his sudden initiation into the cold-minded fraternity of the warrior.

The Virginians hurried their surviving twenty-one French prisoners back to their own camp in a clearing called the Great Meadow. The drama was playing out sixty miles southeast of the Forks of the Ohio, the site of present-day Pittsburgh, where the Monongahela and Allegheny Rivers merge to form the Ohio River. The French had recently ousted the British from this strategic spot and had begun to construct Fort Duquesne.

Robert Dinwiddie, the beefy lieutenant governor of Virginia, had sent Washington and 160 militiamen marching through miles of gloomy, cantankerous forest to defend the critical Forks. Virginia authorities asserted that their territory extended westward to the Mississippi. They were growing increasingly aware of the value of this frontier land and were determined to ward off French domination of the Ohio country.

Following the violence at what would be known as Jumonville Glen, Washington was by turns cocky and nervous. One minute, the young soldier proclaimed that he had "the resolution to Face what any Man durst." The next, he was writing to Dinwiddie that he wished himself "under the Command off an experienced Officer."[4]

He soon learned that the colonel who was to follow him with reinforcements had fallen from his horse and died. This left Washington commander in chief of the Ohio Country and commandant of the makeshift stockade he called Fort Necessity. By July 3, a French attack was imminent. Jumonville's brother, Louis Coulon de Villiers, was leading a force of French soldiers and Indians to avenge the atrocity. Washington's men waited in the shallow trenches they had dug in the boggy Great Meadow.

The French and their Indian allies dispersed along the tree line. Favored by greater numbers, high ground, cover, and mobility, they began to fire at Washington's troops. Fighting in a driving rain storm, they quickly got the better of the inexperienced Virginians. By the time night came on, more than a hundred of Washington's soldiers lay dead or wounded. Others broke into the rum supply and got drunk. Then a small miracle— the cautious Villiers, fearing British reinforcements, offered Washington a chance to surrender. He had little choice but to comply. The next morning, July 4, Washington and his remaining men slunk away from the Ohio Country on parole, leaving behind a brief victory and an inglorious defeat.

Washington could not imagine how far the ripples from these bursts of violence would travel. He could not know that Jumonville's death was the first casualty of the Seven Years' War, a global conflagration that would kill one and a half million. As Horace Walpole, the British man of letters, put it, "The volley fired by a young Virginian in the backwoods of America set the world on fire."[5]

———

His Excellency Major General Edward Braddock came to America to finish the fight with the French that Washington had started. The short, fat, gray-haired general wore a scarlet uniform faced with yellow silk, his shoulders draped in gold braid. He brought an ornate carriage unsuited to the awful roads of America. He brought not one but three suits of polished armor. He brought a dream that he would "conquer whole nations."

Braddock drank, swore, and lacked the manners expected of a gentleman. Yet Crown officials saw fit to make him commander in chief of all British forces in America. They gave him two regular army regiments of about five hundred men each and a wealth of heavy artillery. This was the first substantial force of redcoats most provincials had laid eyes on—rough men in fancy clothes, armed with glittering muskets, shining bayonets, and a cocksure disdain for their enemies.

Braddock had never led troops in combat. Although the son of a general, he had risen through the ranks with difficulty. He was hardly a diplomat. Benjamin Franklin saw in him a "haughty and Imperious Temper." Braddock might do for a European war, Franklin later observed, but "he had too much self-confidence, too high an opinion of the validity of regular troops, and too mean a one of both Americans and Indians."[6]

It was only natural that George Washington should apply for a position with Braddock. Here was his opportunity to go to school with a major general of the most powerful army in the world. The young Virginian wrote, "I wish for nothing more earnestly, than to attain a small degree of knowledge in the Military Art."[7]

To take advantage of Washington's familiarity with the terrain, Braddock allowed him to join the army as a volunteer and attached him to his staff, or military "family." The provincial colonel would serve as aide-de-camp reporting directly to the commander. Washington hoped the resulting connections with top British officers might pay off in a commission from the king as a regular officer himself. First he had to learn.

He began by acquainting himself with the sometimes prickly intricacies of military logistics. In essence, Braddock would have to transport a small city into the wilderness, including a blacksmith's forge to facilitate repairs. The general scoured Virginia and Maryland for wagons but came up short. Fuming, Braddock demanded that the governors of all the colonies meet him in Annapolis, where he treated them, an observer noted, "as if they had been infinitely his Inferiors." This was unprecedented. Each colony had always dealt individually with London—Americans had never thought of themselves as united. Braddock browbeat the governors for failing to support the expedition. He saw "the necessity of laying a tax on all His Majesty's domains in America," one of the earliest suggestions to tax the colonies. He threatened to quarter troops in colonial homes.[8]

Washington also learned about discipline and drill. At Jumonville Glen and Fort Necessity, he had seen how easily undisciplined troops could turn into a mob. In professional armies, the threat of punishment was the prime motivator of men who had been pressed into service by force or economic necessity. Braddock was hard. He ordered a public reading of the Articles of War, which prescribed the severest punishments for a wide variety of offenses. "Any soldier who shall Desert tho he Return Again shall be Hanged without Mercy." Lacerating strokes with the cat-o-nine-tails were the standard punishment for misbehavior. For example, the theft of a keg of beer earned a soldier nine hundred hard lashes.

Americans did not take well to military discipline. Among the most recalcitrant were the civilian laborers, most of them cocky backwoodsmen. To the British, these provincials appeared barely more civilized than the natives. "You see, sir," a British officer wrote home, "what a wild set of Creatures our English Men grow into when they lose Society."[9]

Among the wildest were the teamsters Braddock hired to drive his many wagons westward. They included a twenty-year-old named Daniel

Morgan. A Virginian like Washington, Morgan hailed from the opposite end of the social spectrum. He had strolled into the frontier village of Winchester two years earlier as a footloose teenager and found work at a saw mill, then as a wagon driver. Like Washington, he was a strongly built man, more than six feet tall. He loved handling horses, moving from place to place, gambling, wrestling, hunting, and drinking. He had saved enough to buy his own wagon and team. The Braddock expedition promised him welcome cash and a tempting dose of adventure.

At one point during the expedition, Morgan quarreled with a British officer and knocked the man down. A quick drumhead court-martial sentenced the teamster to five hundred lashes. Morgan was tied to a tree and whipped. In his telling, the number was 499 because the drummer miscounted and Morgan "did not think it worthwhile to tell him of his mistake, and let it go so!" He would bear the scars throughout his life.[10]

The severity of discipline grew out of a concept of war that viewed soldiers as cogs in a machine. The self-willed warrior of the Middle Ages, the knight, had little place in modern fighting. Disciplined troops who followed orders were essential.

Washington learned that the principal actor in battle was not the soldier but the officer, who, by moving units of men as one, amplified and directed the power of their violence. Musket fire, inaccurate at a distance, was most effective delivered in massed volleys. Lines of men standing shoulder to shoulder two or three deep could load and fire in unison and with great speed. Initiative and individual action were counterproductive. Efficiency required drill, an exercise in obedience. As they marched, wheeled, handled their weapons, the men came to resemble a single mechanical mass, their movements automatic, their response to bellowed orders or drumbeats instantaneous.

American militiamen had practiced only a weak semblance of these drills on muster days. Braddock assigned a lieutenant to exercise the provincial troops, "long, lank, yellow-faced Virginians, who at best are a half-starved, ragged dirty Set." In the short time available, the men barely learned the rudiments.

The British soldiers were receiving an education of their own. The intimacy of slavery in Virginia surprised them. "How it strikes the Mind on the first Arrival," an officer observed, "to have all these black Faces with grim Looks round you." Then, when the army finally marched to Fort Cumberland, a primitive stockade at the limit of settled territory in western Maryland, the soldiers first encountered America's indigenous people. The customs and manners of these natives, one of Braddock's men said, "are hardly to be described."[11]

"They paint themselves in an odd manner," he went on. "And the men have the outer rim of their ears cut, which only hangs by a bit top and bottom, and have a tuft of hair left at the top of their heads, which is dressed with feathers. . . . They dance and make a most horrible noise."[12]

Braddock's attitude toward America's natives grew out of his own profound ignorance. Franklin had warned the general that his army, stretched out along a thin line, would be vulnerable to "ambuscades of Indians."

"These savages may, indeed, be a formidable enemy to your raw American militia," Braddock replied, "but upon the King's regular and disciplined troops, sir, it is impossible they should make any impression."[13]

Indians lacked discipline, organization, and the other accouterments of civilization. Braddock assumed they must therefore lack power. A group of chiefs offered their aid to the expedition as scouts and warriors. Braddock was ready to accept, but when the Indians asked for guarantees respecting their own claims to the Ohio Country, he was typically blunt: "No Savage Should Inherit the Land." Most of the Indians departed for good.[14]

Studying bad maps back in London, British officials believed that the trek from Fort Cumberland, Braddock's base, to Fort Duquesne, the French bastion at the Forks of the Ohio, was about 15 miles. The actual distance was 120 miles over mountainous, forested terrain that no English bureaucrat could imagine. In Europe, carriages traveled decent roads and primeval forests had vanished long ago. Braddock's would be the first wheeled vehicles to roll over the Appalachian Mountains.

The expedition started on June 7, 1755, with 2,500 men, far fewer than the 15,000-man amalgam of regulars, provincials, and Indians the plan had called for. The six-mile-long cavalcade would have to climb and descend seven steep mountain ridges before reaching the Forks. Coming down the very first of these heights, three wagons broke away from their drivers and careened downhill, killing the horses and smashing the wagons to pieces. "The very Face of the Country," an officer commented, "is enough to strike a Damp in the most resolute Mind."[15]

As they pushed into the wilderness, Washington complained in a letter that "the march must be regulated by the slow movements of the Train [of artillery and baggage] which I am sorry to say will be tedious, very tedious indeed, as I long predicted, tho' few believed." At times, the expedition became so strung out that the rear guard lagged two days' march behind the van.[16]

Though frustrated at the pace, the young Washington enjoyed Braddock's congenial mess. The general served good wine to his military family, who passed mild summer evenings telling war stories. Washington had a chance to mix with officers like the urbane Lieutenant Colonel Thomas Gage, second son of a viscount. "Honest Tom," then thirty-five, was not given to the usual officers' vices of drinking, gambling, and whoring.

Washington met Charles Lee, an English lieutenant of his own age. The well-educated Lee was a thinker in a profession where deep reflection was not the norm. He loved Shakespeare—Washington was likewise a devotee of the theater. Lee had ordered a copy of Thucydides's *History of the Peloponnesian Wars* in the original Greek to read on the expedition. A great talker, he might have quoted that historian's remark: "Men do not rest content with parrying the attacks of a superior, but often strike the first blow to prevent the attack being made."

Washington also had the chance to know Horatio Gates. The twenty-eight-year-old captain had been born to an English housekeeper. His mother's friend was a maid in the household of the aristocratic Walpole family. As a result, Gates had become the godson and namesake of Horace Walpole. His upper-class connections had helped the young man obtain an officer's commission. Under Braddock, he led a provincial company from New York. He was destined, like some of the others on the expedition, to play a significant role in a war that none of them could yet imagine.

On June 17, heeding the advice of Washington, who "urged it in the warmest terms I was master of," Braddock divided his force. A Falstaffian colonel, Thomas Dunbar, would manage the bulk of the supplies and guns in the rear division. Braddock, freed from encumbrances, would surge ahead with a compact but lethal "flying column."

Daniel Morgan remained with the supply force, which dropped farther and farther behind. Six days later, Washington, too, was forced to join this contingent. Dysentery, dreaded by soldiers as the "bloody flux," had caught up with him. Overcome with violent diarrhea and fever, he could no longer ride but lay in the bed of a jolting wagon. The expedition proceeded into a vast pine forest known as the Shades of Death. A nineteenth-century historian said it was "like the dark nave of some endless, dream-born cathedral."[17] The profound silence went on forever. A feverish Washington caught glimpses of the sky through the black tangle of branches overhead.

On July 8, the main army camped a day's march from Fort Duquesne. Washington came up from Dunbar's supply train, which now lagged thirty-six miles behind. Still weak and suffering an excruciating case of piles, he needed the aid of a cushion to bear sitting on a horse. He was not about to miss the final thrust of the historic expedition.

To reach Fort Duquesne, Braddock had to cross the Monongahela River. Aware that fording would leave his force vulnerable, he ordered Lieutenant Colonel Gage to cross at four o'clock on the warm morning of July 9, 1755, and to secure the high ground on the opposite bank. Gage led an elite force consisting of grenadiers, the tall shock troops of the army, and light infantrymen, its most capable fighters. Braddock then ordered his men to "march over the river in the greatest order, with their bayonets fixed, Colors flying, and Drums and Fifes beating and playing." It was an exercise in intimidation. Over the haughty beat of forty large drums, scores of fifers pierced the forest's stillness with the lilt of "The Grenadiers' March."

Perhaps overly impressed with his own display, Braddock directed Gage's advance guard to give up the high ground and to form a column ahead of the army. Minutes later, Gage's men spotted an enemy force. A small group of French regulars and Canadian militiamen, accompanied by six hundred Indians, had sallied from Fort Duquesne. When they engaged, the two bodies of soldiers stood only two hundred yards from each other in the sweltering forest.

Gage ordered his troops to form a line and fire. One of their first volleys struck the enemy commander, killing him. The French regulars and Indians immediately spread out to seek cover. Their return fire and the unnerving shrieking of the Indians shocked the grenadiers. This was the first taste of combat for many of the redcoats. They ignored Gage's order to fix bayonets and attack up a slope. "Visible terror and confusion," one observer noted, "appeared amongst the men."

The French and Indians fired at the massed troops. The noise was unimaginable. Men groped through smoke, their ears numb. The big guns, which the British had brought across the ocean and manhandled through the wilderness, proved impotent. The Indians, one man saw, "kept an uncessant fire on the Guns," cutting down the gunners before they could load their pieces.

Washington accompanied Braddock into the smoke-clogged chaos, riding forward "on horse-back, tho' very weak and low." He noted the "irretrievable disorder" in the vanguard and the "unusual hallooing and whooping of the enemy." "The yell of the Indians is fresh in my ear," a veteran later wrote, "and the terrific sound will haunt me till the hour of my dissolution."[18]

Washington saw the weakness of an entire system of warfare exposed in an instant. Men trained to act on command as a single unit could not suddenly adopt new tactics. They did not take cover, did not respond to the evolving attack with fluid maneuvering of their own. They fired in volleys as they had been trained to do, even when no target was in sight.

Officers "dropped like leaves in Autumn." Thomas Gage was wounded. Horatio Gates was shot in the breast and arm. Before the battle was over, almost every British field officer would be killed or wounded.

The battle began at one in the afternoon. By four, the British were nearly surrounded. Colonel Dunbar was too far behind to send help. Washington, in spite of his weakness, remained in the thick of the action. Bullets pierced his clothes; two horses were shot from under him.

The line wavered. Civilian wagon drivers, smelling disaster, cut loose the draft horses and fled. A musket ball pierced Braddock's shoulder and lodged in his lung. At around five o'clock on that suffocating afternoon, "as if by beat of Drumm," the whole army turned and ran, "every one trying who should be first."

Washington helped the fallen general into a wagon and off the field. Indians chased down the vanquished, catching some as they tried to recross the river. They "dyed ye stream with their blood, scalping and cutting them." A bonanza of booty distracted the French and Indians, who fell to plundering. The defeated raced on, pursued by their own fears.

That July afternoon, George Washington saw war stripped of all its masks. There was no glory, no dignity, and little honor in the spectacle. The aftermath of the battle stunned him. "The shocking Scenes which presented themselves in this Night's March," he wrote, "are not to be described. The dead, the dying, the groans, lamentations, and crys . . . were enough to pierce a heart."[19]

The soldiers taken prisoner lived through a few hours of mind-scalding terror, imagining what was to come. Then it came. That night outside Fort Duquesne, the Indians lashed them to stakes, prodded them with red-hot irons, tore their flesh, and finally burned them alive, their screams evaporating in the darkness.

As the survivors reached the supply train, General Braddock's condition worsened. He murmured, "Who would have thought it?" The disaster along the Monongahela was the worst defeat that had ever befallen British forces. Fourteen hundred soldiers had taken part, and more than eight hundred had been killed or wounded.

In the second contingent, Colonel Dunbar still had enough men and heavy guns to attack and conquer Fort Duquesne. But as one observer noted, "the Terror of the Indian remaining so strongly in the men's minds," he did not make the attempt. General Braddock, before he died, ordered the precious supplies, gathered and transported at such expense, more critical now than ever for the defense of the frontier, to be destroyed. His object was a faster retreat, although no force was pursuing. Even as the citizens of Philadelphia were raising funds for a victory celebration, Daniel Morgan and the other teamsters were scattering gunpowder and flour and burying the remaining cannon.

Before the expedition returned, Washington had Braddock's body interred not far from the glen where Jumonville had died a year earlier. When the troops reached Philadelphia, Dunbar demanded winter quarters for his troops, inviting the colonists' derision: it was still July.

Washington was quick to criticize the behavior of the British soldiers. He wrote to Lieutenant Governor Dinwiddie, "The Virginia companies behav'd like Men and died like Soldiers." The regulars, he declared, "broke and ran as Sheep before Hounds." The most enduring legacy of Braddock's defeat was the tarnish it left on the British army's reputation for invincibility. "This whole transaction gave us the first suspicion," Benjamin Franklin noted, "that our exalted ideas of the prowess of British regular troops had not been well founded."[20]

Braddock came in for his share of the blame. But Washington, who would remain an admirer of his mentor, simply called him "brave even to a fault."

The defeat affected all of the country's inhabitants. Virginians feared that this demonstration of British impotence might incite a slave rebellion. "The negro slaves have been very audacious on the news of the defeat on the Ohio," Dinwiddie noted. In Philadelphia, nervous inhabitants turned on the Irish, who as Catholics were suspected of sympathizing with the French.[21]

It was not slaves or immigrants whom the Americans had to fear, but the continent's indigenous people. The defeat on the Monongahela touched off a series of violent Indian attacks on frontier settlements, atrocities known as the Outrages. Thousands of pioneers were pushed eastward by the Indians whom they had earlier dispossessed. The frontier regions of Pennsylvania, Maryland, and Virginia lost as much as half their population in the three years after the Braddock catastrophe.

George Washington remained at the head of the Virginia Regiment during the first years of what Americans called the French and Indian War. After early defeats, the British rallied. In 1758, Washington joined General John Forbes on a second expedition to the Ohio Country. That force overwhelmed the French and took Fort Duquesne without a major battle. General James Wolff led British forces in the conquest of Quebec a year later. Having utterly vanquished the French in North America, King

George III, who had assumed the British throne in 1760, emerged from the conflict with the most extensive empire of the age.

Washington showed little enthusiasm for the war he had inadvertently started. Elected to Virginia's House of Burgesses in July 1758, he resigned his militia commission at the end of that year and took no further part in the struggle. He married Virginia's wealthiest widow, Martha Dandridge Custis, in January 1759 and joined the colony's elite.

One of Washington's principal virtues was his ability to learn, and Braddock had been his most important teacher. The Virginian did not take a simple lesson from his experiences in the 1750s. He remained convinced of the efficacy of formal European fighting methods when properly employed, but he saw the need for flexibility and adaptation. Braddock's misfortune showed that the forests of America were not the plains of Europe. Irregular fighting and the use of special forces could be valuable supplements to traditional tactics. It was a matter of balance, and a tendency to weigh and balance was a prominent feature of Washington's mind.

From Braddock, Washington took his concept of how an army should be constituted and managed. In the egalitarian climate that would sweep America during the Revolutionary era, rigid hierarchy, taut discipline, and punishment by flogging would all come into question. But Washington would insist that "discipline is the soul of an army."

Washington learned that a defeat, even a ruinous one like the cataclysm at the Monongahela, could be overcome. Perhaps the most important lesson he took from Braddock was a basic one: how to sustain an army in the field. In war, logistics could often be more critical than any single victory.

Like Braddock, Washington would favor the offensive. Like Braddock, he would scorn Indians as allies, maintain a military family of close aides, and pay close attention to such mundane issues as his troops' hygiene and pay. Like Braddock, he would adopt the honorific "Excellency."

He would not, like his mentor, emulate the studied decadence of the British officer class. He would discourage exorbitant drinking, gaming, and womanizing in the Continental Army, setting a tone that fit his own personality. A contemporary described him as "Discreet and Virtuous, no harum Starum ranting Swearing fellow, but Sober, steady and Calm."[22]

Washington's behavior during the battle on the Monongahela overshadowed and erased the stain of his failure at Fort Necessity. Although a disaster for Braddock and the British, the campaign left Washington "the hero of the Monongahela."

Washington had borne witness to the cost of war. Of 150 Virginia provincial soldiers who marched with Braddock, many of whom Washington had personally recruited, 120 had been killed or wounded. Washington would never again describe bullets as charming. He himself seemed a child of destiny, left untouched when so many others died. The Presbyterian minister Samuel Davis wrote at the time that he hoped Providence had preserved Washington "in so signal a Manner for some important Service to this Country."[23]

And so Providence had. A man who understood something of the military art, a social climber, a slave owner, an athlete, a lover of theater, a determined, self-deprecating man, always wary, subject to anger but not bluster, tempered by early defeats, open to the hard lessons of experience—this was the man whom history had chosen to play the lead role in a drama that would change the world.

TWO

BLOWS MUST DECIDE

1774

Twenty years later, the colonies continued to feel the effects of the war that George Washington had started in 1754. The fighting had left Great Britain with a magnificent empire and a ruinous debt. The government's attempts to tax the colonies had generated more protests than revenues and had goaded the inhabitants to the edge of violent insurrection.

During the tense summer of 1774, two men sat discussing the affairs of the day over pints of ale in the Boston tavern The Bunch of Grapes. One was the tall, paunchy Henry Knox, a well-known city bookseller of twenty-four, given to booming laughter and subtle, insightful analysis. The other was a pudgy, lame Rhode Island businessman named Nathanael Greene. Eight years older than Knox, he still showed the roughness of his country upbringing. But Greene was an avid learner and was in fact one of Knox's best customers. The liberal-minded Knox admired his friend's enthusiasm. To know freedom and not defend it, Greene asserted, was "spiritual suicide."

Knox's shop, the London Book-Store, was stocked with volumes on weapons, strategy, and tactics, ranging from Caesar's *Commentaries* to Maurice de Saxe's influential *Mes Reveries*, on the art of war. British officers frequented the shop to brush up on military theory. It was no contradiction that Knox had transformed himself into an expert on war. Both he and Greene had access to information that was out of the reach of most citizens, who could not afford to purchase books. Knox suggested a reading list for his friend, who was compiling a substantial library.

Knox had grown up during the last war. Greene had experienced the conflict as a teenager, although his Quaker family's strict pacifism discouraged participation. Both men had come of age during the increasingly contentious and tumultuous years that followed the peace treaty of 1763. Both now sensed that the clash of interests between Great Britain and her American colonies was careening toward armed conflict.

His father's bankruptcy and early death had forced Knox to drop out of Boston Latin School, a preparation for Harvard, at age nine. His mother apprenticed him to a firm of booksellers, where an indulgent proprietor let him continue his studies with borrowed tomes. Knox read Plutarch's lives of great men, taught himself French, and absorbed the ideas of Enlightenment thinkers.

He knew violence early. Boston had for decades endured riots touched off by hunger and poverty. Forced impressment into the British navy particularly rankled seamen. The economic bust that followed the French and Indian War brought to the city a declining economy, high unemployment, and a flagrant contrast between rich and poor. Boston would come to be called the "Metropolis of Sedition," a place where inhabitants, British observers noted, had an overblown notion of "the rights and liberties of Englishmen."

A yearly occasion for expressing those rights was Pope's Day, November 5, a date that commemorated the failed 1605 plot by papists to decapitate the English government. The day gave Boston's poorer inhabitants a chance to shake their fists at alien Catholics and generally let off steam. Working men and apprentices like Knox looked forward to Pope's Day as a rare respite from work. It was the annual jubilee of the gangs from the city's North and South Ends. Once, when a wheel came off a Pope's Day float, the prodigiously strong Knox lifted the axle himself to heave the weighty contraption forward.

During the celebration, parading crowds of "servants, sailors, workingmen, apprentices and Negroes" invaded the homes of the well-to-do to beg alms and strong drink. They broke the windows of burghers who stinted them. The day culminated in a monumental brawl, to which boys and young men came armed with "Clubs, Staves and Cutlasses" and fought among themselves with gusto. Afterward, the participants destroyed their floats in a huge bonfire. The teenaged Knox gained a reputation as one of Boston's toughest street fighters, something to brag about in a city populated by fist-hard seamen and muscled dock workers.[1]

In August 1765, when Knox was fifteen, Bostonians turned out for a more pointed purpose. Britain had imposed the Stamp Act. This tax on newspapers, legal writs, playing cards, and other documents was the first direct tax on the colonies. The protests took on many of the trappings of Pope's Day: bonfires blazed and intimidating mobs roamed the city. A "hellish crew" invaded the home of wealthy stamp master Andrew Oliver, smashed a mirror "said to be the largest in North America," and wrecked the place.[2] The mob later burst into the mansion of royal lieutenant governor Thomas Hutchinson and left his home a wrecked shell.

Boston authorities expected new violence when Pope's Day itself rolled around that November. Something more ominous greeted them. The North and South End factions, guided and bribed by radical Whigs like John Hancock and Samuel Adams, had made peace. The gangs marched together and gathered at the Liberty Tree, a celebrated elm on Boston Common. Effigies of government officials replaced those of the pope and devil. Oliver worried that "the People, even to the lowest Ranks, have become more attentive to their Liberties."[3]

Riots and gang fighting melded easily into political protest and what Massachusetts governor Francis Bernard called a "general Levelling, and taking away the Distinction of rich and poor."[4] The mob began to think and reason. Boston became the focal point of growing discontent in the colonies. The gangs came to see themselves as "the people out of doors," the assertive bane of monarchs. The Stamp Act, never enforced, was soon repealed.

Two years later, Knox watched as Bostonians marked King George III's twenty-ninth birthday with a salute from three brass cannon. The concussions, the flashes of fire, and the power of the eruptions kindled his imagination. The seventeen-year-old immediately joined the artillery company, a branch of the provincial militia, and began to drill under Lieutenant Adino Paddock, a chair-maker and staunch Tory.

The unit attracted many of the same young men Knox knew from the South End gangs, the sons of mechanics and shipyard workers. The handling of great guns, as exacting as it was muscular, engaged both his intellect and his physical prowess. The science of artillery incorporated mathematics, mechanics, geometry, and chemistry. The company, known as the Train, became Knox's absorbing interest. Drills were rigorous. Paddock passed on techniques learned directly from British artillery officers. Engineering was part of the gunner's trade, and Knox studied the construction of fortifications and secure gun emplacements.

A new wave of rioting greeted the 1768 import duties known as the Townshend Acts. A British officer called Boston "a blackguard town and ruled by mobs."[5] Patriots began a boycott of British goods. The British government sent four regiments, nearly two thousand soldiers, to occupy Boston. The order was handed down by General Thomas Gage, the agreeable, cultivated officer who had led the advanced guard across the Monongahela thirteen years earlier. Gage, like Braddock before him, now reigned as military commander of all North America.

Knox joined the thousands of Bostonians who watched this "invasion," which contemporary historian Mercy Otis Warren called the beginning of the "American war." The troops marched up from the Long Wharf with fifes screeching and flags unfurled. One regiment featured black Afro-Caribbean drummers in yellow coats with red facings, a bizarre sight to the locals.

Intended to quell unrest, the occupation set off a seven-year slide toward war. Radicals encouraged citizens to arm themselves. Artillery drill took on an added urgency. The Train comprised both Whigs and Tories, designations borrowed from British political parties. In America, *Whig* came to be associated with "patriot," *Tory* with "loyalist." Both factions imagined rolling the great guns into action, one to resist oppression, the other to keep the peace.

In a city of fifteen thousand residents, the presence of so many soldiers became a festering intrusion. On the night of March 5, 1770, Knox was walking home through dark, frigid streets. He encountered a commotion around the Custom House. Bells were ringing as if announcing a fire. Residents were rushing into the street and shouting. He came upon some rowdy youths—a few years earlier he might have been one of them—taunting a British sentry.

The boys, backed up by a growing crowd, threw snowballs and jeered. Knox ordered them back and, seeing the sentry load his musket, told him "if he fired he died." The sentry pointed his gun, the boys dared him to shoot.

Eight or nine men of the British guard, commanded by Captain Thomas Preston, hurried to the sentry's aid, bayonets fixed. Knox, watching the situation spin out of control, grabbed Preston's coat and warned him not to fire on the crowd. "Bloody backs!" the boys continued to scoff. "Lobster scoundrels!" The insult referred to the submission of British soldiers to the lash under the army's draconian disciplinary regime, a degradation for which Americans felt deep scorn.

The scene grew chaotic. Bells continued to clang, more snowballs flew, chunks of ice. There were shouts of "You can't kill us all!" and dares to "Fire!"

The regulars jabbed at the crowd with their bayonets. A soldier slipped. A shot shattered the cold air. After a pause, during which Preston failed to give a decisive command, the rest of the hyped-up soldiers fired a staccato volley. The street became a pandemonium of smoke, shouting, and groans. Five civilians fell dead, six suffered wounds.

Express riders carried word of the "massacre" through the city and out to the countryside. Thousands of citizens prepared to march on Boston. The colony teetered on the precipice of war, but no war came. Henry Knox testified as an eyewitness during the trial, in which lawyer John Adams successfully defended Preston against a charge of murder.

An alarmed British ministry withdrew their soldiers from Boston and repealed the Townshend taxes on all items except tea. Tensions eased. But the anniversary of the Boston Massacre became an annual focus of patriot rallies and an occasion for incendiary orations.

———————

While Knox had known early the rough world of Boston's crowded streets, Nathanael Greene had grown up two miles from his nearest neighbors. He had passed his youth working on the family farm and toiling at his father's successful iron forge on the western shore of Narragansett Bay. Unlike his brothers, he was an avid reader, devoting every slack moment to whatever books he could get hold of.

While a life of hard work built his strength, Greene suffered from several physical ailments. He walked with a limp. Asthma attacks sometimes kept him struggling for breath night after night. He had dared to receive an inoculation for smallpox—the dangerous protective measure remained controversial—but in addition to conferring immunity, the procedure had left him with a scarred right eye prone to inflammation.

The domination of Greene's severe Quaker father shaped his life into his late twenties. At an age when Henry Knox was swinging his fists in street brawls, Greene was still sneaking out to forbidden dances. He did not really come of age until his father died in 1770. That same year, the twenty-eight-year-old Greene fell in love with the well-connected Nancy Ward. She did not return his affection; her indifference broke his heart. He fantasized about winning the lottery: "I intend to turn Beau with my part of the Money," he explained, "and make a Shining Figure."[6]

Greene regretted his upbringing as a "Supersticious" Quaker, and his lack of formal education. "I feel the mist [of] Ignorance to surround me," he later wrote.[7] On his own he read Enlightenment authors like Voltaire and John Locke. Jonathan Swift, whose satires skewered English policies in Ireland, was a favorite. But the demands of the prosperous business that he and his brothers had inherited consumed his time. Politics remained theoretical. In February 1772, that changed.

One of the Greene brothers' ships, the *Fortune*, with cousin Rufus Greene at the helm, was accosted in Narragansett Bay as it transported a load of West Indian rum and sugar. The commander of the British revenue schooner *Gaspee*, a "haughty, insolent" man named Dudingston, had become the scourge of Rhode Island traders. He led a boarding party onto the Greenes' cargo vessel.

The British sailors slapped Rufus around and confiscated the ship. Import duties were one of the few consistent sources of Crown revenue. The government was determined to prevent traders from sneaking past the customs house at Newport. The myriad of coves and islands in the bay made Rhode Island a smuggler's paradise. Greene's cargo may have been legal, but the *Gaspee*'s captain was going to make sure that the cargo had been taxed. When he heard the news, Nathanael erupted. It was piracy, he declared. He brought a court action against Lieutenant Dudingston, making the officer subject to arrest by Rhode Island authorities. New England merchants cheered the defiant Greene, who became obsessed with the affair. The seizure had brought into sudden focus for him the many issues of rights and liberty that had been percolating in the colonies for years.

The crew of the *Gaspee* continued to interdict shipping. In June 1772, chasing a merchantman in the bay, the British schooner ran aground. A gang of citizens, spurred on by the radical patriot group called Sons of Liberty, formed a posse and rowed out in longboats. During their altercation with Dudingston, they shot him in the groin, arrested him, and burned the schooner.

News of the outrage crackled through the colonies. Boston patriot Samuel Adams thought it could touch off a contest between Britain and America that would "end in rivers of blood." The British offered a reward and threatened to send the perpetrators to England for trial. With the *Gaspee*'s captain now in custody, Nathanael Greene, who had a solid alibi for the night of the incident, pursued his lawsuit. He won a judgment of three hundred pounds for the improper seizure of his ship.

Finding himself in the middle of the great issues of the day, Greene changed. By bringing a lawsuit and by taking an interest in armed conflict, he was veering further and further from his pious upbringing. A year after the incident, he was barred from his Quaker meeting, probably for visiting a Connecticut tavern. More and more, he turned his attention to colonial politics. He frequently traveled the fifty miles to Boston and observed firsthand the contentious affairs of that beleaguered city. He formed a friendship with Henry Knox.

The instinct that prompts modern booksellers to install coffee bars was not absent in the eighteenth century. Once he opened his own shop, Knox turned it into "a fashionable morning lounge." His charm and love of humorous stories helped make his London Book-Store one of the most popular hangouts for Boston's smart set. It also became a hub for Boston radicals.

The affable proprietor helped organize a new militia unit known as the Boston Grenadier Corps, which absorbed some of the more Whig-oriented members of the Train. As with the British grenadiers, all the men had to be tall. They dressed in fancy uniforms and drilled in the evenings with musket and cannon. Knox, one of the most knowledgeable as well as the tallest, was elected an officer. The unit drew praise, even from British military men, for its spruce appearance.

In the summer of 1773, while he was hunting ducks in Boston's wet-lands, Knox's gun burst. The explosion blew off the pinkie and ring finger of his left hand, a graphic reminder that a cannon could rupture in the same way, and with much more grievous effects. Henry self-consciously wrapped his mangled hand in a black silk handkerchief. On parade with his militia unit he "excited the sympathy of all the ladies."

One who found Knox intriguing was Lucy Flucker, the plump, comely daughter of Thomas Flucker, royal secretary of Massachusetts, "a high-toned Loyalist of great family pretensions."[8] The seventeen-year-old Lucy was educated, spirited, skilled at chess and card games, and endowed with a wit that matched Knox's own. Their mutual infatuation grew into a passionate, largely secret, courtship.

Relations between Britain and her colonies continued to fray. The one remaining tax sparked a confrontation in 1773, when British ministers handed a monopoly on the tea trade to the East Indian Company. Angry colonists responded with a boycott. Knox was one of those who guarded a British tea ship to prevent the crew from unloading its goods. On December 16, 1773, radicals disguised as Indians famously tossed more than forty-five tons of tea into the harbor in an act of rebellion. The government harshly punished this provocation by passing a series of "intolerable" acts, closing Boston Harbor, renewing the military occupation of the city, and imposing martial law.

In the wake of such unrest, Lucy's parents were reluctant to approve of Knox. They considered him too low class for their daughter and possessed of dangerous political opinions. Lucy, however, loved him "too much for my peace." The Fluckers "gave a half-reluctant consent," but when the lovers were married in June 1774, Lucy's parents refused to attend the wedding. Tension in the city ratcheted ever higher that summer. Lucy's father tried to entice his son-in-law with the offer of a commission in the British army. Knox refused.

Around the same time, Nathanael Greene finally gave up his crush on Nancy Ward and fell for Catherine Littlefield, a teenager with "a snapping pair of dark eyes," whom he had known as a girl. Called Caty, she was thirteen years younger than the thirty-two-year-old businessman. Their romance blossomed quickly—they were married in July 1774.

Like Knox, Greene responded to the growing colonial turmoil by forming one of the many militia units springing up around New England. Soon after his marriage, he began to drill with the group that would become the Kentish Guards. Greene smuggled a black-market musket out of Boston and helped recruit British army veterans to train the battalion. The men marched about in red coats trimmed with green. They drank, socialized, and dreamed of violent action.

Because Greene's knowledge of military theory outstripped that of his fellow militiamen, he expected to be elected an officer. But his comrades could not countenance a lieutenant with a limp at their head. They voted him down. It was, for the sensitive Greene, a "stroke of mortification." "Nobody loves to be the subject of ridicule," he opined. His confidence shaken, he almost quit the unit, but instead decided to soldier on as a lowly private.[9]

Over the winter of 1774–1775, the drills became increasingly meaningful. Showing the fist, the British ministry sent their military commander on the continent, General Gage, to Boston as royal governor. He brought four thousand more regulars with him. The ministers hoped that Gage, with his long experience in the colonies and his American wife, could both intimidate and placate the unruly citizens of New England. But speaking privately of his colonies that autumn, King George III conceded his fear that "blows must decide whether they are to be subject to this country or independent."

Most in Britain were sure of the outcome. Benjamin Franklin, serving as a colonial envoy in London, had overheard an army general claim "that with a thousand British grenadiers he would undertake to go from one end of America to the other and geld all the males, partly by force and partly with a little coaxing." Gage was not so sanguine. He felt that the inhabitants of America had been infected by the "Disease" of rebellion. "Now it's so universal there is no knowing where to apply a Remedy." He wrote to London for reinforcements. "If you think ten thousand men sufficient, send twenty."[10]

In September 1774, he set out to secure Crown gunpowder supplies so that they could not fall into the hands of the seething colonists. He sent 260 British redcoats rowing up the Mystic River from Boston to remove a large supply of the explosive from a powder house north of the city. They faced no opposition.

But Gage had batted a hornet's nest. The action incited wild rumors up and down the colony: War was at hand. Six militiamen had been slaughtered. British ships were bombarding Boston. In response, thousands of armed men took to the roads. The rumors stunned the delegates at the First Continental Congress, then meeting in Philadelphia. "War! war! war! was the cry," John Adams wrote to his wife Abigail back in Boston. He imagined "scenes of Distress and Terror."

The armed men, and later the Congressional delegates, soon found that the rumors were false. But for General Gage the instantaneous mobilization was an ominous sign.

In October, the government forbade the importation of gunpowder and weapons into the colonies. New Hampshire patriots promptly broke into a local fort and removed ninety-seven barrels of gunpowder and fifteen light cannon. Rebels grabbed royal armaments in other cities up and down the New England coast. In February 1775, Gage sent troops to Salem, Massachusetts, to confiscate yet more war supplies. Forty armed militiamen and a crowd of tough fishermen from nearby Marblehead stood in their way. Tense negotiations narrowly averted violence.

"Civil government is near its end," Gage wrote. "Furthermore, conciliation, moderation, reason is over; nothing can be done but by forcible means." Yet Honest Tom's actions remained tentative. "Timid and undecided," a subordinate wrote of him. "Unfit to command at a time of resistance, and approaching Rebellion."[11]

———•·•———

On April 19, 1775, the spring breeze brought to Henry Knox's ears the distinctive, ominous rumble of cannon fire from the west. Word quickly reached Boston of an outbreak of violence at the villages of Lexington and Concord, about fifteen miles northwest of the city. That evening, a parade of bloody redcoats limped into town. The fight that Henry Knox, Nathanael Greene, and thousands of others had dreaded and prepared for had arrived.

It had begun as another powder raid. Gage sent a brigade of grenadiers and light infantrymen into the countryside to confiscate war supplies at Concord. He also instructed them to arrest the notorious rabble-rousers

Samuel Adams and John Hancock, who were correctly reported to be in the area. They were preparing to attend the Second Continental Congress.

Reaching the village of Lexington, the seven-hundred-man British force encountered fifty armed patriots assembled on the Common. The militia captain, farmer John Parker, wisely ordered his men to disperse. The next instant, shots rang out. "Without any order or regularity, the light infantry began a scattered fire," a British officer reported.[12] Eight Americans died, most shot in the back. Nine lay wounded. In this casual manner, on a bright spring morning, a war began.

The British troops marched on to Concord, where patriots had already removed most of the arms. Three British companies tried to secure North Bridge over the Concord River. Hundreds of angry militiamen confronted them. A sudden firefight left six patriots and a dozen regulars dead or wounded. To the surprise of the militiamen, the vaunted British redcoats ran back toward Concord village.

The British commander, the fat, slow-thinking lieutenant colonel Francis Smith, showed "great fickleness and inconstancy of mind." He marched his men pointlessly around Concord, then took time out for brandy and food at a local tavern. After lunch, he put his troops on the road for the perilous return march to Boston. As the tired troops stepped warily along the dirt road, militiamen kept up a hot fire from behind trees and walls. "Cowardly," a British officer called them. "Concealed villains." However, the patriots made up in initiative what they lacked in discipline, and for the British, the march turned into a desperate scramble to reach safety.

As a veteran of the Monongahela debacle, Gage must have felt a sickening sense of déjà vu when he received reports of the fighting. He sent out a relief column under General Hugh Percy, who met Smith's beleaguered force east of Lexington. The energetic Percy got most of the troops back to Boston. The British suffered 73 men killed and more than 170 wounded. Percy noted of his opponents that day, "Whoever looks upon them as an irregular mob, will find himself much mistaken."[13]

General Gage had long known of Henry Knox's Whig sympathies. Early in 1775, he had given orders that the young bookseller was not to be allowed to leave the city. Boston's location on a peninsula connected to the mainland by a 120-yard-wide, fortified isthmus simplified control. Getting out presented a problem for Knox, who was well known and, at 260 pounds, conspicuous.

But the conflict had now turned serious, and Knox knew that if he was to contribute to the patriot effort he had to leave Boston. Shortly after the outbreak at Lexington, Lucy sewed Henry's sword, an emblem of his militia command, into the lining of her cloak. The couple escaped in a small boat, risking prison or hanging if they were discovered fleeing the city. Henry's brother William, then nineteen, took over the bookshop. Lucy fretted that she might never see her family again.

The excitement outside Boston more than matched the apprehension inside the city. Militiamen from all over New England, a total of twenty thousand, were camping in surrounding towns. Military matters were no longer questions of theory and drill. This was real. Men's lives would hang on decisions made by inexperienced officers. Yet it was the age of amateurs. In a time when a retired printer like Benjamin Franklin could make breakthrough discoveries in science, it didn't seem impossible that soldiers armed with book learning could challenge an empire.

Knox was astounded to see his friend Nathanael Greene ride into the bustling bivouac at Cambridge at the head of 1,500 Rhode Island soldiers, his troops among the best dressed and most disciplined of any of those gathering around Boston. Some mysterious alchemy had transformed Greene, a militia private a few weeks earlier, into the commanding general of his colony's "Army of Observation." Was it his political influence? His calm confidence? His book knowledge? No matter. Greene, whose limp had barred his way in the militia, would soon be appointed the youngest brigadier general in the Continental Army. From private to general in a month—his dizzying ascent was a sign of the desperate times.

Moving with energy, Knox designed fortifications to protect the growing patriot army should the British decide to rush out and attack in force. Men set to work piling earthen breastworks and constructing small forts, known as redoubts, in the village of Roxbury, directly opposite Boston Neck. They fortified their camp in Cambridge, on the far side of the Charles River. Knox began training gunners to operate the twelve cannon that Rhode Island patriots had sent.

On June 12, General Gage commanded all the rebels to lay down their arms and swear allegiance to their king or be branded traitors. The zealots outside the city ignored the threat. Charged with an electric sense of anticipation and possibility, they steeled themselves for war. Now blows would indeed decide.

THREE

THE PREDICAMENT
WE ARE IN

1775

It took time for the sound of the shots fired on April 19, 1775, to be heard round the world, but the news flashed through the colonies like a thunderclap. A post rider left at ten o'clock that morning to alert the citizenry of the slaughter at Lexington. He reached Hartford, Connecticut, that night. Word arrived in New London on April 20 and in New York City one day later. The *Massachusetts Spy*, on May 3, was reporting that British troops, had "wantonly and in a most inhuman manner fired upon and killed a number of our countrymen."[1]

Word reached John Stark in New Hampshire at midday on April 20. Within six hours, he was able to recruit four hundred armed men. They responded to his call because of his reputation as a gritty wilderness ranger during the last war. Now a forty-seven-year-old farmer and sawmill owner, Stark hurried his troops to the outskirts of Boston by the morning of April 22. He recruited another four hundred volunteers from those who had raced to the scene of the action on their own. Men from the town of Nottingham had covered the fifty-seven miles to Cambridge in twenty hours, "having run rather than marched."

The dispute over abstractions, over taxation and representation, had given way to grim, bleeding-knuckle reality. All over New England, men threw themselves into the cause with astonishing fervor. The fifty-seven-year-old Israel Putnam heard the "momentous intelligence" the evening of April 19 as he was building a stone wall on his farm in northeastern Connecticut. A well-known fighter during the French and Indian War, Putnam had enhanced his reputation by donating a flock of sheep to struggling Bostonians during the British occupation. The grizzled veteran did not change his clothes. He rode all night, joining others outside Boston the next morning.

None of the men knew what to expect. They just wanted to get at the soldiers who had so offhandedly shot down their fellow citizens. But the British troops did not deploy for battle. General Gage kept his men inside the city, isolated on a peninsula. On the mainland, the threatening mass of militiamen continued to grow.

———————

Three days after Lexington, a Connecticut merchant named Benedict Arnold led his militia company to the New Haven powder magazine, where the colony's arms were stored. He wrangled with one of the city's selectmen, who denied him entry. "Regular orders be damned," Arnold stormed, "None but Almighty God shall prevent my marching!"[2] Cowed, the official handed him the keys. Arnold and his men armed themselves and hurried toward Boston.

The enthusiastic volunteer stayed in the camp that surrounded the besieged city barely two weeks. The Massachusetts Committee of Safety, which now served as a provisional government for the colony, named him a militia colonel and sent him galloping westward. In doing so, they were putting into action an idea that Arnold had himself proposed. He was to gather fighters from the colony's western hill towns and seize Fort Ticonderoga, the largest military bastion on the continent.

On reaching the village of Williamstown, Massachusetts, Arnold learned that the notorious partisan Ethan Allen, leader of a vigilante band known as the Green Mountain Boys, had received exactly the same assignment from Connecticut authorities. The news alarmed Arnold. He left behind his recruiting officers and hurried on to look for Allen at the Catamount Tavern in Bennington, in the territory that would soon be Vermont. There, the patrons told him that Allen had already left. He was even now gathering his men on the east shore of Lake Champlain, opposite the mighty fortress.

Arnold sped on, finally catching up with Allen on the afternoon of May 8, three weeks after the battle at Concord's North Bridge. In a field beside Lake Champlain, two of the most striking personalities of the era came face to face. Allen was more than six feet tall, his massive physique draped in a green coat with oversized epaulettes and gold buttons. His intimidating manner and violent temper could make men cower. The fastidious Arnold wore a fancy scarlet uniform coat. Half a head shorter and cocksure in demeanor, he gazed at his rival with an icy, penetrating stare. Allen was a rough mountain man, Arnold a wealthy and sophisticated trader. An iron resolve and a surplus of self-regard were common to both.

Fort Ticonderoga commanded the water route that led from Canada down Champlain, Lake George, and the Hudson River to New York City. In an era when moving by water was far easier than by land, this corridor was key to controlling the continent. During the last war, the British and French had struggled over the star-shaped fort at the narrow southern end of the lake. Americans understood that Ticonderoga would play a critical role in this conflict, as well. In addition, the patriots desperately needed the artillery and other military supplies stored at the fort.

Arnold knew they had to act before reinforcements reached the remote post. Many members of the Continental Congress, still hoping for a peaceful resolution, hesitated to seize Crown property. But Massachusetts and Connecticut officials had decided simultaneously to order an attempt on the fort. Arnold's credentials gave him greater authority, but Allen had more men. A clash of wills was inevitable.

At first, Allen appeared to accede to Arnold's authority. But he knew his men would not follow the outsider. When Allen's troops threatened to go home, Arnold negotiated a joint command. Together they would launch the first offensive operation of the war.

Ethan Allen had grown up in a remote Connecticut town in the northwest corner of the state. His agile mind marked him as a scholar, but his father's early death ended his studies. He opened an iron forge instead. By the time he was in his mid-twenties, he employed fifty men.

Pugnacious from youth, the huge, work-hardened Allen would strip off his shirt and challenge anyone who dared gainsay him. Yet inside his brawny body was a fierce intelligence. He rejected orthodox religious ideas—his rants about Jesus and Beelzebub led to a charge of blasphemy. A faulty business sense and endless legal disputes left him broke at the age of thirty. On a hunting trip to the north, Allen came under the sway of a new obsession—land speculation.

A dispute about where the border between New York and New Hampshire lay had engendered confusion in the area we know as Vermont. Allen plunged into the controversy with gusto. He bought and sold land and formed an extralegal militia known as the Green Mountain Boys.

If a resident sought to protect his claim by purchasing a New York deed, the Boys were likely to pay him a rough visit.

Allen told people that he "valued not the Government nor even the Kingdom." He walked a fine line, one biographer noted, "between self-aggrandizing land speculator and latter-day Robin Hood."[3]

The outbreak of rebellion in the colonies suited Allen perfectly. He held that his Boys were "a scourge and terror to arbitrary power." The patriots' open defiance had thrown all power into question. The "bloody attempt at Lexington to enslave America," Allen wrote, "thoroughly electrified my mind." As he had battled aristocratic New Yorkers, he would stand up to the British Parliament. "Ever since I arrived to a state of manhood, and acquainted myself with the general history of mankind," he proclaimed, "I have felt a sincere passion for liberty."[4]

In the weeks after Lexington and Concord, Allen gathered perhaps a hundred of his Boys—hunters and trappers, a tavern owner, a poet, three African Americans, immigrants from Scotland and Ireland. Six of them were his brothers and relatives. By the time Arnold found him, he was ready to storm Ticonderoga. He was hopeful because the British, no longer standing guard on a border, had allowed the fort to fall into disrepair. Only forty-six regular soldiers, still ignorant of the violence near Boston, manned the outpost.

Benedict Arnold hailed from the prosperous city of Norwich, at the eastern end of Connecticut. His early life mirrored that of Henry Knox: His sea captain father had fallen on hard times and descended into penury and alcoholism. The family had apprenticed young Benedict to an apothecary. In addition to the intricacies of herbs, plasters, and powders, he had learned the complex strategies of international trade. Coming of age, he had opened up shop as "Druggist, Bookseller &c." He expanded into trading horses and other goods from Canada to the West Indies. With a fleet of ships and a knack for smuggling, he had amassed a substantial fortune.

Now, Arnold and Allen stood in the dark on the eastern shore of the lake and prepared to make a "desperate attempt" to seize the Crown fort opposite them. A storm delayed the operation for hours. With few boats and barely time for two trips across, only 83 of their 250 men made it to the New York side. In the delicate darkness that preceded dawn, Allen cooed three owl hoots to signal the advance. They crept up to the entrance, where a sentry had drifted off to sleep. Arnold and Allen woke him as they rushed to be the first to enter. The guard lifted his musket and pulled the trigger—the gun did not ignite. A second soldier appeared and fired high. The resounding boom echoed through the sleeping fort. The guard thrust his bayonet at Allen, who parried the blow and hammered him on the head with the flat of his heavy pirate's cutlass, knocking him down.

Now all was shouting. The garrison staggered awake, the soldiers scrambled out. Allen acted like a man possessed. He rushed toward the officers' barracks shouting, "No quarter! No quarter!" The fort's commander remained locked in his room as Allen yelled, "Come out of there, you goddamn old rat!"

A contemporary described Allen's oratory as "a singular compound of local barbarisms, scriptural phrases and oriental wildness."[5] Allen claimed that a British officer had asked him by what authority he had broken into His Majesty's fort. "In the name of the great Jehovah and the Continental Congress!" Allen allegedly roared. If he said it, he was wrong on both counts. Neither the Hebrew deity nor the representatives meeting in Philadelphia had authorized any such action. Yet the fort was soon under his command.

When the fireworks, such as they were, ended, the conflict between Arnold and Allen resumed. Arnold made a mighty attempt to stop the Green Mountain Boys from looting, but Allen's men openly defied him. Like Washington at Fort Necessity, Arnold saw what happened when military subordination dissolved.

Ever eager to seize the initiative, Arnold and a few of his men, without any higher authorization, commandeered a small ship, fitted it with guns, sailed the length of Lake Champlain, and passed into the Richelieu River at its northern end. There, they attacked the unwary garrison of the British post at St. John's, Canada, quickly bested the enemy force, and seized a war schooner and supplies.

A dithering Congress, having agreed to hold onto Ticonderoga, decided to relieve Arnold of his authority over the fort and replace him with a Connecticut officer who wielded more influence. Arnold, exasperated by the taint of politics infecting military affairs, resigned his Massachusetts commission and disbanded his regiment. America's boldest and most enterprising officer went home. When he arrived, he found that his wife, Margaret, had died suddenly, leaving him with three young children.

———•─•———

Thousands of patriots, young men drawn by the cause and the excitement, had gathered in camps on the landward side of Boston. They constituted not an army but a collection of militias from the New England colonies. New Hampshire's John Stark commanded his eight hundred men on the left wing north of Boston. Nathanael Greene's Rhode Island troops camped on the right in Roxbury, opposite Boston Neck. Israel Putnam, now a Connecticut general, commanded troops in the center at Cambridge. Fifteen Massachusetts regiments participated on all fronts. Artemas Ward, another French and Indian War veteran, held overall command.

Extensive land filling has radically altered Boston's geography. In 1775, three peninsulas jutted into the shallow harbor, each nearly an island. Skirting the water on the fragment of land to the north lay Charlestown. Behind the built-up area of that village, the land rose to the knolls of Breed's Hill and Bunker Hill. Boston proper occupied the bulging neck in the middle. On the sparsely populated Dorchester peninsula to the south, a ridge joined two more low hills.

On May 25, three scarlet-clad, gold-trimmed generals, the cream of the British high command, joined General Gage in the city. William

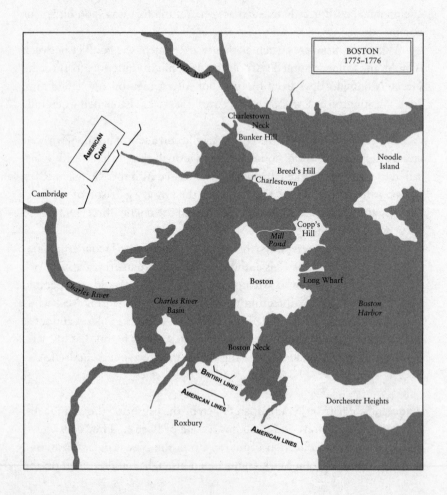

Howe, forty-six, had distinguished himself in the late French war and enjoyed close ties to the royal family. Like Washington he was tall and had bad teeth. Unlike the American commander, he was a hedonist who flaunted his taste for soft living and a pliant mistress. The forty-five-year-old Henry Clinton was a suspicious, closed-mouthed man with bushy black eyebrows who played the violin and described himself as a "shy bitch." The son of a former royal governor of New York, Clinton knew America from his childhood and took a more severe view of the rebellion than Howe did. John Burgoyne, the oldest of the group at fifty-three, brought with him a reputation as a gay blade, a gambler, a successful playwright, and an experienced commander.

The generals were astounded to find the army bottled up in a cul de sac. They had been sent from London to evaluate the tense situation in the colonies before word of the uprising had arrived there. As they surveyed the scene, they saw that the heights to the north and south had to be fortified if the troops were to break out and rout the rebels. In mid-June General Gage, still in overall command, prepared to occupy the Charlestown peninsula. He would use it as a base to move against the rebel camp at Cambridge. Later he would turn his attention to Dorchester, mop up resistance at Roxbury, and finish putting down the rebellion.

Before the attack could get underway, the rebels, led by General Putnam, rushed from Cambridge to occupy Bunker and Breed's Hill themselves. A large, cool-headed northern Massachusetts farmer, Colonel William Prescott, helped Putnam solidify the gains. Through the night, their men dug trenches and erected a redoubt on Breed's Hill. In the morning, they stared defiantly from behind their breastworks.

General Gage could not allow this affront to stand. The next day, a hot Saturday, June 17, guns in Boston and on the warships in the harbor began to heave cannonballs and exploding bombs at the rebel's hastily constructed fortifications. That afternoon, General Howe and three thousand redcoats crossed from Boston to the peninsula, where they prepared to brush aside their opponents and occupy the heights.

Confusion reigned among the Americans. The chain of command was unclear; units marched in the wrong direction; desperately needed supplies and reinforcements went astray. Dressed in his shirtsleeves, the energetic Putnam, known as "Old Put," rode frantically here and there, trying to organize the men who milled idly on Bunker Hill, well behind the American line.

John Stark arrived with five hundred of his men at the narrow neck that separated the Charlestown peninsula from the mainland. He found the air alive with fire from British floating batteries. Stark strolled calmly forward into the killing zone, ordering his men to follow. Captain Henry Dearborn, marching into his first battle, urged him to hurry. Stark, "with a look peculiar to himself," observed that "one fresh man in action is worth ten fatigued ones."[6] They proceeded across at a deliberate pace. When he reached the battlefield, Stark suspected that Howe would try to force his way past the rail fence on the American left. Although manned by rebel musketmen, the fence did not quite reach to the edge of the Mystic River. He ordered his men to reinforce the end of the fence line and to build a protective stone wall on the beach. He set a stake in the mud forty yards in front of their position to mark the spot where his men would first fire on the advancing British.

There was a brief hesitation before the fight began in earnest, a moment of "supremely agonizing suspense." Unaccustomed to combat, the Americans felt their bowels churn and icy sweat flash across their skin. The scene "seemed unreal."[7]

At three-thirty on a sweltering afternoon, the first pitched battle of the Revolutionary War began. Grenadiers and scarlet-clad British infantrymen marched forward in lines, moving step by step toward the tense patriots. "They looked too handsome to be fired at," a militiaman said, "but we had to do it."

As Stark suspected, a key part of General Howe's attack was to sweep along the beach with a column of his best fighters, break into the Americans' rear, and circumvent their efforts at fortification. Spotting the low stone barricade, he did not hesitate to send his light infantrymen charging ahead with steel bayonets thrust forward.

When the redcoats reached the stake on the beach, spectators crowding rooftops in Boston could hear clearly the ripping volley that Stark's men let loose. The approaching infantry men fell to their knees and pitched into the muddy sand, torn by musket balls. The disciplined soldiers were staggered. They hesitated, then kept coming. More volleys, more men dropped.

Remembering tactics from his ranger days, Stark had arrayed two lines of musketmen behind the first. He ordered each line to shoot in succession while the others reloaded, so that attackers had to advance into almost continuous fire. He told them to load their muskets with "buck and ball," a bullet and four bits of shot, for more killing power.

The slaughter stopped the attack along the beach and saved the American line from envelopment. All along that line now, a ferocious fight was under way. The British troops attacked and were driven back. "They advanced toward us in order to swallow us up," one patriot remembered, "but they found a choaky mouthful of us."[8]

The sulfurous air and dripping sweat stung men's eyes. Soldiers on both sides frantically reloaded. Howe, a courageous battle leader, had underestimated the rebels' determination. He regrouped and attacked again. Again his men were repulsed. Then he angled the focus of their charge toward the redoubt. The Americans ran low on ammunition. The British finally broke into the fort and drove the defenders back. Stark's men were among the last to leave the field, fighting to keep the retreat from turning to a rout. Even General Burgoyne conceded that their withdrawal was "no flight, it was even covered with bravery and military skill."

The rebels had killed 282 British soldiers and wounded 800. "A dear bought victory," British general Henry Clinton would declare, "another would have ruined us." When news of the costly battle reached London, the ministers immediately relieved Thomas Gage of his duties. General William Howe was made commander and handed the thorny task of finding a solution to the American rebellion.

———

Three days before the carnage on Charlestown peninsula, the Continental Congress voted to adopt the collection of New England militiamen and transform them into a national army. They turned to one of their own to lead the effort, a delegate who had sufficient knowledge of the military art, the only one of them who had attended the proceedings wearing a uniform: George Washington. The tall Virginian combined a radical devotion to the cause with the ingrained forbearance of a man of property.

Appointed to the job, Washington immediately expressed his fear that "my abilities and military experience may not be equal to the extensive and important trust." His humility combined affectation with genuine modesty. He had never directed the movements of a massed army or mounted a formal siege. He had been away from active military life for sixteen years. He knew almost nothing about naval affairs, cavalry, engineering, or artillery.

Washington appeared "majestic" as he rode into the camp in Cambridge, his boots polished, his silver spurs gleaming. What he found there appalled him. "Confusion and discord" reigned. The soldiers were unseasoned—most had never been more than twenty miles from their homes. Commander Artemas Ward, sick with a bladder stone, had failed to impose a structure on the jumble of militias.

The troops, Washington noted, had "very little discipline, order, or government." He could smell the camp from a mile away, a vast shanty town of wood, turf, and canvas. He found the Yankees viscerally repugnant. They were, he felt, "an exceeding dirty and nasty people." He observed "an unaccountable kind of stupidity in the lower class of these people."[9] Washington had to issue explicit orders for men to use the latrines rather than "ease themselves" where they pleased. Disease had subtracted many from the active duty list, others had simply gone home. Instead of the expected twenty thousand soldiers, a count showed only sixteen thousand.

A twenty-one-year-old captain wrote: "We were all young, and in a manner unacquainted with human nature, quite Novices in Military matters."[10] The men had left their homes, farms, and families to take a stand for a cause. They were independent agents asserting rights that no king or Parliament could abrogate. One observer noted that "the doctrines of independence and levellism have been so effectually sown throughout the country," that soldiers would not respond to the commands of officers. Washington had to grapple with a deep paradox: the spirit that induced men to take up arms for freedom stood in the way of their becoming effective soldiers.

He had learned from Braddock that an army must be based on hierarchy. "Discipline and subordination," he declared, "add life to military movements." To win liberty, the men needed to bend themselves to subservience. Militias might elect unit commanders and allow officers to fraternize with their men—real armies did not. "Great distinction is made between officers and soldiers," an observer wrote about the new tone Washington brought to the camp. "Every one is made to know his place and keep in it."[11]

Helping to assert this tone was Charles Lee, who had pored over Thucydides while traveling toward the Monongahela. During the French war, Lee had extended his military resume in Britain and Portugal, and later had served as a soldier of fortune in Poland and Russia. In 1773, he retired to America, where he had found "a magnificence and greatness . . . not equaled in any part of Europe."[12] Lee now served as third in command after Washington and Ward. In the eyes of many, including his own, this experienced officer should have been the supreme commander.

"He is a queer creature," John Adams noted of Lee. The general had invited Adams's wife, Abigail, to shake the paw of Spado, one of the pack of dogs that always accompanied him. Contemporaries commented on his striking appearance—"extremely thin; his face ugly, with an aquiline nose of enormous proportions."[13] He was "quarrelsome, satirical, and abusive." In an age when officers favored lace, silk, and gold braid, he dressed carelessly. Some made him the butt of jokes, others whispered about "Mad Lee."

The slovenly Lee and the meticulous Washington, both forty-three, became for a time the odd couple of the Revolution. But Lee knew his business. After his appointment, Washington consulted books to brush up on military strategy. Lee didn't need to.

On a tour of the fortifications opposite Boston Neck, both generals were impressed by the efforts of the young artilleryman Henry Knox. They expressed "the greatest pleasure and surprise," Knox wrote excitedly to Lucy, who was sharing the home of a patriot in Watertown, eight miles from Boston. But Knox's breastworks were one of the few elements of the situation that the generals could feel good about. The army's lack of gunpowder was frightening. When he arrived, Washington was informed that he had only 308 barrels of powder for the entire army, a paltry supply. Later, he found that there had been a miscalculation. The amount of powder on hand was 36 barrels, a mere nine rounds per man. On receiving the news, Washington "did not utter a word for half an hour."

"Could I have foreseen what I have and am like to experience," he wrote, "no consideration upon earth should have induced me to accept this command."[14] Some soldiers were equipped only with spears.

What puzzled the American commander was why the British did not simply march out of the city and rout the ragtag army, which would have found it impossible to defend its nine miles of lines. Was it Gage's innate caution? Howe's Whig sympathies? British hopes of reconciliation? The sting of the slaughter at Bunker Hill? Washington found himself "unable upon any principle whatever to account for their silence, unless it be to lull us into a fatal security."[15]

Time was working against the Americans. The men who had marched to Boston on a moment's notice had never expected to stay more than a few weeks or months. They would enjoy some excitement, give the redcoats a thrashing, and go home. Now the drudgery and drill were taking a toll. "The soldiers in general," one noted, "are most heartily sick of the service." In August Washington informed Congress that "the greater part of the troops are in a state not far from mutiny," and feared "the army must absolutely break up."

Patriots were also grumbling. Pamphleteer Thomas Paine thought Washington had "chilled" the revolutionary fire that had flared at Concord and Bunker Hill by adopting a strategy of "cold defense." His criticism stung Washington, who was acutely sensitive to the "esteem of mankind." The commander was in fact constitutionally averse to stalemate. He simply lacked the means to act.

Added to Washington's worries was an epidemic of smallpox. The disease hit Boston in the fall of 1775 and was rampant among troops and civilians by the middle of December. Two-thirds of victims were incapacitated for weeks, the rest killed outright.

The enlistments of the militia units began to run out that autumn. More soldiers would leave in mid-December, all would be gone by the end of the year. Washington cajoled and pleaded with his men, but most were more than eager to go home. Only gradually did he begin to sign soldiers to the new Continental Army, with longer terms of enlistment. For now, Washington found himself in command of a force destined to evaporate before his eyes.

Faced with the task of beating the British on the battlefield, Washington despaired. Militia had shown that they could acquit themselves well when, as at Bunker Hill, they could fight on the defensive from behind fortifications. To ask them to storm the city was to ask the impossible. The lack of ammunition made the prospect even more remote.

Yet on September 11, the commander in chief proposed to his top officers that they row troops across the bay in hundreds of boats to attack the British, a desperate attempt that he admitted was "hazardous." It may be that Washington's boldness was intended to disguise from his own officers their perilous situation. In any case, the others voted for prudence and the attack did not happen.

His Excellency felt the burden of command. "The reflection upon my situation and that of this army," he wrote, "produces many an uneasy hour when all around me are wrapped in sleep. Few people know the predicament we are in."[16]

One thing he knew, as he pondered the standoff through the sleepless hours, was that an effort must be made somewhere, and soon. Benedict Arnold and Ethan Allen had cleared the way up the Hudson-Champlain waterway. To the north lay a vast territory protected by only a few scant regiments. Washington decided to take a chance and embrace a scheme that had been bruited about all summer. The rebels would invade Canada.

FOUR

LEARNING TO BE SOLDIERS

1775

The incursion into Canada, the patriots' first major offensive expedition, would prove to be one of the most extraordinary efforts of the entire war. A critical role in the operation would fall to the itinerant teamster who had years ago followed Braddock into the Ohio Country and been flogged for his insolence.

In the summer of 1775, Daniel Morgan had volunteered to join the first troops specifically recruited for a national army. The hulking Virginian with the loud, twangy voice and the mad gleam in his eye took command of one of ten companies of "expert riflemen." Congress had voted to raise these "continental" troops from the backwoods of Virginia, Maryland, and Pennsylvania to reinforce the siege around Boston. These wild outlanders were experienced in frontier war, accustomed to hard living, and armed with an unusual firearm: the light, long-barreled, frighteningly accurate, uniquely American Pennsylvania rifle.

Now thirty-nine, Morgan was eager to support his "brethren in Boston." Like many of the backwoodsmen, he knew the ways of Indians. His riflemen had a reputation for cunning and savagery that rivaled that of America's natives. Congress viewed them as a secret weapon capable of delivering the British a lethal blow.

After the French war, Morgan had pursued his rowdy life, eager for fights, foot races, and bouts of drinking. He merrily joined in backwoods brawls described as "Biting, Butting, Tripping, Throtling, Gouging,

Cursing," and "kicking one another on the Cods."[1] The sport proved an excellent preparation for war.

During his late twenties, Morgan came under the influence of the teenage daughter of a local farmer. Contemporaries described Abigail Curry as "plain, sensible, and pious." She passed on some of her education and her religious sensibility to the gruff backwoodsman. She bore him two daughters, Nancy and Betsy, during the 1760s, and they finally married in 1773. Daniel went no more a roving. He rented some land in the Shenandoah Valley to grow tobacco and hemp, and did well enough as a yeoman farmer to purchase a few slaves.

The news from Boston reawakened his taste for a fight. Like most participants, he expected the war to be exciting, successful, and short. Abandoning his family and farm for a few months seemed a small price to pay to take part in a drama that might endow its actors with immortality.

Enthusiasm for the cause made recruitment easy. Morgan preached glory and the rights of man in loud, rough terms that made sense to unschooled backwoodsmen. He took his pick of volunteers, selecting the biggest men, the best marksmen, and the hardiest fighters.

Congress had stipulated companies of sixty-eight men—Morgan signed up ninety-six in less than a week. The men possessed the instincts of hunters: deep patience, hair-trigger awareness of their surroundings, and the ability to withstand rain, cold, and hunger. Each was fitted out with a rifle and a tomahawk. Each carried a scalping knife, a nine-inch blade suitable for eating, whittling, or slicing human flesh. Instead of a uniform, the men wore their traditional dun-colored hunting shirts fashioned from heavy fringed linen, along with leather leggings and moccasins. This gear was practical and set them apart as the first of America's special forces.

Morgan trained his men for three weeks in the rudiments of war as he understood it. On July 15, they marched toward Boston. Townspeople turned out to offer them bread, cider, and hearty cheers. Local militiamen marched alongside to show support. Virginia congressman Richard Henry Lee marveled at "their amazing hardihood, their method of living so long in the woods without carrying provisions with them."

"They are the finest marksmen in the world," John Hancock declared. "They do execution with their Rifle guns at an amazing distance." Unlike a musket, a rifle, fully five feet long, had spiral grooves incised along the interior of its barrel. The ridges gave the ball a gyroscopic spin, causing it to fly far more accurately than one from a musket. To impress the locals, one man would confidently hold a five-inch target between his knees for his mates to fire at from forty yards. Then all would strip to the waist, paint themselves like Indians, and put on displays of ferocity.

These intrepid riflemen arrived in Cambridge on August 6, 1775, having tramped a total of nearly six hundred miles in three weeks, an astounding pace. They found themselves in a camp that was suddenly the third-largest city on the continent. Their arrival created a sensation. Their rough language mortified the local descendants of Puritans. They demonstrated the accuracy of their backwoods hunting implements for mystified New Englanders. John Adams thought a rifle "a peculiar kind of musket."

As an elite force, the riflemen were given a separate bivouac and excused from routine camp duties. But a month of inaction wore on them. They drank rum, fought among themselves, and stole from surrounding farms. "They are such a boastful, bragging set of people," an observer noted, "and think none are men or can fight but themselves."[2] When Washington asked for recruits to invade Canada, every one of them volunteered. Morgan's Virginians and two Pennsylvania companies were chosen by lot.

Congress had initially assigned the attack on the fourteenth colony to General Philip Schuyler, commander of the Northern Department. The forty-two-year-old scion of a powerful Albany family, Schuyler supported the patriot cause but remained deeply suspicious of the rebels' egalitarian notions. During the war with the French, he had served as a supply officer, a post suited to an experienced businessman.

He agreed to the operation, then he delayed. In August, with the campaigning season slipping by, Washington turned the Canada invasion into a pincer maneuver. He would send another force north along a little-used route through Maine to threaten Quebec City while Schuyler's men pushed toward Montreal. The British commander in Canada, Guy Carleton, would have to divide his meager force or relinquish territory to defend a single point.

Schuyler finally set out and besieged the British fort at St. John's that Arnold had raided in the spring. While the operation was under way, the commander fell ill with "Barbarous Complications of Disorders." He turned the mission over to his second in command, the former British officer Richard Montgomery. The veteran Montgomery questioned whether Schuyler had the "strong nerves" required for war.

While Montgomery's traditional corps relied on artillery for its heavy hitting, the wing approaching through Maine would embody a new strategic idea. Relieved of the burden of heavy guns, the force would gain mobility.

The lethal fire of the riflemen would, in lieu of cannon, give the force a long-range killing capability. The big backwoodsmen could also serve as shock troops for storming the walls of the city.

As the group was getting organized, Morgan sized up the officer chosen to lead this unique force: Benedict Arnold had returned to the cause. At thirty-four, Arnold was six years younger than Morgan. Both men were self-made, but in different ways. Morgan had spent months wandering through trackless forests with his rifle, sleeping under stars and rain. Arnold had negotiated with sharp-minded merchants and used his wits to turn a profit. In the course of the war, the two would emerge as the patriots' most skilled natural fighters.

Washington told Arnold that "upon the success of this enterprise . . . the safety and welfare of the whole continent may depend."[3] In addition to the two hundred riflemen, Arnold picked eight hundred New England and New York militiamen, many of them veterans of Bunker Hill. In mid-September, the strike force, a total of 1,050 men, marched to coastal Newburyport, Massachusetts, where they would board on a flotilla of small ships for a dash up the coast. Before embarking, they staged a grand parade through town. Amid the cheers, the reality of the great task began to sink in. It dawned on one twenty-two-year-old volunteer that "many of us should never return to our parents and families."[4]

Munching on the ginger that Arnold, the former apothecary, had thoughtfully provided, the men still succumbed to seasickness as they scudded 140 miles along the stormy coast. Yet in a few days they were gathering themselves at the mouth of the Kennebec River, preparing for a trek into the unknown.

The men loaded their supplies into two hundred boats that a local carpenter had slapped together, "very badly," from green wood. Each twenty-foot-long vessel could hold up to a ton of supplies or six men. They carried forty-five days' of food for the expected twenty-day trip— barrels of flour and of preserved beef and pork. Military supplies—powder and ammunition, as well as their own muskets and rifles—added to their load.

Like Arnold himself, most of the leaders were neophytes at war, guided as much by improvisation and guesswork as by experience. Lieutenant Colonel Christopher Greene, a cousin of Nathanael Greene, owned a Rhode Island mill. Major Return J. Meigs was a Connecticut merchant. Captain Henry Dearborn, a twenty-four-year-old New Hampshire physician, had marched his company toward Lexington the very day the news arrived, despite the fact that his wife had given birth that same morning. With John Stark, he had survived the worst of the Bunker Hill inferno.

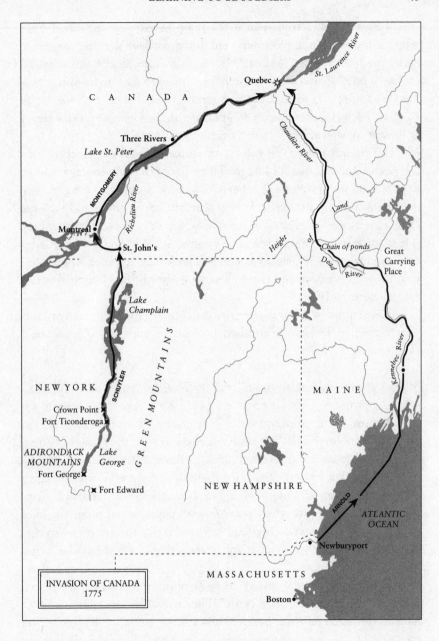

Heading off to Canada, Dearborn took along his black Newfoundland dog for companionship. The oldest and most experienced officer was forty-six-year-old Lieutenant Colonel Roger Enos. He had already been to Quebec with the British army in 1759. His men would haul the bulk of the expedition's reserve supplies at the rear of the march.

At least two men took their wives. Joseph Grier's spouse was a strapping six-footer. Jemima Warner went along because she was concerned about the health of her husband, James. Wives frequently accompanied husbands on military campaigns, but for women to sign on for such a perilous expedition was extraordinary. Another who made the trek was Aaron Burr, a zealous nineteen-year-old graduate of the College of New Jersey at Princeton, who served as a volunteer aide to Arnold.

The riflemen were the core of the force. Arnold put all three rifle companies under Captain Morgan. The experienced woodsmen would go first, blazing the trail for the others. Morgan was suited to commanding hard men. Later portraits show him with the angled nose and battered face of a seasoned pugilist. They downplay an ugly scar he carried on the side of his face. Serving with a ranger corps on the Virginia frontier after the Braddock debacle, he had ridden into an Indian ambush. A bullet had torn through his neck and cheek, knocking out his teeth. He had barely escaped with his life.

"His manners were of the severest cast," one of his men wrote of Morgan, "but where he became attached, he was kind and truly affectionate."[5]

Maine's glacier-clawed landscape, with its three thousand ponds and lakes, offered a grim prospect for travelers. As the Kennebec River stepped toward the sea, it leaped over a series of rapids and waterfalls. At each, the men had to pole, paddle, and push the boats against the tumbling water. Or they had to unload the vessels, haul them out, carry them as far as the next manageable stretch, return for their equipment and supplies, carry that, reload the boats, and go on. Again and again they moved their sixty-five tons of supplies over these punishing portages. At one point, a soldier recorded, the river was "exceeding rapid and rocky for five miles, so that any man would think, at its first appearance, that it was impossible to get Boats up it."

On October 10 they passed the last frontier settlement and plunged into "the greatest forest upon earth." They would not encounter another human habitation for three hundred miles. They could see mountains "on each side of the river, high and snow on the tops." In the brittle evening air, they heard the honking of great wedges of geese heading south. The weather turned severely cold, and they awoke each morning to find their clothes stiff with ice.

"Now," wrote Private Caleb Haskell, "we are learning to be soldiers."[6]

Morgan and his men forged a way over the Great Carrying Place, a series of portages between ponds, to the Dead River, so called because of its easy-flowing water. The crossing took five days. They hauled the boats and supplies through "Spruce Swamps Knee deep in mire." Dysentery ravaged the ranks. Arnold ordered a log hospital thrown up. He was already down to 950 men and twenty-five days' provisions.

On they moved into the "eternal night" of the wilderness. "A dreary aspect," one man wrote, "a perpetual silence, an universal void, form the face of nature in this part of the world."[7] A prolonged, drenching rain caused the river to rise twelve feet and fill with debris. Rifleman George Morison wrote in his journal about "stumbling over fallen logs, one leg sinking deeper in the mire than the other. . . . Down goes a boat and the carriers with it. A hearty laugh prevails."[8]

On October 23, as men tried to dry their sodden clothing around fires, Arnold noted that the increasingly intense cold would freeze the ground and make walking easier. Most of the troops shared their leader's hopeful outlook. Fighting men had an advantage, wrote Private Morison: "Great as their sufferings often are, they are never doomed to endure the miseries of those terrible spectres, spleen and melancholy."[9]

Then came the kicker. Enos and his officers, trailing behind the rest with the bulk of the provisions, decided to turn back. They took food, weapons, medical supplies, and a third of the army. Enos fully justified his decision to disobey orders and quit the apparently suicidal course that Arnold, Morgan, and the others had embraced. He had been defeated not by the enemy but by America's vast terrain and the fear it engendered.

"In an absolute danger of starving," the rest of the men stood one hundred miles from the settlements in Quebec, two hundred miles from those in Maine. "No one thought of returning," a soldier recorded in his diary. "We found it best to endure it patiently." Arnold went ahead in a canoe, promising to send supplies back as soon as he made contact with civilization over the mountains.

The men continued to ascend, now moving along a chain of ponds that were the source of the Dead River. They reached the divide that marked the border with Canada. They watched the mountains close in. "Every prospect of distress," one man wrote, "now came thundering on."

They had survived two weeks on half rations. By October 28, almost all food was exhausted. Each man was allotted a pint of flour and less than an ounce of salt pork per day. Many miles of hard marching lay ahead.

Passing onto the downhill phase of the journey did not make the going easier. Daniel Morgan quickly discovered why the river they needed to follow was named Chaudière, French for "cauldron" or "boiler." Boarding his boat, he hurtled along in the white water until the rapids flipped the craft over. He lost not just food, personal possessions, and guns, but the first man of the expedition to drown.

Still, the unspoiled beauty of the scene moved some of the men. "This place was not a little delightsome," noted Isaac Senter, the expedition's surgeon, "considering its situation in the midst of an amazing wilderness."[10]

They entered a morass of streams and marshes. "After walking a few hours in the swamp," a participant reported, "we seemed to have lost all sense of feeling in our feet and ankles." The men stepped along "in great fear of breaking our bones or dislocating our joints."[11] To be disabled was certain death. On October 30 they waded six miles through a swamp "which was pane glass thick frozen." Mrs. Grier held her skirts above her waist, but none of the men "dared to intimate a disrespectful idea of her."

Their provisions exhausted, they ate moss, candles, and lip salve. They ate "roots and bark off trees and broth from boiling shoes and cartridge boxes." On the first day of November they killed two dogs, one of them Henry Dearborn's Newfoundland, and ate them "with good appetite, even the feet and skins."

As one group prepared to plunge through yet another morass, Jemima Warner noticed that her husband was missing. She went back "with tears of affection in her eyes" and found him lying exhausted along the trail. She sat with him for several days in the cold until he "fell victim to the King of Terrors." She covered his body with leaves and later arrived in camp carrying his rifle and powder horn.

All of this they experienced in the unearthly mental state that accompanies extreme hunger and fatigue. Their minds became taut wires through which they could hear the hum of the stars. The mountains and clouds, trees and rocks, as light as their bodies, seemed to float dreamlike in the cold. The aroma of pine and moss became intense.

"We are so faint and weak, we can scarcely walk," one man noted. Another said, "That sensation of the mind called 'the horrors,' seemed to prevail."[12]

While Morgan and Arnold struggled through Maine, Richard Montgomery and the force marching along the western route to Canada had run into problems of their own. The five hundred British soldiers at St. John's managed to hold off Montgomery's two thousand inexperienced men for two miserable months.

War had seared Montgomery long before the Revolution commenced. The son of Anglo-Irish gentry, the young man had been raised to fight. During the Seven Years' War he had helped the British take Fort Ticonderoga and Montreal. He had endured a full range of slaughter and misery while campaigning in America's wilderness; he had fought through the hellish siege of Havana as the British grappled with Spanish forces. After returning to England, he languished. Europe was exhausted by war. Promotions dried up. His career stalled.

Montgomery himself was exhausted. He sold his commission, left the army and moved to America, seeking the life of a simple farmer. He renewed his connection with heiress Janet Livingston, whom he had met during his period of service. Their marriage in 1773 joined Montgomery to one of the most powerful families in America. The couple settled on a Hudson Valley farm. His wife wanted a child. He did not. Melancholy, the eighteenth-century term for depression, haunted him. "My happiness is not lasting," he wrote. "It has no foundation."

He signed on to defend his adopted country and was appointed brigadier general under Schuyler. He felt it a "hard fate to be obliged to oppose a power I had been ever taught to reverence." Before he left to join his men and to fight against his former comrades, he said, "'Tis a mad world, my masters, I once thought so, now I know it."[13]

The New York soldiers who fought under him at St. John's knew that in Montgomery they had a commander with strong nerves, one of the most competent and inspiring officers on the continent. When they finally overran the post, they also captured a good portion of all British regulars in Canada. Their victory delivered the enemy "a most fatal stab." The men's own nerves were growing accustomed to fire and death. They were sure they could take Quebec and perhaps end the war before winter.

But Montgomery saw that time was slipping dangerously past. The enlistment of a portion of his troops would run out at the end of November. Days were growing shorter. The cold, dirty weather was turning roads to muck.

The British governor of Canada, General Guy Carleton, with only 130 soldiers left to command, abandoned Montreal. He lacked faith in the French Canadians, who had, he thought, "imbibed too much of the American Spirit of Licentiousness and Independence."[14] He hurried back to Quebec, allowing the Americans to take Montreal without a shot.

Yet Montgomery's foreboding continued. In his letters to Janet, he often included the phrase, "If I live . . ." He admonished her not to send him "whining letters" that "lower my spirits."

On November 2, the supplies Arnold had promised began to reach his scattered and famished troops: two oxen, a cow, two sheep, and three bushels of potatoes. The cattle were butchered and eaten on the spot, the bloody hides fashioned into crude moccasins. Soon cornmeal, mutton, and tobacco arrived. It was "like a translation from death to life," one man noted. "Echoes of gladness resounded from front to rear."

The inhabitants around Quebec were astounded to see the bearded, emaciated troops emerge from the wilderness. Of the 1,050 men who started, 675 had completed the miraculous journey. If they had reached the city a few days earlier, Arnold and his men might have taken it. But they found that a corps of loyal Scots Canadians had just arrived to defend the walled city. Arnold chose to withdraw twenty miles and wait for Montgomery. He reported to Washington that his men were "almost naked and in want of every necessity."

In early December, Montgomery arrived, leading only three hundred of his New York men. He had left some to secure Montreal. The rest had departed when their enlistments expired, or had fallen ill or deserted. Arnold's men cheered the arrival of this diminished prong of the grand pincer. They cheered the food, supplies, and winter clothing that Montgomery brought with him. The addition of several hundred Canadian militiamen, who had chosen to join the cause of those they called *Bostonois* or "Congress Troops," raised their numbers to more than thirteen hundred.

General Carleton organized his defenses, but remained pessimistic. "We have so many enemies within and foolish people, dupes to those traitors," he wrote to London authorities, "that I think our fate extremely doubtful."[15]

From outside the city walls, Montgomery sent Carleton word that he was having trouble restraining his hordes from "insulting your works" and taking "an ample and just retaliation." The British commander, who had fought with Montgomery in the West Indies, sneered at the threat.

During the next few weeks, the two sides engaged in a desultory cannon duel. The Americans tried building fortifications of ice, which enemy guns quickly splintered. One cannonball demolished Montgomery's carriage and killed his horses seconds after he stepped down, one of his several brushes with death. Another shot decapitated a woman drawing water from a stream. It was Jemima Warner, who had left her dead husband under leaves back in the mountains.

Morgan's riflemen fired at long range toward any defender who appeared on the walls. After they shot a sentry through the head, a British captain complained about the "skulking riflemen . . . These fellows who call themselves soldiers . . . are worse than savages. They lie in wait to shoot a sentry! A deed worthy of Yankee men at war!"

The soldiers suffered from "lice Itch Jaundice Crabs Bedbugs and an unknown sight of Fleas."[16] Worse—smallpox soon began to prostrate one man after another.

General Montgomery mulled his options. Tall, slender, balding, with a handsome, slightly pockmarked face, he was beloved for "his manliness of soul, heroic bravery, and suavity of manners." Staring at the wintery walls of Quebec, he knew that he must act. Most of the New England troops had enlisted only through December. No pleading could convince them to stay past their promised time. The only course left was to take Quebec by storm. With limited manpower, the key to entering the city was to concentrate on one point. But where?

Montgomery chose the Lower Town, the sprawling waterfront commercial district at the foot of the cliffs on which Quebec stood. "I propose amusing Mr. Carleton with a formal attack, erecting batteries, etc.," Montgomery wrote to Schuyler in the sardonic tone of the day, "but mean to assault the works, I believe towards the lower town, which is the weakest point." Taking the Lower Town would cut off the garrison from the water. A threat to burn the warehouses and places of business might induce the inhabitants to surrender.

On December 16, Montgomery put the question to his officers. They debated the matter: a few staunchly opposed the foolhardy attempt, the majority voted to lead their men against the city's walls. They agreed that the faint of heart could bow out, only volunteers would be included.

"Fortune favors the brave," Montgomery stated. On the evening of Christmas Day, the general gave a rousing address to the troops. "General Montgomery was born to command," one man wrote. He sweetened the prospect of attack, proclaiming that "all who get safe into the city will live well," plundering as they pleased. They would attack using the "first strong north-wester" for cover.

Although Montgomery kept up a brave front for his men, he was feeling the strain. "I must go home," he had written to Schuyler. "I am weary of power and totally want that patience and temper so requisite for such a command."[17]

Quebec sat on a rocky bluff at the end of a peninsula between two rivers: the Charles on the northwest side, the tidal St. Lawrence on the southeast. Montgomery's plan was to set fires at the western gates as a diversion and attack the Lower Town from two directions. He would personally lead an advance party along the path between the bottom of the bluff and the St. Lawrence. Arnold would advance on the Charles side with the main force.

By December 29, it seemed likely the clock would run out before the men could act on the plan. Many of the soldiers were already packing, settling debts, and preparing to return home on January 1. The weather, which had tormented them during the march, now remained frustratingly clear. If they attacked without the cover of a storm, the defenders inside the walls could anticipate and counter every move.

The next evening it began to snow. A screeching gale swept in from the northeast. Word went out for the men to be ready at midnight. They would attack on the last day of 1775.

Doctor Isaac Senter, the battalion physician, remembered that General Montgomery was "extremely anxious" during the preparations. Fortune, Montgomery had written, although it might favor the brave, "often baffles the sanguine expectations of poor mortals."

Waiting in darkness, the troops hunched against the fanged blizzard. At four in the morning, rockets fired to coordinate the separate attacks. Artillerymen working mortars began to lob bombs into the city. The time for action had come.

Montgomery led his three hundred New York musketmen on a mission known as a "forlorn hope." Derived from a Dutch military term *verloren hoop*, "detached troop," it had nothing to do with hope but simply meant an advance assault force. Yet the English words carried their own connotation and fit the tenor of Montgomery's mind.

His contingent descended the steep path to the river. Accompanied by his officers and by workmen equipped with axes and saws, he took the lead. The soldiers strung out behind him. They crept along the narrow ledge between the river and the steep rock cliff on their left. The bitter wind took their breath away.

The river had thrown large blocks of ice onto the path. It took them an hour to scramble two miles. They reached a barricade that Carleton had ordered built to protect the Lower Town. The palisade of stakes was undefended. Carpenters hacked an opening. Beyond, officers made out a two-story blockhouse, its black gun portals staring blankly. Nothing moved.

Every second was precious now. Rather than wait for his straggling men to come up, Montgomery chose to advance with fifteen officers. He drew his short sword with its silver dog's head pommel. He motioned his men forward into the snowy darkness.

On the opposite side of the peninsula, Daniel Morgan and his riflemen were marching into Lower Town at the head of the main body of six hundred soldiers that Colonel Arnold commanded.

"Covering the locks of our guns with the lappets of our coats," Private John Joseph Henry recorded, "holding down our heads (for it was impossible to bear up our faces against the imperious storm of snow and wind), we ran along the foot of the hill in single file."[18] Unseen defenders fired down on them from the walls, which loomed on the rocky promontory to the men's right.

When they reached one of the barricades blocking the road, Arnold ordered Morgan and his riflemen to assault the obstacle. The riflemen surged forward. They ran to the log wall and fired point blank through the loopholes. The shots echoed, the flashes lit the swirling snow. A fragment of a ricocheting ball tore through Arnold's left calf. Unable to stand, his boot overflowing with blood, he allowed himself to be helped to the rear.

Morgan ordered a scaling ladder placed against the barrier and, he later reported, "for fear the business might not be executed with spirit, I mounted myself." A musket blast scorched his face. He fell back. Enraged, he rose and scrambled up again. His momentum carried him over the parapet. He landed on a cannon, "which hurt me exceedingly." As the riflemen swarmed over the top behind him, fifty enemy soldiers fled in panic. Dozens surrendered as the Americans rushed into buildings beyond.[19]

A number of the officers present outranked Captain Morgan, but in the crisis, the younger men deferred to his age, size, and air of cold command. The Virginia rifleman took charge. The moment was ripe. Enemy soldiers, especially the French-Canadian militiamen, were surrendering. Panic was gripping the populace. Some townspeople were welcoming the invaders with shouts of *Vive la liberté!* The tide seemed to have turned. The arrival of Montgomery's contingent from the opposite direction would hammer home the victory.

General Carleton did not panic. He sent his limited force of defenders to the northern walls to fire down on Arnold's men as they streamed into the Lower Town. Amid the chaos, Carleton made two critical decisions. First, he marshaled defenders to rush out and take a stand against the Americans at a second barricade closer to the city walls. Then he sent sixty of his scant remaining men through the Palace Gate on the northwest side of the fortified city. They would tread in the footsteps of Arnold's men to attack them from behind.

General Montgomery had still not arrived. Morgan urged that they should rush ahead and assault the town as planned. But now the others asserted their rank. Leaving a mass of prisoners lightly guarded in their rear would be a mistake. It made more sense to solidify their gains and wait for Montgomery. A frustrated Morgan argued to no avail.

Time ticked away. An impatient Morgan went to look for troops who had gotten lost near the docks. A tepid light was staining the eastern sky. When enemy troops began to congregate at the second barrier, the American officers finally allowed Morgan to attack. Running ahead with

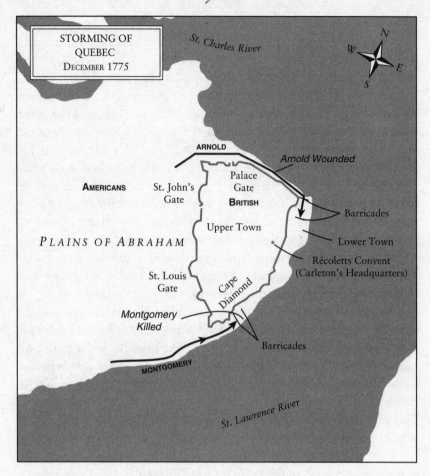

his riflemen, he collided with British regulars. A lieutenant demanded his surrender. Morgan's answer was to shoot him in the head. But enemy fire now forced the Americans to take cover in doorways. They tried to pick off the soldiers firing from the second barricade. Morgan moved among them, encouraging and rallying. From the center of the street, he directed their fire. "Betwixt every peal the awful voice of Morgan is heard," one of the riflemen remembered, "whose gigantic stature and terrible appearance carries dismay among the foe wherever he comes."

The gray light of a snowy day revealed the dire situation: facing defenders far more familiar with the lay of the land, the Americans found the momentum of the battle going against them, and still no sign of General Montgomery. Morgan continued to urge on his troops. "He seems to be all soul," the account continued, "and moves as if he did not touch the earth."[20]

But the attackers' situation continued to erode. The British regulars advancing from behind captured some Americans who had gotten lost in the urban maze. The British took up a defensive position at the first barricade, hemming in the Americans between the two walls. The prospect of victory dissolved as groups of disorganized patriot soldiers began to surrender rather than be killed. Morgan pushed for an immediate escape attempt. The other officers overruled him.

As he saw men throwing down their weapons around him, Morgan "stormed and raged." He broke into tears of angry frustration. He would not give up. He would not concede that the awful ordeal had been for nothing. But surrounded, backed against a wall, he finally had to relinquish his sword.

The attack was over. In three and a half hours, 60 Americans had been killed or wounded, 426 captured. More than a third of the army in Canada had been wiped away. For all they knew, the American cause may have gone down to defeat with them.

Morgan and the others were taken to an improvised prison. A British officer wrote home, "You can have no conception of the Kind of men composed their officers. Of those we took, one major was a blacksmith, another a hatter. Of their captains there was a butcher . . . a tanner, a shoemaker, a tavern keeper, etc. Yet they all pretended to be gentlemen."[21]

The Americans soon learned why General Montgomery had never arrived on the scene that snowy night. As he had rushed through the barricade with the lead unit of his forlorn hope, defenders in the blockhouse had greeted them with the roar of a cannon. The charge of grapeshot, a mass of lead balls that turned the piece into a giant shotgun, "mowed them down like grain," one of the defenders observed. Montgomery and six of his officers were torn apart. The shock induced the others to turn back. Fortune had indeed baffled the expectations of poor mortals.

———————

Montgomery instantly became a symbol of the sacrifice that was required to win Liberty. The fall of a great man testified to the seriousness of the cause. "Weep, America," an officer wrote to Montgomery's brother-in-law, "for thou hast lost one of thy most virtuous and bravest sons!"

America wept. Congress voted to erect a monument in Montgomery's honor. "In the Death of this gentleman," Washington wrote, "America has sustained a heavy Loss."[22]

Janet Montgomery never remarried. She lived for half a century, treasuring the memory of the man she called "an angel sent to us for a moment." Childless, she corresponded with some of the many children named for her late husband, encouraging them to live up to his virtues.

Americans had entered the conflict convinced that free warriors fighting for liberty could vanquish professional soldiers. The notion held both truth and falsehood. At Concord, at Bunker Hill, and in the phenomenal feat of arms that was the invasion of Canada, spirit and patriotism had made up, in part, for discipline and experience. Amateur soldiers and neophyte officers had come close to snuffing out British sovereignty in North America. The men who attacked Quebec had marched with hopeful hearts. They had learned the lessons that Montgomery had understood before they started: that war is cruel, fortune fickle, liberty costly.

Washington sat frustrated before Boston, his army evaporating, recruitment slow, supplies lacking, the first heat of enthusiasm for the cause gone. In the spring, British reinforcements would arrive in numbers. He needed a victory.

FIVE

PRECIOUS CONVOY

1776

With the British fortified in Boston, any patriot victory there was going to require heavy artillery. Washington turned his attention to the cannon at Ticonderoga. "The want of them is so great," he wrote, "that no trouble or expense must be spared to obtain them."[1] He reached into the ranks and chose Henry Knox as the man who might wrestle the heavy guns to Boston.

The commander in chief had an extraordinary knack for reading men and for sensing ability. Having seen experts like Braddock fail, he understood that an officer needed imagination and vision as well as knowledge and experience. Politics would inevitably push mediocre candidates to the fore, but Washington vowed to advance his officers on merit only. Knox was twenty-five and unblooded. Washington gambled by recommending him over more experienced veterans to take charge of all American artillery. He saw a canniness in the young man, a toughness and intelligence that inspired trust, a creativity and initiative that suggested Knox could handle a task most deemed impossible.

From his wide reading, Henry Knox knew that cannon, after their invention during the late Middle Ages, had remained so immensely heavy and cumbersome that they had served mainly as tools to besiege and defend forts and to turn ships into floating platforms of destruction. Gunmakers of the eighteenth century had created lighter, more mobile weapons. Field guns, wheeled into position on carriages, had proven their potency during the Seven Years' War. Canister shot had scythed lines of musketeers, just as it had cut down Montgomery's forlorn hope at Quebec. Big guns sometimes bore the motto *ultima ratio regum*, the last argument of kings. When they were well used, that argument was unanswerable.

On November 16, 1775, while the invasion of Canada still hung in the balance, Knox kissed Lucy, now pregnant, and rode off with his nineteen-year-old brother William on a roundabout trip to Ticonderoga. Neither young man had traveled far from their native town and both excitedly looked forward to seeing New York City, where they arrived nine days later.

Knox wrote to Lucy with a tourist's awe. The brick houses in New York were "three stories high, with the largest kind of windows." The churches, colleges, and workshops were all grand, and the streets wider than Boston's. "The people—why the people are magnificent," he reported, although he found some profane or tending to Toryism. He added: "My Lucy is perpetually in my mind, constantly in my heart."[2]

At Ticonderoga, Knox gazed on war supplies that would make any artilleryman's mouth water. In addition to field guns the armaments included heavy siege pieces larger than any cannon Knox had seen. He examined forty-three guns ranging from 3-pounders, which could do enormous damage at short range, to a huge, eleven-foot-long cannon weighing 5,000 pounds and capable of blasting to pieces any fortification on the continent. The short-barreled mortars and howitzers could heave bombs as big as pumpkins.

Knox understood that a cannon required a great thickness of metal to assure that the explosion did not rip the barrel apart, as it had burst the shotgun that mangled his hand during his innocent duck hunt. Thick metal made the guns dauntingly heavy. All told, Knox figured the artillery he wanted weighed 120,000 pounds. The way to move such behemoths was by boat, but the water route to Boston was closed to him. He had no choice but to do the impossible: transport this massive cargo more than three hundred miles over land. Timing and weather were critical. He had to get the guns down Lake George before the water froze and blocked the movement of boats. Then he had to hope for snow. Only on sleds—"slays" Knox called them—could the heavy guns be moved forward. "Without sledding," he wrote, "the roads are so much gullied that it will be impossible to move a step."[3]

Once crews had manhandled the guns up the short portage from the fort, Knox arranged barges to carry them down Lake George and left William to supervise that phase of the journey. He hurried to Fort George at the other end of the thirty-two-mile-long lake and, improvising as he went, contracted for forty-two huge, custom-built sleds, each designed to hold as much as 5,400 pounds. He rounded up oxen from local farmers and hired experienced teamsters to drive the animals. He managed to procure more than half a mile of three-inch-thick rope for hauling the guns uphill and for keeping them from running away on downgrades.

By December 16, after an arduous trip down the lake, the guns were at Fort George. All Knox needed now was snow. "It is not easy," Knox wrote to Washington, "to conceive the difficulties we have had."[4]

Knox was a muscular man and the Revolutionary War was fought in the age of muscle. Most work during the eighteenth century was accomplished by the exertions of men or draft animals. Building, pumping, cutting, clearing, lifting, gathering, digging, hauling, plowing—all were accomplished by the strength of sinews. Muscle powered war as well. Men marched. Horses carried saber-swinging fighters. Attacking troops killed with bayonet thrusts. Draft animals hauled guns and supplies. Human hands dug trenches and piled breastworks.

But the machine age had begun to enter the military realm, and gunpowder weapons, not muscles, were swiftly becoming the key force on the battlefield. Firearms, simple machines fueled by a highly energetic mixture, significantly extended a man's capacity to kill. When Benjamin Franklin suggested to General Charles Lee that the rebel army, strapped for gunpowder, fight with bow and arrow, the military man smiled at the antediluvian notion.

Muskets could be lethal at short range, but it was the big guns that held the most unprecedented power. Their possibilities, intricacies, and authority appealed to curious and farsighted men like Knox. Artillery pieces represented humans' furthest advance in shaping metal on a large scale. They accelerated projectiles to speeds that surpassed the limits of human vision. The gunner was a new breed of warrior, one who has become familiar today. He fought indirectly, servicing a machine that killed and destroyed at a distance.

But moving guns, Knox knew, depended on the efforts of oxen, horses, and strong men. It depended on muscle. With the guns past the lake, Knox wrote to Washington predicting that he would arrive at Cambridge by New Year and "present your Excellency with a noble train of artillery." To Lucy he wrote proudly, "We shall cut no small figure through the country with our cannon."[5]

A lack of snow stopped the train in its tracks. Knox pushed on to Albany by himself to arrange for more draft animals and teamsters. He needed cold weather to harden the ice on the Hudson River so that his men could safely cross it with the artillery. He was elated when the temperature dropped on Christmas Eve. By morning, three feet of snow covered the ground. On January 6, the guns were in Albany. He wasn't sure the ice would hold, but Knox, anxious to get the guns to Boston, decided to risk crossing the river.

One gun, then another and another made the perilous crossing. A crowd cheered each success. Then a dangerous cracking sound and a huge 18-pounder plunged through the ice. Townspeople spontaneously pitched in to help drag the gun back to the surface. Knox thanked them by naming the piece the *Albany*.

He galloped ahead to scout the road and make arrangements for the caravan. They would wind through eastern New York before entering the Berkshire Mountains and crossing the entire state of Massachusetts from west to east. In addition to presenting a formidable obstacle, the mountains appeared to the untraveled Knox as towering heights. The amazing view prompted him to write that from these peaks he could "have almost seen all the kingdoms of the earth."[6]

Moving the artillery through these mountains, where roads were rudimentary or nonexistent, strained his resources. Eight horses were sometimes needed to drag the largest guns. On descents, the teamsters tied check lines and spread brush and chains under the sleds' runners to control the weight. Men and animals quickly became exhausted. The disheartened teamsters threatened to quit. Knox engaged in "three hours of persuasion," appealing to their patriotism to convince them to continue.

The "precious convoy" wound through mountain passes and thick forests. Sometimes the men traveled forty miles without seeing a house. When they reached Westfield, Massachusetts, twelve-year-old John Becker, the son of one of the teamsters, noted, "Our armament here was a great curiosity. We found that very few, even among the oldest inhabitants, had ever seen a cannon." Knox fired a 24-pounder to impress the locals.[7]

————•—————

"I am in daily expectation of colonel Knox's arrival," Washington wrote in January 1776. The artillery Knox was bringing "is much needed." The commander himself was in need of good news. A paltry number of new troops were signing up to replace the militiamen whose enlistments were expiring. His army remained dangerously vulnerable to a British attack. Word had just reached him through General Schuyler of "a severe check" in the north. The assault on Quebec had failed. Many of the soldiers were in captivity. General Montgomery was dead.

Then Knox arrived at Cambridge to report that his cargo was making good time along the Boston post road. The worst of the long trip was over. He had demonstrated exactly the combination of ingenuity and persistence that Washington knew would be needed to accomplish extraordinary things and to win the war.

Knox learned that Congress had appointed him colonel and put him in charge of the Continental Army's 635 artillerymen and of all its heavy guns, gunpowder, and ammunition. He had soared into the lofty circle of his Excellency's confidants, and on February 1, he and Lucy dined with Washington and his wife. The expectant mother's manners, wit, and enthusiasm endeared her to Martha.

"My charmer," Knox called his wife.

Over in Boston, Lucy's family waited with other loyalists for life to return to normal. Her sister Sally was acting in a cheery romance, *Maid of the Oaks*, written by the debonair British general John Burgoyne and staged to keep up the loyalists' morale in the dismal, besieged city.

The arrival of the guns was a boon for Washington. But how to use them? This was no ordinary siege. Geography favored the British, who were isolated on two virtual islands and in possession of a supply line by sea. Ordinary siegecraft—extending trenches and moving guns steadily closer—could not force them out.

Mounting guns on Dorchester Heights, just south of the city, held intriguing possibilities, but Washington suspected that General Howe had left the position unoccupied as a lure. If the Americans took the bait, Dorchester might become the anvil against which the British hammer would crush the Continental Army. His Excellency kept jumping up and down on the bay ice to see if it could hold assault troops.

What to do? Washington had the machines to deliver a blow against the enemy. But with gunpowder still scarce, he lacked the fuel to operate them. Nevertheless, he preferred to attack. By February, the bay ice was firm. "A stroke well-aimed at this critical juncture might put a final end to the war," Washington told his officers on February 16.[8] He raised the possibility of a night attack led by troops on ice skates. Nathanael Greene calculated that any attack "would be horrible if it succeeded and still more horrible if it failed." The council voted to wait for promised troops and more powder. "Powder!" cried Israel Putnam, the Connecticut veteran and oldest of the generals. "Ye gods, give us powder!"[9]

Two days later, word arrived that 3,000 pounds of gunpowder from Connecticut was on its way. Now Washington's focus had pivoted to Dorchester Heights. General Howe had already declared he would not tolerate an American occupation of that strategic neck. Perhaps the lure could work both ways. If the rebels could put guns on the heights and provoke the British commander, they might defeat his forces in a decisive battle.

Knox gave his opinion. With cannon on the high ground at Dorchester, his gunners could bring the British lines on Boston Neck under fire. They could even hit Long Wharf, two miles away, and harass British ships supplying the troops. The problem was how to shield the guns and gunners from return fire, especially from British warships, or from an assault by enemy troops. To dig trenches and pile breastworks was not feasible—the ground was frozen solid.

The solution came from a book. Lieutenant Colonel Rufus Putnam, a one-time millwright and cousin of Israel Putnam, had been reading *Field Engineer*, a British military manual. He came across the notion of the "chandelier," a heavy wooden frame that could be prepared in advance for easy reassembly. The men could stuff the frame with giant baskets called gabbions and load those with stones and earth to block enemy fire. Knox thought the prefabricated fortifications might work, but only if they could be erected quickly, before the British guns had a chance to sweep the hilltop.

Now experienced at moving heavy artillery, Knox busied himself preparing to transport a portion of his armament onto the heights. His men wrangled the rest of the cannon into emplacements in Roxbury to the south of Boston and Cobble Hill to the north. He distributed ammunition and made sure his men were prepared to service their machines.

This was to be Washington's first great gamble. If it failed, the shaky Continental Army could be crushed, the guns lost, the rebellion extinguished. Even civilians sensed an approaching climax. "Something terrible it will be," Abigail Adams wrote to her husband, John, who was attending to the business of Congress in Philadelphia. "It has been said 'tomorrow' and 'tomorrow' for this month, but when the dreadful tomorrow will be, I know not."[10]

On March 2, tomorrow arrived. As night descended, Knox gave orders to his gunners. They put smoldering matches to the touch holes of their cannon.

Adams went to a knoll near her home in Braintree, ten miles from Boston. She heard "the amazing roar of cannon," a sound she described as "one of the grandest in nature." The concussions plowed the night, the hills echoed in applause. Inside the city, a British colonel wrote, "At nine o'clock . . . they began a pretty hot cannonade and bombardment." Shells "tore several houses to pieces."[11]

Cannonballs could break through stone and reduce wooden structures to explosions of splinters. Knox's short-barreled, high-angled mortars lobbed hollow cast-iron "shells" filled with gunpowder. He taught his gunners to fashion a fuse that delayed the explosion. When the shell came near the enemy, the vessel burst with a spray of lethal fragments and an eruption of flame capable of setting a building on fire.

The mistakes of inexperienced gunners and the fragile condition of some of the Ticonderoga barrels contributed to the explosion of three mortars during the barrage. When a barrel failed, the gun itself became a bomb, blasting metal and flames that lacerated the crew.

The British were astonished at the bombardment—the rebels had always been parsimonious in their expenditure of powder, and General Howe knew nothing of Knox's cavalcade. His own guns in Boston, on Bunker Hill, and on ships fired back. The night sky churned. A British officer wrote, "Their shells were thrown in an excellent direction. . . . Our lines were raked from the new battery they had made and tho' we returned shot and shell, I am very, very sorry to say with not quite so much judgment."[12] It was a high compliment to Knox and his novice gunners.

For the citizens cowering in cellars the bombardment was not spectacle but terror: the helpless, maddening wait for diabolical chance to determine life or death. An American observer noted that "the cries of poor women and children frequently reached our ears." Knox was raining destruction on the landscape of his own boyhood. He knew the buildings, the streets, the homes, the people. A shell that exploded with a sound "like a window frame being smashed" might kill a friend or a teacher. Might set fire to his own shop. Might drop onto members of Lucy's family.

Yet he hurried to fulfill his duty. The guns thumped on until dawn. They commenced again the next evening. The two nights of sound and fury were only a prelude to the bombardment of March 4, when the Americans began their seizure of Dorchester Heights. Abigail Adams was kept awake by "the rattling of the windows, the jar of the house." Under the cover of the continuous roar, American general John Thomas, a doctor from Plymouth, marched three thousand men out Dorchester Neck and onto the high ground. A covering force of eight hundred riflemen took positions along the Dorchester shore. The others began a frenzy of work.

For once, everything favored the rebels. The night was mild and bright under a full moon. A low mist obscured the view from Boston. An easterly wind carried the sound of the bustle and hammering away from the city. The men worked feverishly. They put up the wooden frames and picked out frozen dirt on the heights to fill the gabbions. Knox directed the gunners and teamsters who, with the help of four hundred oxen, hauled the big guns up the hills.

Around ten o'clock, word reached a British general that "rebels were at work on Dorchester Heights." Occupied with the intense bombardment, he chose to ignore the intelligence, perhaps imagining he would have time to deal with the matter the next day.

At three in the morning, three thousand fresh troops relieved the exhausted work crews. General Washington rode among the men, encouraging them. He noted that March 5 was the sixth anniversary of the Massacre that Knox had witnessed on the streets of Boston. "Avenge the death of your brethren," he urged.

In return, an observer noted, his men "manifest their joy, and express a warm desire for the approach of the enemy."[13] By dawn, twenty cannon were in place on the heights, shielded by the prefabricated forts.

All this activity was preparation for the colossal battle that Washington and his officers were convinced would come that very day. Howe had no choice but to challenge the rebels' possession of Dorchester, as he had challenged their occupation of Bunker Hill nine months earlier. But during those months, Washington had shaped the men whom Charles Lee had called "the worst of all creatures" into the Continental Army.

When the British attacked, Washington was prepared to launch an immediate counterstrike. He positioned Generals Greene, Putnam, and Sullivan at the head of four thousand men on the north shore of the bay, ready to assault the city the moment Howe made a move toward Dorchester. The ice gone, they would have to attack from small boats. All knew that an amphibious landing against regular troops manning a fortified position would be a bloody affair.

Before the operation got under way, Washington had emphasized its serious nature, insisting that each man "should prepare his mind, as well as everything necessary for it. It is a noble cause we are engaged in." Any man who would "skulk, hide himself, or retreat from the enemy," he declared, would be "*instantly shot down.*"[14] In the hospitals, workers prepared thousands of bandages and beds for the anticipated casualties. A call went out for nurses to tend the wounded.

When dawn broke, the British soldiers in Boston saw the black mouths of guns gaping at them from forts that had not been there the night before. They could not believe their eyes. The structures had been put up "with an expedition equal to that of the genie belonging to Aladdin's wonderful lamp."

"My God," Howe was said to have marveled, "these fellows have done more work in one night than I could make my army do in three months."[15]

He faced a dilemma. If he allowed the rebel move to stand, it would leave him with "the necessity either of exposing the army to the greatest distresses by remaining in Boston, or of withdrawing from it under such straitened circumstances."[16]

Against the advice of many of his officers, the man who had led the storming of Bunker Hill chose to attack. The climactic battle that Washington had hoped for was on. British captain Archibald Robertson thought it "the most serious step ever an army of this strength in such a situation took." He was sure "the fate of America" was at stake.

The attack had to come quickly. The rebels were still working, their position on the heights growing stronger by the hour. The Americans, for their part, eagerly awaited the action. As at Bunker Hill, it was the British who would have to march uphill into fire. This time, a serious array of artillery would await them. "We were in high spirits," one of the defenders noted, "well prepared to receive the threatened attack."[17]

The British troops remembered the June slaughter. As they marched to the wharfs to board the transports that would carry them against Dorchester, they appeared "pale and dejected."

"The hills and elevations in this vicinity are covered with spectators to witness deeds of horror in the expected conflict," one observer noted.[18] A full-scale battle was the event of a lifetime, not to be missed.

Then circumstances took over. The fine weather changed abruptly. A southeast wind kicked up in the faces of the British vessels. It turned into a fierce storm, "driving the ships foul of each other, and from their anchors in utter confusion."

No landing was possible in such weather. The gale blew all night, pelting the defenders and tossing the miserable attackers around the harbor. The tempest, Howe wrote later, "gave the enemy time to improve their works." He called off the attack. Boston was lost.

As a teenager, Henry Knox had watched British troops march into Boston eight years earlier. Now, the frustrating, fruitless occupation ended quite suddenly. Howe sent a message under a flag of truce saying that if his men were not fired upon while leaving, he would not burn the town. Washington agreed. The victory gave the rebels "unspeakable satisfaction," their first real thrill of the war.

The redcoats looted with abandon while they waited for sufficient ships to gather in the harbor. Many loyalists chose to endure exile rather than remain under the rebels. Few had ever lived anywhere but Boston, and they did not know where they were headed now. They would have to leave almost everything behind. John Lovell, who had taught young Henry Knox at the Boston Latin School, joined the exiles. So did Lucy's mother, Hannah Flucker. Her father had departed earlier. As she had feared, Lucy would never see her family again. One gentleman reported that passengers on the transports were "obliged to pig together on the floor" in steerage.[19] Hundreds of ships carried 9,000 British soldiers and their families and 1,100 loyalists out of Boston.

On March 17, a boy ran across the isthmus of Boston Neck with the news. The last of the redcoats were gone. Americans crept up to the

British lines on Charlestown peninsula, only to discover "the Centinels to be images dressed in the Soldiers Habit." The congenial inscription on the mannequins read, "Welcome Brother Jonathan," using the familiar nickname for a New Englander.[20]

"The more I think of [it], the more amazed I am," wrote Abigail Adams, who had expected that regaining Boston would cost the lives of many of her countrymen. John Hancock praised Washington for forging "an undisciplined band of husband men" into soldiers. Even the modest Washington could not help crowing in private, "No man perhaps since the first institution of armies ever commanded one under more difficult circumstances than I have done."[21] Harvard awarded an honorary degree to the man who had never attended college.

Washington had won his first victory as commander since the fifteen-minute battle of Jumonville Glen almost twenty-two years earlier. That he had prevailed through maneuver, imagination, and inspired leadership rather than bloody fighting made the success even more commendable. That this result had emerged from the desperate predicament of the winter months seemed miraculous.

Henry Knox, who had just lived through his first real military action, basked in glory. With ingenuity, perseverance, and muscle, he had defeated an enemy even more formidable than the British army: the rugged mountains and bad roads of inland America. When Washington rode victorious into Boston, the young gunner was at his side. He would remain there until the war's end.

The liberation of Boston was a crucial juncture in a conflict that would see many turning points. But the fighting was far from over. Howe took his army to Halifax to regroup. Everyone knew that the British were going to hit back. They assumed that the blow would be a massive one and they guessed exactly where it would fall.

Washington wrote to his brother Jack, "We expect a very bloody Summer of it at New York."[22]

SIX

SUDDEN AND VIOLENT

1776

"Whoever commands the Sea must command the town," Major General Charles Lee wrote Washington from New York.[1] The British commanded the sea—the guns of the warship *Asia* already glowered at the city from the harbor. With more ships, the enemy could pulverize defenses and land troops at will. "Should they get that town and Command of the North River," Washington worried, "they can Stop the intercourse between the Northern & Southern Colonies upon which depends the Safety of America."[2]

Last autumn's Canada expedition had aimed to secure the northern end of the critical Hudson-Champlain corridor. The prospects of victory there were now dashed. New York City, Washington declared, was "the place that we must use every endeavor to keep from them." To assess the situation, he sent Lee, whom he valued as "the first officer in Military knowledge and experience we have in the whole army."[3]

A commercial hub ever since the Dutch merchant Peter Minuit established a trading post there for the West India Company in 1626, New York City occupied a cramped square mile at the southern tip of Manhattan Island. The spindle-shanked General Lee recognized the dilemma: New York must be held; New York could not be held. The loss of the colonies' second largest city and major commercial port would strike the rebellion a critical blow; defending an island without naval superiority was futile. The best he could advise was to erect fortifications that would make it "expensive" for the British to prevail. He quickly laid out plans for gun batteries on the East River and the Hudson, also known as the North River. Barricades would block the ends of the streets and forts would guard key locations around Manhattan and adjacent Long Island.

The work had to be done quickly. Spring was coming and British regulars were certainly on the way from England. They would be accompanied, rumor had it, by legions of professional soldiers hired from the principalities of King George's relatives in Germany.

Just as Lee began to organize work parties, he discovered that General Henry Clinton had left Boston and was headed toward the southern colonies, intent on establishing a base of operations in Virginia or the Carolinas. Three thousand additional troops from Ireland commanded by Lord Cornwallis would join him. Together, they would open a new front in a poorly defended territory that was rife with loyalists.

Congress turned frantically to General Lee. "We want you at N. York—We want you at Cambridge—We want you in Virginia," John Adams wrote.[4] With work under way in New York, the South took precedence. Lee rode off to shore up the defenses of cities there. He handed over command to an inexperienced local officer who was almost as eccentric as Lee himself.

———————

William Alexander had grown up in New York. His father, a Scottish immigrant, had prospered as a lawyer and investor. His Dutch mother, an astute businesswoman, had amassed her own fortune. The doting parents had given young Billie a first-rate education. His aptitude for science impressed his teachers. His marriage to Sarah Livingston cemented his connection to one of New York's most influential clans—Sarah's cousin Janet was the widow of the martyred Richard Montgomery.

The French and Indian War broke out when Alexander was in his late twenties. He served briefly as secretary to a family friend, William Shirley, the provincial commander who replaced General Braddock. Having botched the early phase of the war, Shirley was called to London to explain himself. Alexander decided to go along in order to defend his mentor and to garner payment for some of his own cash outlays.

He had planned to visit England for a few months. His stay stretched to five years. The reason: William Alexander had fallen in love with British aristocracy. He could not get enough of lords and ladies, of elegant conversation, country estates, and riding after hares and hounds. He lived on fatted geese and fortified wine. He came to know bluebloods like Lord Shelburne, the Duke of Argyle, and Lord Bute, who would become prime minister under George III. Styling himself an expert in colonial affairs, he murmured advice into the ears of the ruling class.

Then one day it dawned on him that he was just as worthy as the worthies. A bit of digging in the archives would surely prove his connection to that distant Alexander whom King James I had dubbed the Earl of Stirling in Shakespeare's day. The title would give him a claim on the American lands the king had promised to the bygone earl: ten million acres across Canada, Maine, and Long Island, enough to support a lavish life. One of his friends laughed when Alexander revealed his plan, thinking it a joke.

It was no joke. In Edinburgh, Alexander and a team of solicitors strained their eyes over ancient documents. Soon they compiled a tangled family tree that, yes, did seem to indicate that the young American was in line for the title. The Scottish Lords approved, but British peers, whose nod was needed to pursue the land claim, scoffed.

No matter. Homesick at last, Alexander returned to America, where he would ever after remain Lord Stirling. His wife was Lady Sarah, his daughters Lady Mary and Lady Kitty. They rode around in the most sumptuous, the most vulgar coach on the continent. In Basking Ridge, New Jersey, thirty-five miles west of New York, the new lord built himself an opulent country home. Famous for his hospitality, Lord Stirling tippled and dined as became a lord. He pursued his interest in science, publishing a paper on his observation of a transit of Venus across the sun. His spending so far outpaced his income that his lordship soon found himself bankrupt. He sponsored a lottery to raise money. It failed. Sheriffs began to sell his household possessions at auction. Then came the Revolution.

A debauched, forty-nine-year-old patrician born to privilege, a self-styled nobleman, Lord Stirling would seem to be the archetype of the American Tory, steadfast in his loyalty to the Crown. Instead, he wholeheartedly embraced the cause of the rebels. Some accused him of using the rebellion to slip out from under his debts, but any such relief could hardly be worth the enormous risk he ran in siding with treason. His motives were sincere—Lord Stirling, in spite of his fascination with aristocracy, was a child of the Enlightenment.

He energetically recruited New Jersey militiamen, boosting the cause in that wavering colony. In spite of his scanty military experience, he soon found himself in command of the entire body of troops raised there. Congress commended his "alertness, activity, and good conduct" after he led a raid on a British cargo ship in the harbor. The representatives made him a brigadier general in the Continental Army.

Stirling certainly looked the part. Red-faced and bald, he was "a man of noble presence," who presented "the most martial Appearance of any general in the service."[5] General Lee summoned Stirling and his regiments to New York to help prepare the city's defenses. Lee considered him "a great acquisition" and on departing gave him command of the single most critical location in America.

Lord Stirling followed General Lee's defensive plan to the letter. He enlisted a thousand citizens to help, including members of the patriotic gentry, who toiled so hard with their delicate hands that "the blood rushed out of their fingers."[6] By March 20, Stirling, who had described himself as a "young beginner" when he was appointed, could report that the effort was hurtling ahead. Ever optimistic, he thought it would be an "easy summer's work" to secure the whole continent. He did not yet know that General Howe, now in the process of abandoning Boston, was determined to take New York.

———————

George Washington arrived in the city in late April 1776. Looking over the situation, he wrote, "The plan of defence formed by General Lee is, from what little I know of the place, a very judicious one."[7]

Command at New York had passed from Lord Stirling to Israel Putnam, one of the original major generals in the Continental Army. Putnam, whom a historian described as looking like a "cherubic bulldog," wore the aura of a folk hero.[8] As a young man, he had crawled into a cave to kill a dangerous wolf. He had fallen prisoner to Indians who nearly roasted him alive. During the French war, Putnam had held General Howe's dying older brother George in his arms after the fighting near Fort Ticonderoga. Later, Putnam had survived a hurricane and a shipwreck in Havana.

The fifty-eight-year-old was still game. He declared martial law in New York and imposed a curfew. On his own initiative, he led a thousand militiamen to occupy Governor's Island, at the mouth of the East River, a thrilling reprise of his seizure of Bunker Hill. When Washington arrived, Putnam became his second in command. The experienced Horatio Gates, another former British officer who had enlisted in the patriot cause, served as adjutant general, the army's chief administrative officer.

Washington commanded nearly ten thousand men. To New Yorkers, the soldiers were rustics. "They have all the simplicity of ploughmen," an urbanite observed. For their part, the New England militiamen were awestruck: "This city York exceeds all places that ever I saw," one said.[9]

Across the East River, the western end of Long Island rose to form the modest highlands now known as Brooklyn Heights. Lee had seen the necessity of holding this ground and Lord Stirling had started building a four-sided citadel there. The cannon of Fort Stirling would threaten British ships in the river and protect the city from the east.

To lead the forces defending Long Island, Washington turned to another inexperienced officer. He saw something of himself in the young Nathanael Greene: a certain solidity, an attention to detail, a modest equanimity. Like Washington, Greene had missed the chance for a formal education, but also like Washington, he was a learner with a mind grounded in practicality.

On Long Island, Greene set his troops working to finish Lee's defensive plan. In addition to Stirling's citadel, he constructed a string of forts meant to seal off the area facing New York. Ditches and ramparts would join the strong points across the thick peninsula. The men erected a tangle of sharpened tree branches, a structure known as an abatis, the eighteenth-century equivalent of barbed wire. These veterans of the spade transformed Greene's book knowledge into formidable defensive works.

Greene issued strict orders for the men to perform guard duty according to the book and to avoid wounding "the Modesty of female decency" when bathing nude in local ponds. Even coarse language he deemed "unmanly and unsoldier like."[10]

Brooklyn was then a small hamlet in the agricultural expanse of Kings County. The word derived from *breuckelen*, Dutch for "broken land" or "marsh." Large areas were drowned with salt water at high tide. Living in close quarters near swamps, surrounded by flies and mosquitos, the men soon began to fall to typhoid and typhus, known collectively as "putrid fever."

"The air of the whole city seems infected," wrote an American doctor. Many complained of "the stench that rose from the American camps." Illness spread, killing some and leaving many groaning in barns and sheds. By July, every third man was laid low.

Washington's senior officers, exercising the privileges of rank, tried to maintain a semblance of civilized life. They occupied the mansions of the city's departed loyalists and visited each other's headquarters for dinner. Washington had brought Martha to New York; Knox and Greene invited their wives, as well. The pretty, vivacious Caty Greene's sharp wit and flirtatious nature at times unsettled her insecure husband. Caty enjoyed the excitement and formed a close relationship with the motherly Martha Washington, who had turned forty-five in June. Knox's daughter, named Lucy after her mother, had been born during his wife's trip from Boston in April. Henry doted on her, but he also fretted about the presence of the pink infant in an armed camp.

Knox had established his headquarters in a luxurious house abandoned by a loyalist at the southern tip of the city. He and Lucy liked to breakfast in the second-floor room where arched windows offered a panoramic view of the harbor. On Saturday, June 29, they caught sight of ships sailing into the lower bay. Ships and more ships. And still more. The white sails of forty-five warships and transports soon fluttered above the water.

The arrival of the British fleet sparked an uproar. American guns boomed warnings. Troops sprinted to their posts. Imagining Lucy and their baby in the line of fire, Knox nearly panicked. "My God, may I never experience the like feelings again!" he later wrote.[11] To disguise his fear, he scolded Lucy "like a fury" for having stayed against his advice. Now she had to go, as did most of the remaining women and children in the city.

Knox hurried to make sure his guns were ready. He thought his large cannon would intimidate any invader, but he had not imagined a force like this one. Just five ships of the line, the massive battleships of the day, wielded more guns than Knox could muster to defend the entire city. The naval guns would be handled by experts; Knox had to entrust his pieces to inexperienced infantrymen drafted from the ranks. One neophyte subordinate was a twenty-one-year-old Kings College student named Alexander Hamilton, whom Knox assigned to the Battery at the south end of the island.

Within four days, 130 ships had anchored in the outer harbor, many of them troop transports. The redcoats of General Howe's army were disembarking on Staten Island without opposition—the island's militia had collectively gone over to the enemy. The British set up camp and waited for yet more troops. Rather than let the American rebellion smolder, King George's ministers had decided to extinguish it with unanswerable power.

Washington, with Lee's warning about command of the sea echoing in his mind, was dramatic in summing up what was at stake. "The fate of unborn millions," he wrote, "will now depend, under God, on the courage and conduct of this army."

Then urgent news arrived at New York from Philadelphia. In a letter, John Hancock, the president of Congress, was understated: "That our affairs may take a more favorable turn, the Congress have judged it necessary to dissolve the connection between Great Britain and the American colonies."[12] It was the monumental step that Washington, Knox, and other military men had been urging for months. On July 9, Washington had the Declaration of Independence read to all his men.

An excited John Adams declared, "We are in the very midst of a revolution, the most complete, unexpected and remarkable of any in the history of nations."[13] In New York City, jubilant rebels pulled down the

4,000-pound gilded lead statue of the king, hacked off his majesty's head, and hauled away the metal to make musket balls.

A few days later, Knox wrote to Lucy, who was living in yet another temporary home in Connecticut, "I thank Heaven you were not here yesterday." On a lovely summer afternoon, two British warships, the *Rose* and the *Phoenix*, accompanied by a schooner and two tenders, broke away from the fleet and headed north. They entered the Hudson River, firing at American defenses as they went. They even unloosed a broadside into the city itself, sending civilians screaming in terror.

Knox's artillery corps fired two hundred cannon rounds without seriously damaging the vessels. The captain of the *Rose* and his officers sipped claret on the quarterdeck as the ships skimmed unscathed past the guns of Fort Washington, the Americans' last line of defense at the north end of Manhattan. By the end of the day, the British ships were anchored thirty miles above the city, ready to cut waterborne supplies and to incite local Tories.

The foray dismayed and embarrassed Henry Knox. Some of his men had been drunk, more were incompetent. They were too "impetuous" around the guns, Knox observed. Their carelessness had caused several cannon, including two of Alexander Hamilton's, to explode, killing six men.

If two ships could skim past the American gauntlet, so could the entire fleet. The British demonstration had suddenly drained New York City of its military value. The city had become a trap. If the British army were to secure a beachhead to the north, Washington's own force, arrayed on two islands, would be cut off. His tentative optimism evaporated. Militarily, the best bet was to abandon the city, but Congress would not allow him to cede it without a fight.

Another group of warships now dropped anchor in the lower bay. They included the *Eagle*, the sixty-four-gun flagship of Admiral Richard Howe. Known as "Black Dick" because of his swarthy complexion, he was the dour older brother of General William Howe. He had come to America not only as naval commander but also as peace commissioner. The British ministers, blanching at the potential cost of another prolonged war, were willing to make concessions. A negotiated settlement would be a feather in the caps of the Howe brothers. Such a course seemed eminently practical even after Howe heard about the Declaration of Independence. That measure, said one of his aides, simply pointed up "the villainy and the madness of these deluded people."[14]

Black Dick, fifty years old and a veteran of two wars, sent over his adjutant with a letter addressed to "Mr. Washington, Esq., etc. etc., etc."

Washington, whom John Adams would call one of the great actors of the age, was in his element. His bearing and gravity could not fail to impress. The general insisted on being referred to by his appropriate title. The *et ceteras*, the adjutant declared, implied everything. "Or anything," Washington rejoined, "or nothing."

Howe was authorized to pardon the rebels' treason. Washington pointed out that "those who have committed no fault want no pardon." If the admiral wanted to negotiate, he should apply to Congress, which spoke for the new nation. Knox attended the meeting and wrote that he "lamented exceedingly the absence of my Lucy" to enjoy this historic repartee. The British officer "appeared awe-struck, as if he was before something supernatural. Indeed, I don't wonder at it. He was before a very great man."[15]

The British military build-up around New York continued. Arriving troops moved into well-ordered camps on Staten Island and enjoyed the ripening melons and peaches. They raped local women—a young officer named Lord Rawdon complained that the wenches didn't tolerate the assaults "with the proper resignation," resulting in "most entertaining courts-martial."[16]

On August 1, General Henry Clinton arrived with nine more warships, thirty-five transports, and three thousand veteran troops. He and Lord Cornwallis had attempted to capture the important southern port at Charleston. American general Charles Lee had arrived just before the British attack to help the citizens of Charleston prepare their defenses. Patriot guns had prevented the enemy from gaining the harbor. Unsuccessful in their southern adventure, a chastened Clinton and Cornwallis joined the main British army for the attempt against a much more important prize.

They were followed by yet another fleet of ships carrying Hessian soldiers. The Germans had been thirteen weeks at sea and were glad to step onto dry land. Now General Howe had assembled his army: thirty-two thousand trained and disciplined soldiers, along with four hundred warships and transports to move them at will. "A Force so formidable would make the first Power in Europe tremble," was how the commander of a British escort frigate described it.[17]

To counter this host, Washington commanded twenty-eight thousand men in New York, only twenty thousand of them fit for duty. Many of the reinforcements who had streamed in during the summer were militiamen, eager but inexperienced. "Let their Force be what it will," General Howe declared, "it can never stand against the veteran Troops commanded by the best Officers in Europe."[18]

Washington struggled to guess Howe's intentions. Why the maddening delay? Why did he not attack? There was, he wrote, "something exceedingly mysterious in the conduct of the enemy." Tedious guard duty and continual false alarms abraded the nerves of Washington's men and officers.

Then a grievous misfortune. The disease that had depleted Washington's force struck Nathanael Greene, who had spent the summer preparing the fortifications on Long Island. On August 15, he reported being "confined to my Bed with a raging fever." Five days later he was "sick nearly to death."

A reluctant Washington replaced Greene with General John Sullivan. The former New Hampshire lawyer had been one of the first to respond to the crisis at Boston. Enthusiasm and political connections had won him high rank in the army. Earlier in the summer, the intense, dark-haired Irishman had led troops north to reinforce the crumbling American army in Canada, the remnants of the invasion led by Richard Montgomery and Benedict Arnold. Sullivan had blindly sent his men against a superior British force, then managed a chaotic retreat. Replaced by Horatio Gates, he had rushed to Philadelphia in a fit of anger to resign his commission. His friends convinced him to stay in the service.

Asked his opinion, Washington described Sullivan as "active, spirited, and Zealously attach'd to the Cause." But, he said, Sullivan "has his wants, and he has his foibles. The latter are manifested in a little tincture of vanity, and in an over-desire of being popular."[19] Nevertheless, Sullivan's political allies in Congress had promoted the ambitious soldier to major general. He lacked Greene's innate judgment, as well as his familiarity with the geography of Long Island.

Two days later, on August 22, drums in the American camp beat "to arms." The sound, after four months of waiting, sent an electric charge through the men. British transports were sailing across the placid waters of the bay to deposit eight thousand troops on the shore of Long Island. The redcoats quickly shoved back the rebel riflemen screening the shore. Now hidden from American eyes, boatmen ferried another fifteen thousand troops, the bulk of Howe's army, across the bay. The British lined up in an eight-mile arc along the plains of southern Kings County.

Washington, still in New York, was told about the landing of the advanced guard. He decided it was a trick. Howe was trying to get him to commit his forces to Long Island before striking the main blow elsewhere, probably at Manhattan. The cautious Washington sent four more regiments across, but held his best troops in New York.

The next day, he went over himself to ride the ground with Sullivan. He concurred with a significant alteration that Sullivan had made in the plan laid down by Lee and implemented by Stirling and Greene. He would align three thousand men along a rocky, wooded ridge that ran ten miles obliquely in front of the fortified line. The steep, densely wooded, sixty-foot-high obstacle would serve as its own defense, preventing the passage of artillery or massed troops. Sullivan would station most of his own men at the three roads that cut through the ridge, one by the Gowanus marshes in the west and two more near the villages of Bedford and Flatbush in the center.

"The hour is fast approaching," Washington wrote that day, "on which the honor and success of this army, and the safety of our bleeding country depend."[20] Trepidation suddenly swarmed Washington's mind. Doubting the judgment of the vain and callow Sullivan, he abruptly named Israel Putnam overall commander on Long Island. Sullivan would assume responsibility only for the soldiers on the ridge; Putnam would direct the defense from inside the Americans' fortifications.

For the second time that summer, the prickly John Sullivan saw himself superseded. For the second time that week, the defenders of Long Island came under a new commander. Yet Sullivan's inexperience was a trait shared by all officers, including Washington. Directing a skirmish was one thing. Moving masses of troops over a wide area was a far more intricate matter. "The limited and contracted knowledge which any of us have in Military Matters," Washington admitted, "stands in very little Stead." They were, in fact, amateurs at war. Their resources were "some knowledge of Men and Books" and an elusive quality that Washington called "enterprizing genius."[21]

That same day, 4,300 Hessians marched off transports to take up positions on Long Island opposite the center of the American line. Howe's total force on the island had reached twenty thousand men.

On Sunday, August 25, Washington sent six more regiments to Long Island. He had divided his force almost in half in the face of a superior enemy, something all military textbooks condemned. Convinced the enemy was on "the point of striking the long expected blow," he crossed to Long Island once again to survey the American position. With Putnam and Sullivan, he rode along the ridge that now formed the first line of defense. "At all hazards prevent the Enemy's passing the Wood and approaching your Works," he told Putnam.[22] He warned that when the attack came, it was likely to be "sudden and violent."

———————————

Sullivan commanded the center of the ridge in person. He stationed a force of riflemen to his left and assigned Lord Stirling to guard his right.

On the night of August 26, Stirling was sleeping in his camp behind the line. His troops were arrayed across the Gowanus Road at the western end of the American front. Two of the best units in the Continental Army manned this important position. The First Delaware Regiment, under Colonel John Haslet, was the largest battalion in the army, eight hundred men outfitted in identical blue coats with white waistcoats. Colonel William Smallwood had recruited his First Maryland soldiers from some of the best families in Baltimore. The men of both units carried good English muskets fitted with bayonets. Unfortunately, the two colonels had been detained in the city that night to serve on a court-martial.

At midnight, a smattering of musket fire broke out—some British scouts had raided a watermelon patch near the Red Lion Inn just beyond the pass. Then the night settled into deep quiet. A couple of hours later, sentries on the Gowanus Road, their eyes tired from staring into darkness, spotted three hundred British regulars marching toward them like a bad dream. The guards ran for it. Awakened inside the fortifications, Putnam rode out to Lord Stirling's camp and ordered him to meet whatever enemy force was advancing toward his position and to "repulse them."

Stirling roused his young men at three in the morning, the hour of nightmare. Through keen blackness, with no experience of combat, they marched to meet the enemy. If this was to be the "grand Push," it would be their first battle, the first battle fought by soldiers of the newly independent United States, and the first time that Americans faced the enemy without stone walls or breastworks for protection.

Stirling met Colonel Samuel Atlee and his Pennsylvania musket regiment retreating along the Gowanus Road. It was more than a skirmish, Atlee told him. They faced a large body of troops commanded by General James Grant, a fat Scotsman who had earlier bragged about the ease with which he would whip the Americans. His men were advancing in full force. "Indeed I saw their front between us and the Red Lion," Stirling noted. He quickly issued orders.[23]

"The enemy advanced towards us," wrote Major Mordechai Gist, the ranking officer with the Maryland battalion, "upon which Lord Stirling, who commanded, drew up in a line and offered them battle in true English taste."[24] Stirling posted his men in formal battle array and ordered them to face the enemy in the open. This time, it was the British who took cover behind trees.

Lightning from field guns and muskets flashed in the darkness. Quiet became din. The battlefield took on the jagged confusion of a dream. Rather than rush the American line, the British "began a heavy fire from their cannon and mortars," wrote Gist, "for both the Balls and Shells flew very fast, now and then taking off a head." For men who had never endured organized violence, the sudden decapitation of a comrade was a rude introduction to the hallucinatory world of combat. "Our men," Gist added, "stood it amazingly well."

They stood it and stood it. The concussions of British artillery and the zinging musketballs stripped the world of all safety. The deafening percussion went on hour after hour.

All of New York came awake to the desperate struggle that had erupted. As dawn brightened the eastern sky, Stirling rode up and down his lines, adjusting, encouraging. General Washington came over from New York—he could do little but observe from Cobble Hill, a high point

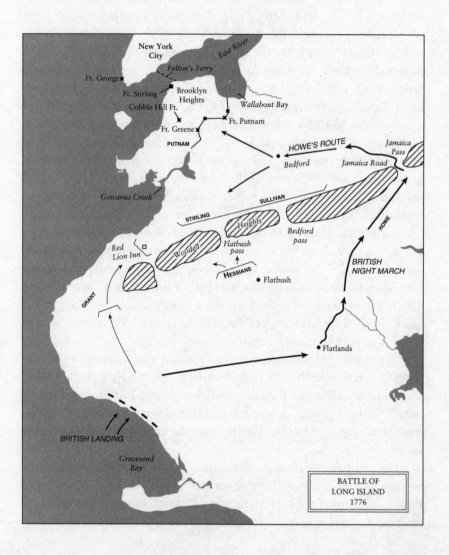

BATTLE OF
LONG ISLAND
1776

inside the American fortifications. At nine o'clock, amid the din, Stirling's ears picked out the firing of a single cannon. Could it be? Yes, the boom sounded a second time—from behind him. What could it mean?

An instant later—for Stirling, for Sullivan and Putnam, for Washington and the whole Continental Army—the veil dropped. The attack against Stirling was a diversion. While Grant's cannon banged away at the American right, General Howe had marched his army through the darkness to a distant pass where the Jamaica Road went around the end of the American line. The pass, Howe noted, had, through "unaccountable negligence," been left undefended. His men captured the five mounted sentinels stationed there and slipped around to the north of Sullivan's men. They marched down the length of road that led straight toward the main American fortifications.

Now the whole tenor of the battle changed. The Hessians, who had been exchanging a sporadic fire with Sullivan's men in the center, formed for an attack in earnest. The green-jacketed jaegers, German hunters, scrambled through the woods, firing with short-barreled rifles. The huge, brass-helmeted grenadiers came tromping forward, their drums pounding an angry tattoo. The Americans, accustomed to clean-shaven faces, had never seen the like of the fierce black mustaches the men wore. These fairytale giants from the German woods, smelling blood, thrust their eighteen-inch bayonets into any American flesh that came within reach. They had no mercy.

Caught in a vice between the Hessians in front and Howe's infantry to their rear, Sullivan's men threw down their muskets and sprinted to gain the relative safety of the fortified lines two miles away. Fear gave their feet wings. "The rebels abandoned every Spot as fast, I should say faster, than the King's Troops advanced upon them," General Howe's secretary noted.[25]

Sullivan did what he could, which was nothing. "The last I heard of him," one of his officers reported, "he was in a corn Field close by our Lines with a Pistol in each Hand." He was captured by three Hessians.[26]

The American outer line collapsed. Lord Stirling, with his Maryland and Delaware regiments, stood alone outside the fortifications. They now faced the all-out attack of Grant's brigade at their front, the Hessians sweeping down the ridge from the east, and General Cornwallis leading the British advance guard against their rear. Stirling "encouraged and animated our young soldiers with almost invincible resolution," Major Gist wrote. Watching the action beyond the American fortifications, Washington was reported to have sobbed or yelled, "Good God! What brave fellows I must this day lose." It apparently had not occurred to him or to Putnam to order these troops to retreat. Lord Stirling had been directed to repulse the enemy and he had received no further orders. He fought on.

Finally, pressed on three sides, Stirling saw that the only escape was through the marshy Gowanus Creek. He detached 250 Marylanders as a rear guard and sent the rest of his regiments toward the water. Wading through the tidal muck under fire, most of them made it across, emerging inside the American lines "looking like water rats."

Sword in hand, Lord Stirling led his Maryland contingent in a sharp counterattack to the north against Cornwallis. Flung back, the Americans regrouped and tried again. And again. They came very close to breaking through and gaining the fortified line. Their commander, a soldier noted, "fought like a wolf." [27]

After five charges, Stirling saw that it was "impossible to do more than to provide for safety." His men ran for it the best they could—all but nine were killed or captured. Stirling was cornered and forced to surrender. As his biographer duly noted, no one could have predicted that this amateur, "this overweight, rheumatic, vain, pompous, gluttonous inebriate," would shine so in battle.[28]

By noon, the largest battle that would be fought during the entire war was over. It seemed to officers on both sides that the rebellion itself was finished. The Americans had been utterly defeated. William Howe had outthought, outmaneuvered, and outfought George Washington. Nathanael Greene, who had yet to participate in a battle, lamented his absence. "Gracious God! to be confined at such a time." He suggested that the outcome "would have been otherwise," had he been in command.[29]

And the cost. Captain Joseph Jewett lingered in agony from bayonet wounds to his chest and stomach—a day and a half later he was "sensible of being near his End, often repeating that it was hard work to Die."[30] Three hundred other Americans had been killed, hundreds wounded, and hundreds, including three generals, taken prisoner.

The rest of the bedraggled force was now trapped inside their perimeter. The victorious British and Hessian troops might have instantly overrun them, but Howe followed, a historian noted, "the dictates of prudence rather than those of vigor."[31] Sure of victory, he called his men back and began a classic siege. The cocky General Grant opined that "if a good bleeding can bring those Bible-faced Yankees to their senses, the fever of independency should soon abate."[32]

———•—•———

With half his army trapped in a cul de sac, George Washington had full cause to despair. Yet he did not despair. He did not flinch. The next day, as the fine weather turned cold and rainy, Washington did the unexpected: he ordered two more regiments over to Long Island. The sight of 1,200 fresh men marching up from the Brooklyn ferry landing with drums beating did wonders for the morale of the weary army manning the fortifications.

The drenching rain developed into a cold nor'easter. The storm dampened the spirits of the soldiers, but the contrary wind kept the British navy from getting up the East River and cutting them off. American riflemen popped away at the enemy from the forts and from forward skirmish positions as often as their damp gunpowder would allow. The British began digging ditches that would soon bring their cannon within range of the forts.

By the following day, some Americans stood waist-deep in water-logged trenches. Washington had not slept the past two nights. He displayed no anger, frustration, or panic. He thought out his situation and ordered men to confiscate all available boats along the Manhattan shoreline. They would be used, he let on, to bring more troops over from New Jersey.

In the late afternoon, with the boats assembling, he called a war council of his officers. Retreat was the only option. Washington was going to try to slip the army on Long Island, 9,500 men, over to New York. The move would test the nerves of every man in the force. As each regiment withdrew, the others would have to spread out to maintain the illusion of a strong defensive line. Down at the Brooklyn ferry landing, John Glover, a stocky, redheaded member of the Massachusetts "codfish aristocracy," commanded a regiment recruited from rugged Marblehead fishermen. These watermen would row the army across an estuary churning with contrary currents.

As a drizzly darkness fell and the wind died, the silent evacuation began. Orders were passed in whispers; wheels were muffled; the men were warned not even to cough. The fishermen began rowing their makeshift ferries, the gunwales inches above the water. Over and back, over and back. Washington personally supervised the loading. Henry Knox directed his gunners in hauling and ferrying across almost all his critical cannon. For those left in the lines, the danger steadily grew. If the British got wind of what was going on, the men who remained would be instantly overrun and slaughtered.

Dawn came and hundreds of men remained on the Brooklyn side. Luckily, a dense fog formed along the waterfront and continued to obscure the movement from British eyes. By seven in the morning, all the troops had escaped. None had died in the effort. Washington stepped into the last vessel to cross.

An hour later, British officers appeared on the empty Brooklyn shore. They peered across in astonishment. Washington, who bore most of the blame for the calamitous defeat three days earlier, had pulled off one of the most delicate exploits of the war. But the escape could not erase the rout. British experience had bested American enthusiasm. "In general," John Adams noted wryly, "our generals have been out-generalled."[33]

The British were exuberant. Having easily triumphed over Washington's amateur army in battle, they now had his troops on the run. Lord Cornwallis was sure that "in a short time their army will disperse and the war will be over." Soon after the battle, British general Henry Clinton, who had devised the brilliant flanking march that had beaten the Americans, wrote home to his sister. He ended with that perpetual, poignant soldier's cliché: he would, he assured her, be home by Christmas.

SEVEN

VALCOUR ISLAND

1776

On a long twilight evening in midsummer 1776, as rebels rushed to fortify New York City, the curtain dropped on the last scene of the Americans' dramatic effort to conquer Canada. Benedict Arnold sat astride his horse at the north end of the Hudson-Champlain corridor witnessing the tragedy's end. The town of St. John's, which Arnold had raided the previous May, which Richard Montgomery had captured after an exhausting siege in November, was in flames. It would soon return to British control. Sparks danced into the gathering darkness. Arnold and his aide James Wilkinson spotted the forms of enemy grenadiers emerging from the trees.

Arnold's trek through Maine, Montgomery's sacrifice, the loss of five thousand American lives, all had come to naught. A force of British regulars and hired Hessians had landed in Quebec during the spring. Their goal was to retake Canada, drive south, meet with Howe's huge army, and end the uprising. Governor Carleton had gone on the offensive. The Americans had scurried away from Quebec. "In the most helter skelter manner, we raised the siege, leaving everything," noted Dr. Isaac Senter, who had marched over the mountains with Arnold and who had removed the bullet fragment from his leg after the failed attempt to storm the city.[1]

During May, they had retreated up the St. Lawrence. The men had become, Arnold wrote, "a great rabble." Their commander, General John Thomas, died of smallpox on June 2. John Sullivan, arriving on the scene with 1,400 more men, took command. The New Hampshire lawyer had ordered an attack on the British at Three Rivers, ignorant of the fact that additional British reinforcements had arrived at this outpost halfway between Quebec and Montreal. Blindly crashing into the superior army, Sullivan's men were routed in confusion. Arnold, recuperating from his wound at Montreal, understood the situation. "The junction of the Canadians with the Colonies—an object which brought us to this country," he wrote, "is at an end."[2]

Sullivan reluctantly hurried south along the Richelieu River, with the enemy close on his heels. He blamed his "dispirited Army" for his inability to hold back the British. Panic gripped men and officers. On a rumor of approaching Hessians, some troops ran off and "could not be Stopt." Arnold abandoned Montreal and led his own force to join Sullivan's men at St. John's. Still limping, Arnold volunteered to command the rear guard while the patriots departed.

Now, the vanguard of the enemy army was bearing down on him. Arnold and his aide turned and spurred to the waterfront. The last of the Americans were piling into boats on the river, which flowed north from Lake Champlain, for the escape.

When Arnold had led the initial invasion northward, Canadian authorities had sneered at him as a "Horse Jockey" because he had traded the animals before the war. Although he loved a good mount, Arnold was determined to leave nothing behind for the victors. He put the barrel of his pistol to his horse's head and killed it. He ordered a reluctant Wilkinson to do the same.

The two men scrambled to a waiting bateau. Arnold, the first American officer to arrive in Quebec, "pushed the boat off with his own hands" and climbed in, the last to leave. Canada fell entirely into British hands.

Hearing that his troops had almost captured Arnold, Lord Germaine, the British secretary of state for America, regretted the failure. Arnold, he wrote, "has shown himself the most enterprising man among the rebels." George Washington was relieved. "It is not in the power of any man to command success," he advised Arnold, "but you have done more—you have deserved it."[3]

Lake Champlain, the long carrot-shaped glacial gouge with its south-pointing tap root, had for months served as the supply route for the northern army. Now it had become a potential path of invasion. Because the British could not sail their ships past the twelve-mile rapids north of St. John's, they were temporarily blocked from falling on the fleeing Americans. But it was only a matter of time before they attacked southward along the lake.

During the first year of the war, Horatio Gates had helped to guide Washington through the jungle of administrative details required to organize an army from scratch. Striving and ambition came naturally to this man who had, against the odds, climbed the British officer ranks. He wanted a command of his own, and in June 1776, with the Canadian expedition in a shambles, Congress had raised him to the rank of major general and appointed him to head the American army there. When he arrived at Fort Ticonderoga early in July, he was dismayed to discover that there was no army in Canada. He began to give orders anyway. A miffed General Schuyler, still commander of the northern department, complained. John Hancock, the president of Congress, informed Gates that he would have to serve under the patrician, who was six years his junior and far less experienced in military affairs.

The men at Ticonderoga and nearby Crown Point were not fit to resist the British force that would inevitably advance along the lake. Smallpox had prostrated thousands and was claiming thirty lives a day. "The most descriptive pen cannot describe the condition of our army," Schuyler wrote. "Sickness, disorder and discord reign."[4] An observer noted that it was "not an army but a mob."

But Benedict Arnold had a plan. The rebels already possessed four armed warships on the lake: Arnold himself had grabbed the *Enterprise* and the *Liberty* during his campaign to capture Fort Ticonderoga. Montgomery had seized the *Royal Savage* the previous fall. Workmen at Ticonderoga had just finished building the *Revenge*. If the Americans could construct and arm more ships, they might keep control of the lake and block a British invasion. Lacking north-south roads, the enemy would have to build their own fleet to protect troop transports. This naval arms race would give the rebels a chance to rally, dig in, and reinforce. It would buy time.

The logic of the plan was obvious to Schuyler and Gates. Arnold, a nautical professional, was the man to make it a reality. Now a brigadier general, he had become intimate with the sea during his days as a merchant and smuggler. The experience had also shaped his personality—a sea captain needed backbone and dauntless self-mastery to exert his will over the rough men of a ship's crew.

Schuyler had already directed the building of several gondolas. These open, flat-bottom gunboats, fifty feet long, were maneuverable, powered by both sails and long sweep oars. He had planned to use them as transports to supply the army in Canada.

In addition, Arnold wanted seventy-foot galleys, a common type of coastal warship fitted with a gun deck and a raised quarterdeck at the stern. They carried about two dozen powerful cannon that could fire a coordinated broadside. They were likewise propelled by oars as well as sails.

Arnold began to oversee the construction of the Champlain fleet at Skenesborough, a tiny village at the southern limit of the lake (now Whitehall, New York). At Ticonderoga, twenty-five miles north, workmen would fix the masts and install sails, rigging, and arms. The fleet was to be stationed at Crown Point, site of another fort on the lake ten miles north of Ticonderoga, ready to take on any British incursion.

Constructing ships at a post two hundred miles inland presented knotty problems. Sawyers worked their mills around the clock to shape the needed beams and planks. Everything else had to be scavenged, improvised, or begged for: canvas for sails, blocks and pulleys, rope, nails, oakum to caulk the hulls, and all the devices and fittings unique to the nautical trade. Arnold aptly summed up his frustration with the creaky supply system: "When you ask for a frigate, they give you a raft; ask for sailors, they give you tavern waiters; and if you want breeches, they give you a vest."[5]

The shortage of experienced workmen frustrated the project. Arnold tried to teach house carpenters nautical construction. He pleaded with Congress to offer salaries sufficient to induce skilled shipwrights to venture to the interior. Even harder to come by were sailors. Few were willing to give up the potentially lucrative privateer trade to man oars on an inland lake.

Yet Arnold thrived on adversity, on inducing others to go beyond apparent limits. He had exercised this knack for leadership during the harrowing march to Quebec. He now threw himself into a frenzy of activity, moving from Skenesborough to Ticonderoga and Crown Point, ordering, urging, instructing, browbeating, and improvising. Slowly, the work advanced. Shipwrights finally arrived. They scrounged supplies from shipyards as far away as the Hudson River port at Poughkeepsie. Half-finished warships kept splashing down the ways into the lake.

The feud between Gates and Schuyler sputtered along all summer. Gates had grudgingly accepted Schuyler as overall commander in the north, then blamed the New Yorker for the shortages. He wrote peremptory letters to his superior, demanding supplies like powder, lead, and flints. "Pray hurry it up," he added.

Arnold's personality was another lightning rod for resentment. His men loved him; fellow officers often found him abrasive and arrogant. While Arnold had held sway in Montreal, he had requisitioned supplies needed by the army, sometimes at bayonet point. These transactions came back to haunt him during a complicated court-martial in late July, during which Arnold was accused of mishandling goods from a Montreal warehouse. Forced to deal with such pettiness during this critical period, Arnold erupted and challenged the judges to meet him on the dueling ground. Gates was alarmed when the court moved to have Arnold arrested, and he ordered the tribunal dissolved.

All summer, Arnold had been itching to find out about British preparations at their own shipyards in St. John's. He decided to make his way there and see for himself. This wasn't exactly what Gates had in mind. As cautious as Arnold was impetuous, Gates had written to John Adams in the spring: "Our business is to defend the main chance, to attack only by detail, and when a precious advantage offers."[6] He reiterated the message to Benedict Arnold. "It is a defensive war we are carrying on." He advised his aggressive subordinate to keep to the south end of the lake and avoid "wanton risk." His job was to shield Ticonderoga from attack, a duty Arnold might find "monotonous."

Arnold put his own interpretation on Gates's orders. On August 24, with several of his galleys still under construction, he took the rest of the small fleet—a schooner, a sloop, one galley, and nine gondolas—and sailed north. A headwind and storm slowed his progress, but by the first week in September the fleet lurked at the very mouth of the Richelieu, barely a mile from the Canadian border.

As the forests took flame with autumn color and sailors shivered in the cramped open boats, Arnold tried to determine British strength and guess the intentions of Carleton, the smart, careful strategist who had gotten the better of him at Quebec. He sent out scouting parties to investigate the fleet the British general was assembling to protect his invasion force. He knew that the world's leading naval power would have a full cohort of shipwrights and stores of nautical supplies in the holds of their ships on the St. Lawrence. But before they started construction, they would need to haul the material around the rapids to St. John's.

While he awaited word, Arnold received a letter from his sister Hannah, who had taken over the care of his three sons after the death of his wife. He had not seen them in more than a year. She sent him several pairs of stockings, and reported that "Little Hal sends a kiss to Pa and says, 'Auntie, tell my Papa he must come home, I want to kiss him.'"[7] He also found out that George Washington's army had been crushed on Long Island and was reeling before Howe's massive invasion force.

As he awaited the British, Arnold demanded that Gates send the supplies that had been lacking all summer: ammunition, anchors, caulking irons, sail needles, pitch and tar, pine boards. Also "Rum, as much as you please; Clothing, for at least half the men in the fleet who are naked" and "One hundred seamen (no land-lubbers.)"[8]

His scouts returned to give Arnold a daunting picture of British strength: A 10,000-man invasion force, 27 war ships, 250 bateaux to carry the troops. With his own puny navy—barely 500 men on a dozen ships—he had no hope of stopping them.

Yet Arnold remained in his forward position, his men enduring the raw weather and the icy spray the lake spat at them. By October 7, three more galleys had joined the fleet. Arnold transferred from the schooner *Royal Savage* onto the galley *Congress* in order to command from a more maneuverable vessel. Always thinking, Arnold had his men erect screens of tree branches along the gunwales of the ships to protect them from small arms fire.

Any battle in the open water would favor the British, who wielded twice as many guns as the Americans. But Arnold had studied the lake thoroughly and sounded many of its bays. He now retired with his fleet to a haven twenty miles south of the Richelieu. He tucked the vessels into a channel three-quarters of a mile wide between the New York shore and Valcour Island. His ships could ride there out of sight from the lake. Shoals to the north would help protect him from a superior enemy. He planned to surprise the British armada as it passed.

On the brisk, windy morning of October 10, General Carleton's ships, directed by Commodore Thomas Pringle, finally emerged from the river onto Champlain. Carleton had spent the summer and early autumn completing two ships that were guaranteed to give him mastery of the lake. One was the man-of-war *Inflexible*, a full-rigged battleship resplendent with three masts, tiers of square sails, and rows of powerful cannon. The other, the floating gun barge *Thunderer*, carried six massive 24-pounder guns that could outshoot any armament in Arnold's fleet. Carleton, like General Howe, had assembled an overwhelming force.

His ships nudged south by a cold wind, Carleton probed carefully along the lake's clutter of islands and coves, expecting to meet with Arnold's fleet around every headland. He went to anchor for the night about fifteen miles south of the river, five miles north of the Americans' concealed ships.

The brisk north breeze continued the next morning. Snow whitened the peaks of the Adirondack Mountains to the west. Arnold called a council of war on the *Congress*. His second in command, General David

Waterbury, a Connecticut militia leader, argued that the channel behind Valcour was a trap, the British fleet too powerful to oppose. He favored a fighting retreat to the south, where they could protect the bastion at Ticonderoga as ordered. Arnold overruled him. He would fight where he was.

Arnold had an uncanny ability to inspire men. The heat of his passion kindled their own. Neither he nor his nervous subordinates could imagine the wild ferocity of an all-out naval battle, yet he made the coming fight appear to them something that no man would want to miss.

Carleton's fleet came down the lake that morning, ready for battle but still unsure where they might encounter the Americans. His flagship *Maria* led the flotilla, followed by the majestic *Inflexible* and three other warships. Weighed down by a single large cannon in the bow, each of the two dozen gunboats nodded to every wave. Bringing up the rear were more than four hundred Indians paddling thirty-foot-long war canoes. Sailors rowed longboats loaded with provisions. The squadron stretched out as the wind hurried the warships southward and the rowers strained their backs to keep up.

Carleton came even with Valcour Island. Where were the Americans? Arnold kept his fleet arrayed in an arc across the hidden channel, ready to aim all his firepower on any vessel that entered. When the first British ships were two miles past, he sent a small squadron onto the lake to incite the fleet. Spotting the American schooner *Royal Savage*, the British vessels immediately came about. Now they had to beat back into the wind to join battle, a difficult feat for the square-rigged *Inflexible*, nearly impossible for the flat-bottomed *Thunderer*. But the forty-foot-long gunboats were able to pivot nimbly and open fire.

The *Royal Savage* never regained the channel. Blasted by British guns, she lost part of her rigging and ground to a halt on a submerged rock ledge at the end of the island. She would be captured and recaptured several times during the day.

Powerful in the open water, the *Inflexible* was a helpless giant when attempting to thread a narrow channel. The more maneuverable schooners *Maria* and *Carleton* approached to within a few hundred yards of the American line and opened fire. The British gunboats joined in, their ordnance operated by skilled German artillerymen.

Eighteenth-century naval battles were unimaginably violent. Ships could support the weight of huge cannon and carry them to an intimate range. Guns with the power to throw a cannonball a mile blasted enemy vessels from less than a hundred yards. The confined interiors of the ships turned hellish. The firing in close quarters numbed men's ears; smoke burned their eyes. Cannonballs punched through hulls with an explosion of splinters, lacerating limbs. Decks turned slippery with blood.

As the air screamed, Arnold, his face blackened by gunpowder, ran from gun to gun on the *Congress*, carefully aiming the cannon. He pointed one heavy piece and barked the order to fire. The explosion sent a five-inch iron ball hurling across the water. It passed directly between two men on the quarterdeck at the *Maria*. The shock wave knocked Guy Carleton's younger brother Thomas to the deck and left him bleeding from both ears. This was no fluke—men were sometimes killed by near misses. Carleton himself, although unhurt physically, was stunned by this supersonic angel of death. He allowed Commodore Pringle to direct the ship back down the channel. The *Maria* did not stop until she was safely two miles up the lake.

Carleton had neglected to draw up any plan of battle in advance. Each British captain was left to improvise. As the afternoon progressed, the fight turned into a waterborne melee, with British gunboats and American galleys and gondolas darting forward to fire, returning to the line to reload. By now, Indians were shooting from both banks, waiting to capture or tomahawk any American forced ashore.

The enemy "continued a very hot fire with round and grape-shot," Arnold reported.[9] Smoke wafted on the wind. The noise of the firing echoed down the lake. The raw militia fifty miles away at Crown Point knew from the distant booms that the fate of the lake—and their own fate—hung in the balance.

At five o'clock, Arnold watched as the captain of the mighty *Inflexible* finally managed to zigzag his ship into the channel. The firing from both sides reached a mad crescendo as the ship's big guns pounded the American line.

Only darkness brought an end to the shrieking madness. Carleton's ships and gunboats pulled back and formed a line across the mouth of the channel. For a time, Arnold could make them out in the light of the flames that had engulfed the *Royal Savage*. Then all faded to blackness. An autumnal fog unrolled a deep quiet over the water.

———— · + · ————

Arnold called his captains to a war council in his cabin. A makeshift surgery during the fighting, the room still reeked of human blood. The reports were all bad: Every ship had been damaged, one gondola was sinking, a dozen cannonballs had pierced the *Congress*. The men had expended three-quarters of their gunpowder during the seven-hour battle. Crewmen and officers lay dead. The survivors could not continue the fight.

The battered fleet, all summer in the making, was doomed. They had to surrender.

No, Arnold told them. They would escape. As the fog thickened, he ordered every captain to mark the stern of his craft with white chalk and to hang a shrouded lantern so that its light fell only on this smudge. By following the boat in front, the ships could maintain a line, hug the shore and perhaps sneak past the enemy.

The escape resembled Washington's daring retreat after the Battle of Long Island six weeks earlier. The rowers muffled their oars. The men held their breath. As they glided through the dark, they could hear voices and laughter from the enemy ships. By morning they were seven miles south of Valcour Island.

Carleton awoke to the amazing news that Arnold had "given us the slip." His naval officers were humiliated. They struggled south against a head wind, determined to finish the upstart American fleet.

As darkness fell on the day after the battle, Arnold's fleeing crewmen continued to row through stinging sleet. Weary muscles could not propel the heavy craft fast enough. The British armada bore down on them the next day. General Waterbury, aboard the galley *Washington*, wanted permission to remove his wounded and blow up the ship. Arnold refused. But as the *Inflexible* came within range and its guns began to pound his vessel, Waterbury lowered his flag in surrender.

Arnold was determined not to give up. He traded shots with seven enemy ships as he worked his galley southward. Finally, he steered the *Congress* and the remaining gondolas into a bay too shallow for the pursuing vessels. The British continued to fire. Seeing the war suddenly arrive on his doorstep, local farmer Benjamin Kellogg decided to flee with his family. Rowing a boat into the bay, they "fell in between Arnold's fleet and the British fleet," his daughter Sally later remembered, "but happy for us the balls went over us. We heard them whis." The family made it to Fort Ticonderoga.[10]

Arnold's men dumped their guns overboard and ran the boats onto the beach. He ordered them to set fire to the vessels with their flags still flying defiantly. He organized the 150 men who had escaped and took off through the woods, carrying the wounded on litters cut from sails. The next day, he reached Crown Point, indefensible against the approaching navy. He ordered the docks and barracks burned and the position abandoned. By four o'clock, he was at Fort Ticonderoga, having endured three days without sleeping or eating.

Benedict Arnold had been beaten. Eighty men were dead, many more wounded, one hundred and twenty taken prisoner. Most of the fleet was gone, only five vessels remained afloat. The British, in just a few days, had taken complete control of Lake Champlain. Some criticized Arnold for what they saw as a costly disaster. One officer wrote a facetious letter noting that "General Arnold, our evil genius to the north, has, with a good deal of industry, got us clear of all our fine fleet."[11]

But battles are not decided by comparing casualty lists—they are won and lost in the minds of the commanders. Arnold's ambitious effort to build a fleet on the lake had forced Carleton to do the same. The battle at Valcour Island, like the cannonball that had skimmed past his head, had rattled the British general's nerves. The fighting had damaged the British fleet and checked his momentum. Instead of looking forward toward Albany, he now looked back to his supply line from Canada. Instead of dreaming about trading war stories with General Howe in New York City, he imagined himself caught in a prolonged winter siege of Fort Ticonderoga. After two weeks of indecision, the cautious Carleton called off the invasion. He would wait until next year.

In order to buy time, Arnold had first built, then sacrificed, America's first navy. The crushing blow from the north, though painful, had glanced off. Relieved of the pressure, Gates could now release needed troops to aid Washington's beleaguered army in New York.

History was kinder to Arnold's effort at Valcour Island than were some of his contemporaries. The nineteenth-century naval strategist and historian Alfred Thayer Mahan wrote: "Save for Arnold's flotilla, the British would have settled the business. The little American navy was wiped out, but never had any force, big or small, lived to better purpose."[12]

The war would go on.

EIGHT

AN INDECISIVE MIND

1776

Nathanael Greene was for burning New York City to the ground to keep it from falling to the British. Congress would not stand for such a move. After the devastating loss on Long Island, Washington had to decide whether to hold the city or relinquish it to the enemy. He saw the military logic of a retreat before a superior force. "On the other hand, to abandon a City, which has been by some deemed defensible . . . has a tendency to dispirit the troops."[1] He worried about his own reputation, noting that "declining an engagement subjects a general to reproach."[2]

During the second week in September 1776, even as he tried to monitor the fraught events unfolding on the border of Canada, Washington admitted that his army had to clear out. He started the bulk of the men marching toward Harlem Heights, a defensible ridge across Manhattan Island ten miles north of the city limits.

Part way up the island, nervous, untried troops were guarding an inviting landing spot along the East River at Kips Bay. They watched as four massive British warships made their way up the river and dropped anchor two hundred yards away. They could count the black holes of seventy-four large cannon scowling at them from the ships' sides. Crowds of British and Hessian soldiers were gathering on the opposite shore.

The next morning, September 15, these same recruits peered over their ramparts as the thousands of enemy soldiers embarked in a flotilla of rowboats. The late-summer day turned sultry and stagnant. Sailors began to maneuver the crowded boats into the river, pausing near the center of the channel. The defenders could make out the faces of their enemies.

"All of a sudden there came such a peal of thunder from the British shipping that I thought my head would go with the sound," remembered Joseph Plumb Martin, one of the privates waiting in the shallow trenches the troops had dug to defend the beach.[3]

"So terrible and incessant a roar of guns," another observer declared, "few even in the army and navy had ever heard before."[4]

Cannonballs tore into the mounds of earth in front of the troops, lifting spouts of sand and plowing great gaps. The guns' mind-numbing detonations deranged the defenders' senses and shattered their determination to resist. They panicked. "The demons of fear and disorder," Martin remembered, "seemed to take full possession of all and everything that day."

The German and British invaders stepped ashore under a pall of heavy smoke without losing a man. "I saw a Hessian sever a rebel's head from his body," a British officer reported, "and clap it on a pole in the entrenchments."[5]

Washington came galloping down from his headquarters four miles to the north. Five thousand of his men remained in New York City, along with tons of supplies and scores of heavy cannon. If the defenders allowed the British to march across the island and block the army's retreat, the loss would be fatal. The enemy must be stopped.

"I used every means in my power to rally and get them in some order," he reported to Congress, "but my attempts were fruitless and ineffectual." This was an understatement. Washington's usual tight control slipped and his "ungovernable passions" took over. He became a "harum Starum ranting Swearing fellow." He screamed orders. He dashed his hat onto the ground. "Distressed and enraged," an observer noted, he "drew his sword and snapped his pistols" to check the fleeing men. "Are these the men," he shouted, "with which I am to defend America?"[6] As advancing enemy troops came within musket range of the American commander in chief, Washington's alarmed aides had to yank the reins of his horse to rush him to safety.

"I could wish the transactions of this day blotted out of the annals of America," wrote a patriot officer. "Nothing appeared but fright, disgrace, and confusion."[7]

Washington sent orders to hurry the evacuation of troops up the west side of the island. Israel Putnam, by means of "extraordinary exertions," organized a hasty departure, forcing Henry Knox to leave behind some of his cannon. Fortunately for Washington, General Howe moved at his usual cautious pace. Rather than rush the advance guard across to the Hudson and cut the island in half, he waited until another nine thousand of his troops could be ferried across the East River. The delay gave Old Put the time he needed. The American troops managed to reach the safety of their lines at Harlem Heights just before night descended and the British sealed the largely empty trap.

Washington blamed the rout on the "disgraceful and dastardly conduct" of the troops. Others recognized that it was not the men but the officers who were to blame. "The bulk of the officers of the army are a parcel of ignorant, stupid men," Henry Knox wrote to his brother, "who might make tolerable soldiers but bad officers."[8] He began to push for the establishment of an academy to train professional military leaders, a cause he would champion for years to come.

The loyalist residents of New York City welcomed the redcoats enthusiastically. Some carried British soldiers on their shoulders and acted like "overjoyed Bedlamites" at the return of legitimate authority to the city.

The day after the Kips Bay fiasco, a skirmish south of Harlem Heights suddenly flamed into a full-scale battle. The clash provided Nathanael Greene with his first taste of combat. After years of studying and dreaming about war, after listening to the roar of the battle of Long Island from his sick bed, he now found himself in the middle of a chaotic, nerve-jangling fight. He and General Putnam rallied their men. The British fell back and were soon running up a slope opposite the Heights, seeking protection under the guns of British warships on the river. Washington gave orders for his troops to break off the chase lest they should stray too close to the main British line. In the fight, they had killed or wounded almost 400 enemy soldiers, losing only 150 of their own men.

The Americans came back elated. For now, they had stopped running, had given the enemy a beating. "They find that if they stick to these mighty men," Knox noted, "they will run as fast as other people."[9] Washington wrote of the engagement, "It seems, to have greatly inspired the whole of our Troops."

For the next few weeks, the two armies stared at each other from lines that stretched across Manhattan. From Harlem Heights, the Americans watched New York City burn on September 21, the fire touched off by "Providence—or some honest fellow," Washington noted. The blaze reduced nearly a quarter of the town to ashes. Daniel Morgan and some of his companions from the Quebec expedition, on their way to being exchanged for British prisoners, watched the inferno from ships in the harbor. They saw the towering steeple of Trinity church, erected in 1698

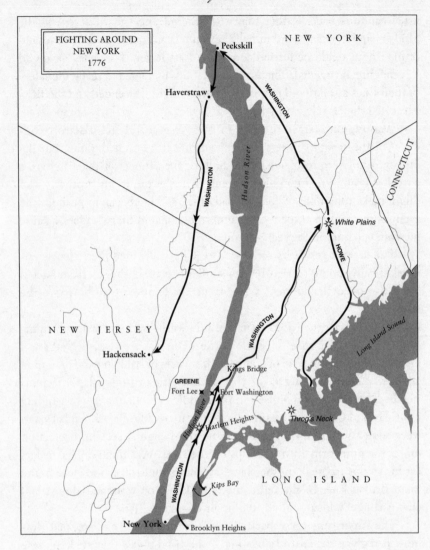

FIGHTING AROUND
NEW YORK
1776

with the help of the pious pirate Captain Kidd, turn to a "pyramid of fire"
before it crashed to the ground.

Washington now made the odd decision to hold his position on Harlem Heights. If the enemy were to land troops north of Manhattan and
cut off the Americans' escape route over Kings Bridge, the army would
again be trapped. They could be surrounded and defeated or isolated and
starved to death. Nathanael Greene, for one, wanted to get out: "Tis our
business to . . . take post where the Enemy will be Obligd to fight us and
not we them."[10]

The burden of command weighed on Washington. "In confidence," he wrote to his cousin Lund, "I tell you that I never was in such an unhappy, divided state since I was born." He was, he admitted, "wearied to death."

Desertions, expiring enlistments, illness, and battle casualties had cut his army in half since midsummer. After a brief hiatus, the violence resumed. On October 9, three British warships sailed up the Hudson River, straight through the barriers that the rebels had constructed in the water, past the guns of Fort Washington on the eastern and Fort Lee on the western heights. "To our surprise and mortification," Washington wrote, "they ran through without the least difficulty." Three days later, Howe landed troops on the mainland, threatening to trap Washington's forces.

General Charles Lee had just returned from helping thwart the British attack on Charleston. His appearance relieved many in the army who valued his experienced opinion. Alarmed, he pointed out that remaining in Manhattan was worse than folly. The troops must withdraw north before the enemy cut them off. They had to start now.

A council of war agreed. The officers decided to abandon all but the narrow northern tip of Manhattan, which was safely dominated by the guns of Fort Washington. Lord Stirling, who along with General Sullivan had returned to the army in a prisoner exchange, immediately led an occupying force to White Plains, fifteen miles north of Manhattan.

On October 28, Howe attacked the Americans dug in on high ground near White Plains village. Fall foliage filled the limpid day with gold, vermilion, and bright orange. The British and German soldiers had seen nothing like a northeast autumn. Their own scarlet and blue coats added to the spectacle. Their polished bayonets glittered in the harvest-scented air.

The battle began with a thunderous bombardment. "The air groaned with streams of cannon and musket shot."[11] It ended with Hessians pushing the Americans off a nearby hill and chasing them through a forest of burning leaves. The British won, but endured 250 casualties, twice as many as the rebels. The Americans pulled back and awaited a renewed attack that never came. On November 5, the British withdrew. Where were they headed now?

Washington divided his army. General Lee would remain with seven thousand troops near White Plains, ready to react to British movements. Another four thousand men would guard the strategic Hudson Highlands to the northwest in order to prevent the enemy from moving up the river. They would also protect the ferry crossings essential to coordinating the American forces. Washington and Lord Stirling would cross to the west side of the Hudson and march two thousand men south, joining Greene's brigade at Fort Lee. Washington suspected that New Jersey, and ultimately the capital at Philadelphia, were Howe's targets.

———•—•———

Commanding Forts Lee and Washington, which straddled the Hudson at the north end of Manhattan, Nathanael Greene had anticipated his superior's concern. He had directed his men to establish a string of supply depots on the road to Philadelphia, which ran south through Newark to Brunswick, then straight across the state to Trenton, which lay a day's march from the capital. It was the type of initiative and foresight that heightened Washington's confidence in the young general.

That confidence was about to be put to the test. The British had proven they could run ships up the Hudson past the guns overlooking the river. Howe's army was now ranging north of Manhattan. Yet Greene still insisted that Fort Washington be held. He figured the British would never dare to thrust into New Jersey with an armed post at their rear. If they besieged Fort Washington, it would take them until December at the earliest to prevail against its high dirt walls and guns. If worse came to worst, Greene could easily ferry the garrison across the river.

Washington was not so sure. When more British ships slipped up the river in early November, he wrote to Greene, "If we cannot prevent vessels passing up, and the Enemy are possessed of the surrounding country, what valuable purpose can it answer" to hold the fort? Then he conceded, "But, as you are on the Spot, I leave it to you." Greene was confident. "I can not conceive the garrison to be in any great danger," he wrote back. "The men may be brought off at any time."[12]

Within days, Howe was massing fourteen thousand troops around upper Manhattan. In response, Greene sent more men across the river from New Jersey, bringing the total American force around Fort Washington to 2,800. This was reckless folly, but Greene could not see it. The immediate commander of the fort, Colonel Robert Magaw encouraged Greene in his error. "We have labored like Horses and completed a Fort said to be one of the Strongest in America," he boasted.[13] A thirty-five-year-old bachelor lawyer from the Pennsylvania frontier, Magaw loved to fight. But like Greene, he had only been soldiering for a year. Both men consulted wishes rather than reality in assessing the situation.

On November 13, Washington arrived to look over the terrain in person. He would later speak of "warfare in my mind," but he did not countermand Greene's strategy. Two days later, catching up on paperwork at his headquarters in Hackensack, the commander received an urgent message. The British, under a flag of truce, had delivered Magaw a demand to surrender Fort Washington in two hours. If he refused, all the defenders would be put to the sword. Such threats were traditional intimidation tactics in sieges and were allowed under the customs of war.

Washington galloped the five miles to Fort Lee. He was starting to cross the river under a darkening sky when he met Generals Greene and Putnam returning. Magaw had refused to surrender. "Activated by the most glorious cause that mankind ever fought in," the fort's commander had written to Howe, "I am determined to defend this post to the last extremity." There was nothing to do for the moment.

The next morning, Washington went over to the fort named for him, accompanied by Greene, Putnam, and Hugh Mercer. The fifty-year-old Mercer, a Scottish immigrant and physician, was a fellow Virginian and close friend of Washington, a comrade during the French and Indian War. While the generals were taking stock of the situation, the British began to attack American positions from three sides.

Four thousand infantrymen approached the American lines from the south. The loud, contemptuous Hessian colonel Johann Rall led a five-hundred-man regiment of grenadiers up the precipitous north slope of the heights on which the fort stood. Scottish Highland troops attacked from the east.

The four American generals had made their way to the Morris House, Washington's former headquarters south of the fort. "There we all stood in a very awkward situation," Greene later recorded. "As the disposition was made, and the enemy advancing, we durst not attempt to make any new disposition; indeed we saw nothing amiss."[14]

Suddenly, enemy troops came rattling through the woods. The generals had to get Washington away instantly. Fifteen minutes later, the Morris House was in British hands.

At the north end of the heights, a regiment of Pennsylvania riflemen fired down at the German grenadiers who were scrambling up the steep cliff. They were backed by the fire of two cannon. A gunner's mate named John Corbin stepped in front of the barrel to ram home a cartridge. The Germans fired their own guns from a nearby hill and killed him. Corbin's wife, Margaret, who had celebrated her twenty-fifth birthday a few days earlier, stepped up to take his place. She was a child of the frontier, her father having been killed and her mother kidnapped in the raids that followed Braddock's defeat on the Monongahela. Knowing the routine of the gunners, she helped service the piece until canister shot ripped into her breast and shattered her arm. Captured, she would survive her wound and receive a soldier's pension.

As Corbin lay wounded, she watched the German grenadiers begin to emerge over the lip of the heights, driving the riflemen before them. Colonel Rall was known as "The Lion" for his ferocity. The Germans had suffered many casualties during the climb and were in a mood for revenge. The Americans ran for the fort. There an eighteen-year-old Connecticut soldier was moving down a passage with two comrades to defend an outer breastworks. "There came a ball," he noted, "and took off both their heads, the contents of which besmeared my face pretty well."[15]

Soon a white flag appeared over Fort Washington. All the defenders, 2,800 soldiers from Washington's rapidly dwindling army, became prisoners. The British were surprised to see that many of them were old men and boys younger than fifteen. All were filthy and lacked military bearing. "Their odd figures frequently excited the laughter of our soldiers."

Their fate was no laughing matter. Like other American captives, most would die in British hands. Some starved to death in excrement-layered New York churches and warehouses. The rest were packed into the hell of black ship holds and sent to Gravesend Bay, off Long Island, where disease and exposure finished them off.

"I feel mad, vext, sick, and sorry," Nathanael Greene wrote to Henry Knox after the surrender. "Never did I need the consoling voice of a friend more than now."[16] Insecure by nature, he pressed Knox for news of how the loss was seen by other officers. Would Greene be sacked?

Washington was certainly upset. Some said he wept as he watched from the New Jersey shore. An aide recorded that he "hesitated more than I ever knew him on any other occasion."[17]

"I am wearied almost to death with the retrograde motions of things," he wrote to his brother Jack. "What adds to my mortification is, that this post after the last ships went past it, was held contrary to my wishes and opinions."[18]

What? It was Washington who had approved the dispositions of his inexperienced subordinate. A military leader does not express himself in wishes and opinions. He gives orders. His Excellency was still learning.

Having taken Fort Washington, General Howe moved with uncustomary dispatch. On a rainy night three days after the surrender, he sent five thousand men rowing across the Hudson River on flatboats. It was the first independent command for Lord Cornwallis, the most enterprising officer in England. This thirty-eight-year-old son of privilege had joined his majesty's army at seventeen and was prized for his competence. He landed his force at the base of the sheer Palisade cliffs on the west side of the river. His men trudged up a steep, four-foot-wide trail, expecting a fight at the top. General Greene had neglected to station guards there. The British winched eight field guns up the cliff. They were not discovered until daylight.

Fort Lee, more of an armed camp than a fortification, was doomed. All Greene could do was to order an instant retreat. The British marched into the fort to find fires burning, cooking pots bubbling. They found hundreds of tents, cases of entrenching tools, and scores of cannon. When a German officer recommended a spirited attack against the fleeing Americans, Cornwallis replied, "Let them go." The beaten, disintegrating army of rebels was not even worth pursuing.

———•—•———

Now came the great retreat that Washington had feared. First to Newark. Then to Brunswick, near the southern tip of Staten Island. Then across the narrow waist of New Jersey toward Trenton. Washington's iron determination became the army's backbone. "A deportment so firm, so dignified, but yet so modest and composed," wrote eighteen-year-old James Monroe, "I have never seen in any other person."[19]

Cornwallis, under orders from Howe, followed Washington across the state without trying to crush his force. Washington called upon General Lee, still camped near White Plains, to bring his troops and help defend Philadelphia. Lee, who claimed he "foresaw, predicted, all that has happened," failed to respond.[20] In the midst of the army's worst catastrophe, Washington now faced a crisis of leadership. His second in command, who led more troops than Washington himself, was heeding his own notions about the proper way to execute the war.

Lee's resistance to Washington was based on more than mere vanity. He was concerned about his troops, many of whom lacked shoes. Politically more radical than most of the other military leaders, Lee believed in a war fought by militia drawn from an "active vigorous yeomanry." He was sure that "a plan of Defense, harrassing and impeding can alone Succeed." The army, he thought, should keep a presence in New Jersey to rally local militia and reinforce their efforts. If Washington abandoned the state, loyalists would reign.

Others were hinting that Lee, not Washington, should be in charge. On November 21, Washington's secretary and aide Joseph Reed wrote to Lee, "I do not mean to flatter nor praise you at the Expense of any other, but I confess I do think that it is entirely owing to you that this Army & the Liberties of America . . . are not totally cut off. . . . You have Decision, a Quality often wanting in Minds otherwise valuable."[21]

Washington continued to urge Lee to hurry forward with his men. In deference to the style of the day and to Lee's superior military experience, he did not issue a flat-out order. Lee continued to resist.

A week later, Washington accidentally opened a letter from Lee to Reed. "I . . . lament with you that fatal indecision of mind which in war is a much greater disqualification than stupidity," Lee wrote. He listed some excuses for his failure to comply with Washington's request. He asserted that he would set his troops in motion when ready because "I really think our Chief will do better with me than without me."

The word "indecision" must have bitten Washington as deeply as the evidence that his trusted secretary had criticized him behind his back. Indecision, his indecision, had cost the army at every step.

The recalcitrant Lee was writing in private letters that "the present crisis" required a "brave, virtuous kind of treason."[22] He stationed his force in Morristown, directly west of New York and fifty miles from Washington, who was now at Trenton. General Horatio Gates, freed from danger by Arnold's sacrificial battle at Valcour Island, had brought some of his troops to reinforce Washington's men. He received an invitation from Lee to join forces and "reconquer . . . the Jerseys." It was Gates, his former comrade in the British army, who had urged Lee to come to America. Like Lee, Gates thought highly of militia. He was not, however, prepared to subvert the chain of command.

On December 8, Washington sent Lee an unambiguous order to advance. "The Militia in this part of the Province seem sanguine," Lee replied three days later. "If they could be assured of an army remaining amongst 'em, I believe they would raise a considerable number."[23]

The situation in New Jersey was actually deteriorating. On November 30, the Howe brothers had offered a "full and free pardon" to anyone who would take an oath of allegiance to the king. Thousands, afraid of losing their property, hurried forth to swear. Loyalists began to take reprisals on patriot neighbors.

British and German troops contributed their own savagery. Nathanael Greene, in a letter to Caty, claimed that "the brutes often ravish the mothers and daughters and compel the fathers and sons to behold their brutality." The rape of girls as young as ten was reported.

The news grew even darker. Howe had sent General Henry Clinton to Providence to secure that important port against rebel privateers. He had taken the city easily and now dominated Rhode Island. During the first week in December, Washington, ceding New Jersey, transferred his army to a defensive position on the west bank of the Delaware River, which divided that state from Pennsylvania.

Prospects were bad. Two thousand of Washington's troops, their enlistments having run out, had limped off toward home. Another three thousand men were too sick to report for duty. At the end of the month, when almost all enlistments would expire, the Continental Army would effectively dissolve.

On December 13, General Lee was still refusing to join Washington. That morning, ensconced with a small guard at an inn several miles from his camp, he was finishing up some paperwork. In a letter to Gates, he facetiously referred to "the ingenious manoeuvre of Fort Washington." He went on: "*Entre nous*, a certain great man is damnably deficient. He has thrown me into a situation where I have my choice of difficulties."[24]

Suddenly, a squadron of British cavalry came pounding up to surround the inn. One of their officers, a twenty-two-year-old subaltern and military prodigy named Banastre Tarleton, threatened to burn the building and those in it if Lee refused to come out. Lee, still in his slippers and night clothes, surrendered.

Lee's capture delighted the enemy. A Hessian officer said that Lee was the only rebel general they had reason to fear. "This is a most miraculous event," Tarleton wrote home to his mother. "It appears like a dream." He was sure his coup would put an end to the campaign.[25]

For Washington, the surprising turn of events may not have been entirely unwelcome. "Unhappy man!" he wrote, "taken by his own Imprudence." His back against the wall, he had little time to dwell on the loss.

Nathanael Greene, who had spent the autumn learning the hard, bloody lessons of being a general, clung to a shred of optimism. "I hope this is the dark part of the night," he wrote home to Caty, "which generally is just before day."[26]

Washington also dared to hope. Perhaps the British were a bit too overconfident. Perhaps his men could still pull off a counterstroke. Perhaps he could then hold out long enough to recruit a new army. Perhaps. If not, he wrote to Lund, "I think the game will be pretty well up."[27]

NINE

HE THAT STANDS
BY IT NOW

1776

As the dwindling Continental Army limped across New Jersey, a Connecticut officer wrote: "Never was finer lads at a retreat than we are."[1] They had reached Trenton and were preparing to cross the Delaware River. New Jersey was lost. In the heat of the previous August, the eight hundred men of Colonel John Haslet's crack Delaware regiment had faced British cannon on Long Island. Now only one hundred shivering soldiers remained to clamber into boats for the escape.

Howe and his redcoats barged into the shabby riverfront village soon after the Americans scrambled ashore on the Pennsylvania side. Washington deployed his troops along the west bank of the Delaware, expecting the British to pursue. "I tremble for Philadelphia," his Excellency wrote on December 11. The members of Congress were not going to stay to see what happened. They decamped to Baltimore the next day, leaving Washington to act as dictator during the crisis.

The short, dark days whispered of winter. British scouts reported that the east side of the river had been stripped of boats. General Howe decided to end the year's campaign. He would quarter his troops through central and western New Jersey, where the army could forage, discourage patriot recruiting, and maintain a solid base from which to continue the war in the spring—assuming the rebel army did not collapse over the winter.

Three Hessian regiments squeezed into Trenton, only a mile from Washington's headquarters on the opposite bank. Their commander was Colonel Johann Rall, the "Lion" whose tough grenadiers had scaled the heights and taken Fort Washington in November. Howe returned to a warm life of ease with his mistress in New York.

An exhausted Washington contemplated the expiration of his men's enlistments at month's end. He wrote Congress about how poorly clothed his troops were, "many of 'em being entirely naked and most so thinly clad as to be unfit for service." He admitted, "I am almost led to despair."[2]

Almost. He still yearned to take the offensive. He hoped, he wrote to Connecticut governor Jonathan Trumbull, "to attempt a Stroke upon the Forces of the Enemy, who lay a good deal scattered." He was sure that "a lucky Blow . . . would most certainly raise the Spirits of the People, which are quite sunk by our late misfortunes."[3]

Since mid-December, Washington had been receiving encouraging reports from units of Pennsylvania and New Jersey militia who were harassing the Hessian occupiers. Familiar with the terrain, they ventured back and forth across the river to skirmish with patrols and foraging parties.

On December 20, Generals Sullivan and Gates rode into camp with four undermanned regiments from the north. They found officers and men reading a tract called *The Crisis*, which had been published the day before in the *Philadelphia Journal*. It was an exhortation by Thomas Paine, well known author of the pamphlet *Common Sense*, published a year earlier. Paine, an English corset maker turned journalist, had accompanied the army during the long retreat, serving as a volunteer aide to his friend Nathanael Greene.

"These are the times that try men's souls," Paine had written. "The summer soldier and the sunshine patriot will, in this crisis, shrink from the service of their country; but he that stands by it NOW, deserves the love and thanks of man and woman."

He went on to give details of the retreat, to rail against Tories, and to whip up enthusiasm for what many had written off as a lost cause. "Let it be told to the future world, that in the depth of winter, when nothing but hope and virtue could survive, that the city and the country, alarmed at one common danger, came forth to meet and to repulse it."

Paine's electric words crackled through the colonies. They gave voice to a popular spirit, which defeat had prodded awake rather than dampened. "We require adversity," said Benjamin Rush, a Philadelphia physician and signer of the Declaration of Independence, "and appear to possess most of the republican spirit when most depressed."[4]

"Read in the camp, to every corporal's guard," *The Crisis* had a dramatic effect. It became both a catalyst and a symbol of a fresh seriousness in the minds of the beleaguered patriots. "The great revival did not follow the battles of Trenton and Princeton," writes modern historian David Hackett Fischer. "It preceded them, and made those events possible."[5]

Something had to be done. Washington called a council of war to discuss a plan he had been mulling. Secret preparations followed. On Christmas Eve, another war council met over dinner at Nathanael Greene's headquarters. The following day, officers issued their troops three days' food and told them to be ready to march by evening. They did not say where.

The cold and snowy weather had eased. Ice floes sped down the Delaware. On Christmas night, troops marched toward two ferry landings ten miles north of Trenton, where the river was barely three hundred yards across. Colonel John Glover's Marblehead mariners had gathered as many boats as they could find, including high-sided cargo boats and flat-bottomed ferries. As evening descended and a full moon rose in the east, Henry Knox began barking orders. He was to manage the complicated task of moving 2,400 men and eighteen field guns, along with horses and equipment, across the tusked river.

"Floating ice in the river made the labor almost incredible," Knox later wrote to Lucy.[6] The strong current, high winds, and speeding chunks of ice turned the crossing into a slow, Herculean task requiring "the stentorian lungs and extraordinary exertions of Colonel Knox." Delaware colonel John Haslet fell into the icy water, but continued on in his sopping clothes.

"Perseverance accomplished what first seemed impossible," Knox wrote.[7] By about two o'clock in the morning the troops were on the Jersey side and ready to march. During the crossing, the weather had turned dirty. A snarling nor'easter brought snow, rain, and hail. Sharp winds drove needles of sleet against exposed flesh.

The delays during the crossing left Washington in a quandary. Intent on surprise, he had planned to reach the town just before daylight. But by the time the men marched and dragged their cannon ten miles to Trenton, it would be light. In addition, thick ice had blocked the landing of additional militia troops below the town. The main body would have to attack without support.

It was all up to Washington. Call off the attack? Go back to safety? Or risk his whole army? He decided to plunge on. "The troops marched with the most profound silence," Knox noted.[8]

Slashed by hail and icy rain, in ruined shoes or no shoes at all, through a mauling wind, carrying heavy muskets and packs, the soldiers plodded into the darkness. Some reported an elation at odds with their surroundings. "I felt great pleasure," one remembered later, "more than I now do in writing about it."[9]

As they approached the town from the north, Washington divided his force. General Sullivan would attack along the river. Greene's men would sweep to the inland side and push down the two main streets of the village. Later, a myth gained traction that the Hessian troops had been celebrating Christmas and were too drunk to fight effectively. The truth was they had been on high alert for days, ready to turn out at any alarm. Rall had posted guards on all the roads and sent out frequent patrols. Warned of a possible attack, he had responded, "Let them come."

But in spite of these preparations, Washington was able to achieve almost complete surprise when his men reached the first guard post. The storm helped. Torrents of snow and sleet continued to claw the watery light, reducing visibility and encouraging the enemy to remain indoors. The rebels attacked with the bare-toothed savagery of creatures too long beaten down. "I never could conceive," an American colonel recorded, "that one spirit should so universally animate both officers and men to rush forward into action."[10]

Sullivan began his charge just as Greene's men came pounding into the village. Henry Knox unlimbered his artillery and pointed the barrels down the high street. When the Hessians came running out, his gunners blasted canister shot along the pavement, cutting men to pieces. Knox was "cool, cheerful and was present everywhere." The fight, within the confined streets of the compact village, stunned the troops of both sides with its noise and hellish chaos. "There succeeded a scene of war of which I had often conceived," Knox wrote to Lucy, "but never saw before." He compared it to the end of the world.[11]

"The sight was too much to bear," a sergeant wrote. A musket ball tore into the shoulder of an eighteen-year-old American lieutenant. A surgeon saved his life by clamping a severed artery. The soldier, James Monroe, would live to be elected president in 1816.

The battle lasted two hours. The Americans pressed the Hessians back and surrounded them in an orchard beside the town. Colonel Rall, cantering on his horse to rally his men, was shot and mortally wounded. The remaining 886 enemy soldiers surrendered.

Washington singled out his young artillery officer for praise in his report on the battle, an honor Knox was delighted to relay to his wife. "This I would blush to mention to any other than you, my dear Lucy."[12]

The troops gathered up the spoils, which included six field guns and 1,200 muskets. They hurried back to the west side of the river. They had accomplished something remarkable.

———•••———

Washington immediately faced another critical decision. The next day, December 27, he learned that the Pennsylvania militiamen, who he had hoped would join him in the Trenton attack, had finally made it across the icy water. The inexperienced troops were determined to fight, and their leader, John Cadwalader, urged Washington to join him. Perhaps they could push the remaining invaders out of western New Jersey.

The commander in chief knew that his men were tired. Many were sick. Should he risk another crossing? He called a council of war. His officers raised "some doubts." Washington steered the meeting toward a consensus. Yes, they would go over the river again with the entire army.

The thickening ice floes made the crossing on December 30 more treacherous than the first. With reinforcements, Washington now commanded five thousand men. As they took up positions in Trenton, he learned that they would have more of a fight than they had bargained for. General Cornwallis was rushing across New Jersey with eight thousand British and Hessian soldiers.

Washington found himself in a precarious position. The enlistments of most of his men would run out at midnight on the 31st, freeing them to go home. Few had signed up for another stint. Like Richard Montgomery before Quebec, the commander in chief was about to see his army evaporate.

A master of the theatrical gesture, Washington addressed his assembled troops from astride his horse. "My brave fellows," he shouted. "You have done all that I have ever asked you to do, and more than could be expected; but your country is at stake, your wives, your houses, and all that you hold dear." His speech, and a ten-dollar bonus, convinced 3,300 men to reenlist.[13]

Washington aligned these troops on the south side of a creek that joined the Delaware at Trenton. He sent out a strong force to meet Cornwallis on his advance along the main road from Princeton, twelve miles away. Their core was a battalion of Pennsylvania riflemen led by Colonel Edward Hand, a tough, Irish-born frontier physician. His men slowed Cornwallis's advance. When they finally arrived in Trenton, the British pushed the Americans toward a bridge that would bring them across the creek. The fighting became intensely violent. Benjamin Rush, who treated the wounded, wrote that "for the first time war appeared to me in its awful plenitude of horrors."[14]

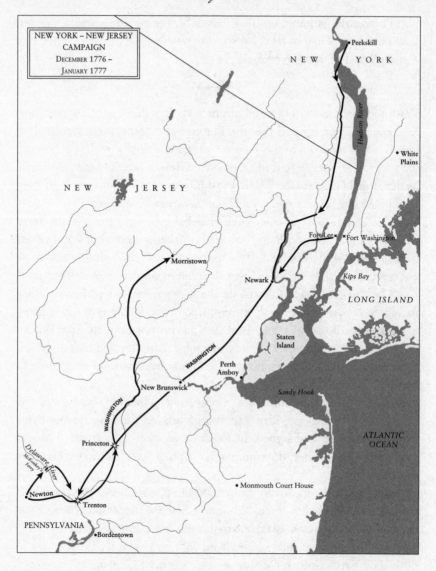

As the mass of British troops kept pouring into the town, the enor-
mity of the situation dawned on the patriots. They were outnumbered.
They could no longer retreat across the Delaware. Their position along
the creek, strong for the time being, could be outflanked by Cornwallis's
superior force.

"If there ever was a crisis in the affairs of the Revolution," an American officer affirmed, "this was the moment."[15]

Fortunately, the early darkness gave Cornwallis pause. He decided to wait until daylight to renew the fight. He was reported to have said, "We've got the Old Fox safe now. We'll go over and bag him in the morning."

In a council of war that night, Henry Knox, who had just learned that Congress had promoted him to brigadier general, argued that the next day's battle would be a disaster. The army, he noted, was "cooped up" like a flock of chickens. Why not break out and attack the enemy's rear at Princeton?

Washington, the Old Fox, weighed his options. He wanted to avoid "the appearance of a retreat." He had to think of "popular opinion." He wanted "to give reputation to our arms." He decided to attack.

Leaving behind a small force to make noise and keep campfires burning along the creek, he quietly led his army onto a country road and hurried them toward Princeton. A sudden invasion of bone-chilling air froze the mud and allowed the Americans to lug their cannon along the rutted lane.

By morning, they were approaching the village of Princeton, home of one the colonies' premier colleges. The limpid day was "bright, serene, and extremely cold, with a hoarfrost that bespangled every object."[16]

Washington led the main force along the back road, intent on surprising the British in the village. General Hugh Mercer, his physician friend, veered left with 350 men to secure a bridge on the main road. Before Mercer reached his objective, a flash of light alerted the Americans. It was the glint of the rising sun on the bayonets of British reinforcements hurrying down the turnpike toward Trenton.

Rushing to secure the high ground, Mercer's men smashed directly into two enemy regiments commanded by British colonel Charles Mawhood. Neither force had time to dig in or to array in formal battle lines. They mingled in a wild, hand-to-hand melee as the crystalline morning erupted in violence.

During the fighting, a cannonball shattered the leg of Mercer's horse. A British infantryman swung his musket butt and knocked the general to the ground. Mercer refused to yield and was fatally bayoneted by British soldiers. Delaware colonel John Haslet, who had earned a master of divinity degree in Glasgow, Scotland, stepped up to rally the American forces. A musket ball struck him in the head and killed him.

"The ground was frozen," one observer noted, "and all the blood which was shed remained on the surface."[17] The rising sun turned the battlefield into a sparkling crimson horror. British troops charged with bayonets. Mercer's men retreated. But now American soldiers were turning back from the road to Princeton village and rushing onto the field of battle. Henry Knox's gunners began to rake the enemy with cannon blasts. A thousand untrained Pennsylvania militiamen could not form a line until Washington himself cantered in among them on his white horse. "Parade with us!" he screamed in his reedy voice. "There is but a handful of the enemy, and we will have them directly!" His words trumped fear. He waved his hat. The men rushed forward. The tide of battle turned. Providence again preserved the general amid the flying bullets.

Cornwallis, realizing that Washington had gulled him, rushed his men from Trenton back toward Princeton. By the time they arrived, the Americans had already left.

Washington wanted to hurry on to Brunswick, sack the enemy's main supply depot, and "put an end to the war." But his men were entirely spent. He led them to the high ground around Morristown, where they could safely spend the winter.

"Lord Cornwallis is, I believe, a brave man," a British officer commented, "but he allowed himself to be fairly outgeneralled by Washington."[18]

The battles at Trenton and Princeton had deep consequences. They forced the British to pull back to a shrunken perimeter around Brunswick. Foraging parties that ventured farther into New Jersey were set upon by roaming patriot militia units.

"Our affairs at present are in a prosperous way," Washington wrote with a sigh of relief. "The country seems to entertain an idea of our Superiority—Recruiting goes on well."

He would never be a military genius, but when it mattered most, his Excellency had cast off indecision, taken a heart-stopping risk, and conquered. He had met his crisis. He had stood by his country and repulsed the enemy. In a bemused afterthought, Washington concluded, "a Belief prevails that the enemy are afraid of Us."[19]

TEN

A CONTINUAL CLAP
OF THUNDER

1777

Far from being afraid of Washington's feeble army, the British were now determined to crush the rebellion during the 1777 fighting season. Conciliation had not worked. The overwhelming British victories at Long Island and New York had not convinced the rebels to yield. Only unrelenting violence would decide the matter.

General John Burgoyne had convinced the ministry in London to adopt a bold plan. He would haul men and guns down from Canada, overwhelm the fortress at Ticonderoga, continue on to Albany, secure the Hudson-Champlain corridor, divide the New England rebels from the rest of the colonies, and thus "do the business in one campaign."

Fort Ticonderoga, the mighty "Gibraltar of the north," had been left vulnerable when the British destroyed Arnold's fleet the previous autumn. Burgoyne's engineers hauled several cannon up a nearby mountain, forcing American general Arthur St. Clair to abandon the poorly located fort without firing a shot. Early in July, the Americans snuck out of the bastion in the middle of the night and headed south. The loss, a rattled George Washington wrote to Schuyler, was "an event of chagrin and surprise not apprehended nor within the compass of my reasoning."[1]

As the Americans fled Ticonderoga, the Green Mountain Boys, now incorporated into the Continental Army, took up a rearguard position at the Vermont crossroads of Hubbardton. Ethan Allen, their former leader, had earlier been captured by the British. Vermont farmer Seth Warner, almost as large as Allen but of quieter demeanor, now led the Boys. He and his men fought a sharp battle that slowed the British pursuit.

Slowed but did not stop. Burgoyne marched on. When King George heard of the capture of Ticonderoga, he blustered, "I have beat them! I have beat all the Americans!"[2]

Having expected a long siege at Ticonderoga, Burgoyne was as confident as his king. In Skenesborough, at the southern tip of Lake Champlain, the invaders paused to regroup. Burgoyne decided to continue overland rather than backtrack to Ticonderoga, where he could have portaged his artillery and supplies to Lake George. A few days' march would bring him to Fort Edward. He would follow the Hudson River south and, in a few days more, arrive in Albany. The war would be as good as won.

Celebrating his impending victory, Burgoyne ordered choice bottles drawn from his traveling wine cellar. The man whom Horace Walpole called "General Swagger," who saw war as a grand drama, cavorted with his mistress, his mind fizzing with champagne.[3] He had already decided that he would not accept a mere knighthood, like the ones awarded to generals Howe and Clinton. Only a hereditary title, a baronetcy, would suffice. He wanted to be a lord.

––––––––

It hardly seemed that the death of one young woman could play a major role in derailing his dream. Yet two days before Burgoyne reached the Hudson at Fort Edward, Indians allied with the British killed twenty-five-year-old Jane McCrea, known as Jenny.

The young woman had lived with her older brother outside Fort Edward. He was a patriot; Jenny and some of her other siblings were loyalists. Such divided families were not unusual in northern New York, where sentiment was sharply split between Whigs and Tories.

The lovely Jenny—her beauty purportedly enhanced by long reddish hair—had fallen in love with and become engaged to a local man named David Jones, also a loyalist. Jones had traveled to Canada and signed on to fight with Burgoyne. Now a lieutenant in a provincial battalion, he was marching south with the invasion.

As Burgoyne approached, Jenny's brother fled with other patriot refugees. Jenny stayed behind at the home of an older woman. When the British came close enough, she planned to join her fiancé and be married.

McCrea's brother had good reason to depart. A month earlier, in Burgoyne's camp at Skenesborough, soldiers had fired a salute to welcome five hundred Indian warriors. Some were Mohawks, the fiercest fighters among the Iroquois. Others were strapping Ottawa warriors, who had come from as far away as the upper Great Lakes, drawn a thousand miles by the promise of scalps, prisoners, and booty. The Canadian Indians who had come south with Burgoyne averted their eyes when they encountered these large, ruthless men from distant forests. To settlers, they were demons from Hell.

The details of what happened to Jenny McCrea would never emerge entirely from the fog of legend. On July 27, Indians abducted her and her hostess. The women became separated. Two chiefs may have argued about whose prisoner Jenny was, each coveting the expected ransom. One of them shot or tomahawked the young woman. One of them slit her scalp with a knife and ripped off her hair with his teeth. One of them stripped her, mutilated her body, and tossed her into a ditch. One of them headed back to camp with her scalp. As her killer, oblivious to sentimentality, danced around the fire with his prize, her horrified lover recognized the distinctive hair.

Burgoyne resolved to execute the offending brave. Cooler heads prevailed. Such a penalty, the general was warned, would prompt the Indians to desert. On their way home, they would kill many more white settlers. Burgoyne, who needed a cloud of Indian scouts to feel his way through the forest, relented. He granted the warrior a pardon. In war, "we must wink at these things," a British officer said about the murder.[4]

The crime was one of hundreds of atrocities committed by Burgoyne's native allies. Indians had butchered an entire local family just two days before the McCrea killing. Yet it was the girl's fate that most ignited the imaginations of patriots. Americans were infuriated that she had been "scalped and mangled in a most shocking manner," as Horatio Gates wrote, while "dressed to receive her promised husband."[5] Her lovely hair, said to trail to the ground, instantly found a place in settlers' gossip and nightmares. Her death "caused quite an uproar" even among Burgoyne's own troops. The event, an American captain noted, "added much to the numbers of the American Army."[6]

Although General Henry Clinton had earlier spoken of the need "To Gain the Hearts and Subdue the Minds of America," British officers often acted in ways certain to do the opposite.[7] Word of the incident, spread through lurid newspaper accounts, curdled the hearts and ignited the minds of settlers across the northern frontier.

———

John Stark was one who could understand Jenny's plight. He had become intimate with violence long before he led his New Hampshire troops into the inferno at Bunker Hill. In his twenties—he was now nearly fifty—John and his older brother William, along with two companions, had traveled deep into the Indian country of northern New Hampshire to hunt. A band of Abenaki Indians had emerged from all sides and taken him prisoner. He could still remember the "sharp, hissing sound" they made, "as of a snake." They had killed one companion and captured another—William escaped.[8]

Back at their village, the Indians forced Stark's friend, Amos Eastman, to run a gauntlet. Lines of young braves with sticks and paddles beat him severely as he stumbled between them. When urged toward the same punishment, Stark, who had known Indians from childhood, grabbed a paddle from one of the men and began swinging. He boldly swore he would "kiss" all their women. According to the often-told story, this show of impertinent courage impressed the tribe's sachems. So did Stark's refusal to labor in the fields, his shunning of "squaw's work." After holding him for several months, the Indians exchanged him for a ransom.

Later, during the French and Indian War, Stark fought with the charismatic Robert Rogers. Rogers's Rangers attacked Indian style, ambushing French war parties in the forest. Stark became Rogers's right-hand man and acquired a reputation across the New England frontier as a fierce fighter. After playing a critical role at Bunker Hill, he led a regiment to Canada, faced the Hessians at Trenton, and battled the British at Princeton. Returning home to rest, he quite naturally expected a promotion for his strenuous efforts.

Congress had other ideas. In February 1777 they handed out brigadier general commissions to several officers, but Stark was not among them. New Hampshire's generalship was allotted to Enoch Poor, a younger man with less experience than Stark but more political clout. Stark could not ignore the implied insult. A month later, "extremely grieved," he resigned from the Continental Army. "I am bound on Honour to leave the service," he declared, "Congress having tho't fit to promote Junr. officers over my head."[9]

Such fits of pique were common among officers in an army where favoritism and regional interests played a role in decisions about rank. Officers were forever parsing distinctions of precedence and merit. There was no avoiding this touchiness. Their individual sense of honor was what spurred them to fight—or to find quarrel in a straw.

To some, the failure of an expected promotion was enough to drain their faith altogether. Stark's brother William, initially a patriot, had joined the British after being passed over for promotion. The two never spoke again. Stark's old leader Robert Rogers had also sided with the Tories and had briefly led a regiment of Queen's Rangers against his countrymen.

Stark, still committed to the cause, returned to his New Hampshire farm, to his wife, Molly, and to his lumber business. Like Achilles, he chose to brood in his tent.

———•—•———

Now the Champlain Valley, which Stark knew well from the French war, had become the route of an invasion that threatened all of New England. The blow that Benedict Arnold had deflected with last year's delaying action was falling with full force on the northern frontier.

John Stark could not ignore the threat. Burgoyne could easily pivot his eight-thousand-man army toward the east and rampage into New Hampshire and Massachusetts. The rebellion had originated in the New England colonies and could be extinguished there. In July, the New Hampshire General Court, the state's legislature, named Stark a general of the state militia and authorized him to raise as many men as he could. So popular was he that 1,500 men reported for duty over the next six days.

The new recruits were spurred on by more than just Stark's popularity. The heartbreaking news of Jenny McCrea's killing had been reported in graphic detail by almost every colonial newspaper. Settlers across the frontier were already primed for outrage by Burgoyne's own statements. Before he captured Fort Ticonderoga, the British general had warned those in his path that cooperation was in their best interest. "I have but to give stretch to the Indian Forces under my direction," he declared in a pompous proclamation, "to overtake the harden'd Enemies of Great Britain and America, (I consider them the same) wherever they may lurk."[10]

Burgoyne hoped that the natives' reputation would make wanton violence unnecessary. He privately said that he wanted to "spread terror without barbarity." It was a fine distinction. The inhabitants of the region knew far more about Indian raids than the general did. His proclamation enraged patriots. They could hardly believe that a British officer, a civilized man, would unleash on them a horde of what they considered ungovernable savages. The death of Jenny McCrea confirmed their fears and proved that Burgoyne was unable to protect even loyalists from the Indians under his command.

———•—•———

It had taken Burgoyne an entire month to move his expedition the twenty-two miles from Skenesborough to Fort Edward on the Hudson River. Like General Braddock a generation earlier, he was dragging a massive train of artillery and supplies along rutted forest trails, moving through territory that offered little food or forage. He was also bringing thirty additional wagons loaded with his fancy uniforms and fine china, his Madeira and champagne.

Directed by General Schuyler, the rebels did everything they could to hamper his movement: they downed trees, diverted streams, rolled boulders onto roads. Burgoyne's men, "almost devoured by musketoes of a monstrous size and innumerable numbers," had to work like devils to remove the obstacles. The delay gave the patriots time to catch their breath.

In early August, John Stark sent a thousand militiamen from New Hampshire to Manchester, Vermont, forty miles east of Burgoyne's Fort Edward camp. They were to join other militiamen, along with those of Seth Warner's Green Mountain Continentals who had survived the battle at Hubbardton, to oppose Burgoyne should he shift eastward. Stark ordered kettles, ammunition, bullet molds, cannon, wagons, and plenty of rum, "as there is none of that article in them parts where we are a going."[11] A few days later, Stark headed west himself.

In Manchester, the flinty New Hampshire general was amazed to see the men he had sent ahead parading under the orders of Benjamin Lincoln, a Continental Army general whom George Washington had sent to aid Philip Schuyler's efforts. Desperate for troops, Schuyler had directed Lincoln, a fat Massachusetts farmer, to bring the New Hampshire militia to join him on the Hudson to block Burgoyne's path south.

Lincoln was a political officer, five years younger than Stark. The steely-eyed veteran answered only to the New Hampshire legislature and would not serve under Lincoln or give up his troops. Lincoln recognized that Stark was "exceedingly soured and thinks he hath been neglected and hath not had Justice done him by Congress."[12] He diplomatically concurred with Stark's plan to threaten Burgoyne from Vermont. Congress grumbled that Stark had become a rogue general, "destructive of military subordination."

Stark didn't care. He marched most of his men twenty-five miles south, placing them directly east of Schuyler. They would camp near Bennington, a small town just over the New York border in southern Vermont.

The patriots were still falling back—Schuyler's men lacked tents and provisions, and they could muster only two artillery pieces. Burgoyne's army, heavily supplied with cannon, continued to press them south along the Hudson River. "Desertion prevails," Schuyler lamented, "and disease gains ground."[13]

In late July 1777, Burgoyne faced supply problems of his own. Flour and meat had grown scarce. The expedition especially lacked horses. Hauling

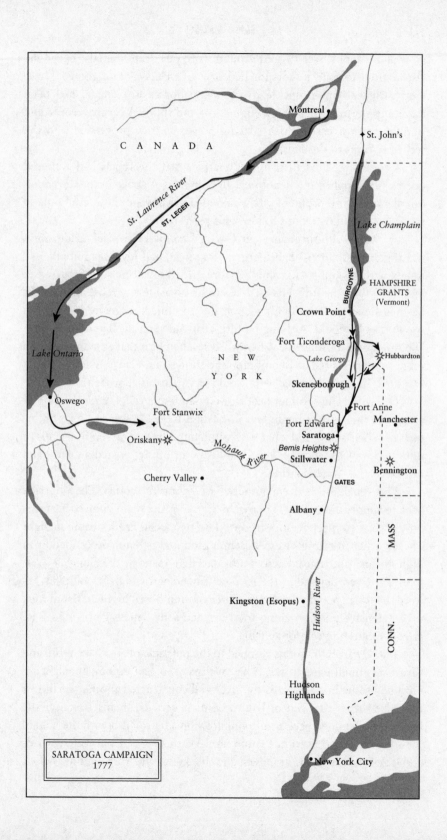

Montreal

St. John's

C A N A D A

St. Lawrence River

ST. LEGER

Lake Champlain

BURGOYNE

HAMPSHIRE
GRANTS
(Vermont)

Crown Point

Lake Ontario

Fort Ticonderoga

Hubbardton

Lake George

N E W

Y O R K

Skenesborough

Oswego

Fort Anne

Fort Stanwix

Fort Edward

Manchester

Oriskany

Saratoga

Mohawk River

Bemis Heights

Stillwater

Bennington

Cherry Valley

GATES

Albany

MASS

Kingston (Esopus)

Hudson River

CONN.

Hudson
Highlands

SARATOGA CAMPAIGN
1777

New York City

guns and wagons over rugged ground wore out draft animals. Burgoyne also wanted to find mounts for his corps of Brunswick dragoons. These German cavalrymen, unable to round up horses in Canada, had been marching south in their thigh-high boots and spurs. A cavalry arm would significantly increase British striking power as they proceeded into the settled regions to the south.

A rumor reached British headquarters that the rebels had gathered horses and supplies at a depot near Bennington. A strike in that direction might prove very profitable. It would also discourage the New England states from sending troops to block his path south.

On August 9, Burgoyne sent German colonel Friedrich Baum eastward with 1,200 men—half German dragoons, half loyalist militiamen—armed with several small cannon. More armed loyalists were expected to join him along the way. His goal was to brush aside any rebels that might be guarding the Bennington depot and to collect as many horses and supplies as he could. Although a fifty-year-old veteran, Baum knew little about fighting in America. When word reached him that as many as 1,800 rebel soldiers waited at Bennington, he showed no alarm. They were, he was sure, "uncouth militia" who would vanish at his approach.

The withering summer heat slowed Baum's march. He reached a mill about ten miles from Bennington on August 14. He scared off a contingent of rebels and found what he was looking for: seventy-eight barrels of flour and tons of wheat. He set a miller to grinding, posted a guard, and moved on, his hopes soaring.

The rebels he had encountered were Stark's scouts. They hurried back to report the enemy's approach. Stark put the main body of his force on the road to meet Baum's troops. The two small armies came in sight of each other four miles west of Bennington just as Baum descended from high ground and started across a bridge that spanned the sluggish Walloomsac River. Beyond it, the road continued across a flat flood plain toward the town. Seeing that Stark's force outnumbered his own, Baum took up a defensive position along the river and sent a message back to Burgoyne, requesting reinforcements.

The German dragoons climbed to the pinnacle of an adjacent hill and threw up rough earthworks. The loyalists who had accompanied Baum occupied some houses across the river and constructed another small fort on a rise there. The rest of Baum's soldiers arrayed themselves near the bridge. Stark pulled back a mile and drew up a battle plan with the help of Seth Warner, who lived in Bennington. Warner was "given to few words and circumspect with strangers, but he knew the surrounding woods intimately."[14] He sent word for his battalion of former Green Mountain Boys to hurry down from Manchester. Stark's own force consisted entirely of militiamen. Many officers, including George Washington, thought these citizen soldiers unreliable at best. They would soon be given a chance to prove themselves.

———•———

The next day, a heavy rain prompted Stark to hold off his attack. The wait was a nervous one, since he rightly suspected that a larger enemy force would be arriving soon. In spite of the damp, his skirmishers, firing through the trees, managed to pick off thirty of the enemy.

Reverend Thomas Allen, a militia leader known as the Fighting Parson, complained to Stark that his volunteers were continually being called out but not given a chance to fight. "If the Lord gives us sunshine tomorrow and I do not give you fighting enough," Stark promised, "I will never call on you to come again."[15]

In the morning, a warm drizzle softened the air. A German relief column led by Colonel Heinrich von Breymann was dragging two substantial 6-pounder guns along the muddy roads from the west. Baum now knew that he only need hold out a few more hours and the combined force could deal handily with the rebels.

As the morning advanced, the rain slackened. The humid day was drenched in late-summer green. Stark sent a battalion of three hundred men around the hill to his right and another on a long hike across the plain, over the river and up the far side. He planned to lead a force against Baum's center by the bridge himself. By noon, the day was brightening. Tropical humidity clogged the air. Most of the rebels stripped to their shirtsleeves. They tucked corn leaves in their hats or pockets to distinguish themselves from the loyalists. An intense, nerve-stretching quiet settled on the valley.

The two flanking wings of Stark's army, a total of 650 men, met in Baum's rear at three o'clock. They burst out of the woods and attacked the Germans in their log and earthen redoubt. The dragoons fired back, blasting grapeshot from their small cannon.

The enemy troops fought desperately. They "fired by platoons and were soon covered with smoke."[16] The rebels hid behind trees and picked off targets of opportunity. Then, with "the coolness of veterans," the American militiamen rushed the improvised fort.

"For a few seconds the scene which ensued defies all power of language to describe," remembered one of the German survivors. "The bayonet, the butt of the rifle, the sabre, the pike, were in full play, and men fell, as they rarely fall in modern war, under the direct blows of their enemies."[17]

The militiamen prevailed. The dragoons gave way and ran for their lives down the hill.

The whole valley was now quaking with the banging clamor of battle. Stark sent militiamen down a sunken road that allowed them to reach the loyalist redoubt without being seen. He led his own men toward Baum's soldiers near the bridge. The struggle became feverish. Relentless. Stark, the Bunker Hill veteran, admitted the fight was "the hottest engagement I ever witnessed, resembling a continual clap of thunder."[18]

The fighting around the Tory fort was particularly vicious. John Peters, the leader of a loyalist brigade that had accompanied Burgoyne from Canada, watched one of the attackers fire and run at him with his bayonet. "Peters, you damned Tory," the rebel screamed, "I have got you!" His bayonet stabbed into Peters's body below his left breast just as Peters finished reloading. He recognized his attacker as "an old schoolmate and playfellow." A half second of hesitation. "Though his bayonet was in my body," Peters remembered, "I felt regret at being obliged to destroy him." He fired.[19]

A rebel named William Clement drove his bayonet into a Tory's eye with such force that it stuck and detached from his musket as the man dropped dead. The sight so shocked Clement that he refused to touch the bayonet to retrieve it—his victim would be buried with the steel still jutting from his head.

In less than two hours, the fight was over. Colonel Baum had been wounded and captured. Stark's men had shot down many and taken hundreds more prisoner. As the ears of the patriots continued to ring, some sank down to rest, others scavenged for souvenirs. Many were reeling in the heat, having fortified themselves with rum throughout the desperate fighting.

At this point, about four-thirty in the afternoon, Colonel Breymann's relief column came marching up the road. They ran into a band of militiamen a few miles west of the battlefield. A hot firefight alerted Stark. He gathered as many of his spent soldiers as he could and rushed up the road.

Seth Warner's troops had not reached the scene of the action until the fighting was winding down. Still fresh, they stormed toward the sound of the guns and slammed into Breymann's grenadiers. Surrounding the Germans' two field pieces, they managed to turn the guns around and fire them at the enemy. Twenty more Germans died in the fight and 140 fell prisoner before Breymann extracted his force and headed back toward the main army.

Darkness forced Stark to call off the fighting. "Had day lasted an hour longer," he stated, "we should have taken the whole body of them."[20] His raw militia force had beaten trained German mercenaries. They had scored a victory whose repercussions would echo down history. "Undisciplined freemen," Stark would say much later, "are superior to veteran slaves."[21] George Washington praised the "great stroke struck by Gen. Stark." A patriot proclaimed it "the compleatest Victory gain'd this War."[22]

Burgoyne still led a potent force, but he had, in one day, lost a thousand men he could not replace. Vermont, he worried, "abounds in the most active and rebellious race of the continent and hangs like a gathering storm on my left."[23]

The previous autumn, young Sally Kellogg had listened to the whiz of cannonballs as she and her family had rowed away from their home directly through Arnold's Lake Champlain naval fight with the British fleet. They had taken refuge at Bennington. Now she witnessed the blood-soaked aftermath of another battle. It was "a sight to behold," she wrote. "There was not a house but what was stowed full of wounded."[24]

ELEVEN

FIGHT AS WELL AS BRAG

1777

"He will never make a scholar," young Anthony Wayne's schoolmaster wrote to his father. "He may perhaps make a soldier, he has already distracted the brains of two-thirds of the boys under my charge, by rehearsals of battles, sieges, etc."[1] It was the late 1750s and Wayne's playmates were reenacting the clashes of the French and Indian War then raging in the hinterlands.

Now, on the morning of September 11, 1777, a month after the patriots' Bennington victory, the thirty-two-year-old Wayne was a soldier in earnest, a general hungry for the glory he had dreamed of as a boy. With a thick body and assertive black eyebrows, he stood sweating in the late-summer heat along the Brandywine Creek, a small river about twenty miles west of Philadelphia and only a short distance from the scene of his pretend skirmishes. The massed army of British general William Howe was marching toward his position. Now he would face musket balls and bayonets instead of clots of dirt and wooden swords, death and horrific wounds instead of mock charges and bloody noses.

The peace that followed the French and Indian War had dried up career opportunities for a military-minded youth like Wayne, so he learned the trade of surveyor. The Waynes had prospered for three generations in the agricultural enclave a day's ride from Philadelphia. Anthony married Mary Penrose, known as Polly, and had a daughter and a son with her. He ably managed the family farm and tanning business. During the run-up to the Revolution, he plunged into Whig politics, winning a seat in the Pennsylvania Assembly. He eagerly read the military classics, drilled militia, and dreamed of martial fame.

When war came, Colonel Wayne recruited a regiment and found himself working on the defense of New York City. Henry Lee later noted that Wayne "had a constitutional attachment to the sword."[2] Wayne and his men were soon ordered to join the corps that General Sullivan was taking north to support the faltering invasion of Canada. Wayne acquitted himself in battle, but found little glory in the long retreat that followed.

He ended up at Fort Ticonderoga, his men weak, tattered, and disease-ridden. Yet the Pennsylvanian was an optimist. "Our country can absorb much & still rise," he declared.[3] He and his troops manned the fort during the summer of 1776, while Benedict Arnold furiously constructed the fleet that would protect them on Lake Champlain. After Arnold ended the threat, Horatio Gates left Wayne in charge of the fort. Commanding a sick, undersupplied garrison in a freezing wilderness far from the action was onerous duty. Wayne's only consolation was that Congress raised him to brigadier general that winter.

In May 1777, Washington called Wayne back to help organize militia units near his Chester County home. It was the first time he had seen his wife, children, and mother in a year and a half. Wayne's relationship with Polly, at first affectionate, had grown cold. Long separation and Wayne's admitted "fondness for ladies' society" contributed to the estrangement. Flirtatious as he was with women not his wife, Wayne's real love was war itself.

The patriots spent much of the summer waiting to see what General Howe would do. The British commander remained entrenched in New York City, leaving George Washington in "a State of constant perplexity." In the middle of July, Howe loaded sixteen thousand troops, heavy guns, and horses onto the ships of his brother's fleet and headed out to sea. The Americans scratched their heads and laid bets on where he was headed. On August 22, word arrived at Washington's New Jersey headquarters that the British fleet was sailing up Chesapeake Bay and would soon land sixty miles southwest of Philadelphia, threatening the capital. Washington put his army into motion.

The commander in chief choreographed a grand parade through Philadelphia to buck up the morale of local patriots. Anthony Wayne, who rode at the head of his brigade of Pennsylvania Continentals, reveled in the display. Some of his troops referred to him as Dandy Wayne. He was, an observer noted, "somewhat addicted to the vaunting style." He readily admitted the predilection. "I have an insuperable bias in favor of an elegant uniform and a soldierly appearance," he wrote to Washington. But Wayne was no popinjay. He could, it was said, "fight as well as brag." Washington noted that Wayne was "more active and enterprising than judicious and cautious."[4]

The ardent Wayne had suggested to his Excellency a plan to send out troops, including Wayne's men, to strike the British hard on both flanks. He modestly admitted that the tactic was not his own—Caesar had used it against the Gauls. Washington decided to adopt a more conservative, defensive stance.

Wayne waited along the Brandywine early on that hot morning, listening to American riflemen sniping at the advancing British. The firing grew closer. Given the position of honor opposite Chadd's Ford, Wayne had posted his Continentals on a rise that looked down on the waist-deep water. They stood in the center of the American position, ready to take the brunt of the enemy advance.

A red sun squinted through fog, promising a day of oppressive heat. The men fidgeted in bowel-loosening anticipation. Eager to fight, Wayne could only wait. Soon, forces led by Hessian general Wihelm von Knyphausen pushed the skirmishers back and approached the creek directly opposite Wayne's position. General Knox's cannon sang hosannas. The Germans blasted back with their own field guns. Wayne's men kept up a rattling of musket fire. The enemy advanced no further.

Then a rumor: Scouts sent out by General Sullivan on the American right had spotted a large body of enemy troops moving northwest, left to right, along the river. Thousands of men, the reports said. Sixteen heavy guns. Generals Howe and Cornwallis, conspicuous in gold braid, at the head of the column.

Washington and his aides were mystified by "the very magnitude of the blunder." For the British to divide their army directly in front of an enemy force was unorthodox and dangerous. It invited the Americans to fall upon and defeat one part of the force, then turn their attention to the other. That was just what Washington decided to do.

Wayne was thrilled. He was about to enact the type of soul-stirring head-on charge that had excited him since boyhood. Washington ordered his entire division across the creek.

But no. Another scouting mission had detected no movement on the opposite bank. The first move was likely a feint. Washington would not be fooled—he called off the attack. Wayne's troops resumed their defensive positions and continued to trade shots with Knyphausen's Hessians.

At two in the afternoon, a farmer showed up at the American headquarters with urgent news. He had seen two British brigades and the dust of a larger force approaching the Americans on their side of the Brandy-wine. Further investigation made the truth snap into clarity.

In a close replay of the battle on Long Island, General Howe had again outthought and outmaneuvered both Sullivan and Washington. Just as British general Grant had toyed with Lord Stirling at the beginning of that battle, Knyphausen had been "amusing" Wayne at the ford. Howe had marched seven thousand men twelve miles up the Brandywine and come over at a ford that Sullivan had left unguarded. Washington had missed a chance by recalling Wayne's men. Howe had gambled on the American commander's cautious indecision.

The British host now attacked the hasty lines manned by the brigades of Lord Stirling and Adam Stephen. Sullivan's own men came up late. The roar of the enemy's heavy field guns was heard in Philadelphia, twenty-five miles away.

General Greene's troops, who had been standing behind the line as a reserve, rushed to the scene of the main fighting, covering the four miles in forty-five minutes. Wayne's men waited nervously on the riverbank, ready to handle the Hessians even as they listened to fierce musketry explode to their rear.

All over the field, the fighting was "almost Muzzle to Muzzle," as "small arms roared like the rolling of a drum." A Pennsylvania militiaman reported that "bombshells and shot fell around me like hail, cutting down my comrades on every side, and tearing off the limbs of trees like a whirl-wind."[5] The Americans began to give way before the merciless attack.

"Our way was over the dead and dying," a retreating American soldier reported, "and I saw many bodies crushed to pieces beneath the wagons, and we were spattered with blood." A private described the battle as "Cannons Roaring muskets Cracking Drums Beating Bumbs Flying all Round, men a dying."[6]

In front of Wayne's troops, a hammering artillery duel filled the field with smoke. The Hessians took advantage of the thick haze to come pouring across the Brandywine. Wayne saw glory leak away. His men fought well in a losing cause. Like the rest of the army, they were forced back. They had to relinquish their field guns as the enemy overran them. The Americans backpedaled toward Philadelphia, having lost more than a thousand men.

———•◦•———

Derogatory rumors about Washington's qualities as commander began to circulate just as they had a year earlier when Howe drove him from New York. The grumbling was justified. Washington had shown that he could organize and sustain an army, but on the battlefield he seemed an inept tactician. Even Nathanael Greene was reported to have commented, "The General does want decision. For my part, I decide in a moment."[7]

Through "a variety of perplexing Manoevres" over the next couple of weeks, Howe kept the American army off balance and continued to threaten Philadelphia. The American troops, "nearly without shoes or winter clothes and often without food," marched 140 miles in eleven days.[8] One British feint sent the members of Congress fleeing the city in the middle of the night.

Anthony Wayne's game performance along the Brandywine impressed Washington, who sent him out with a 1,500-man brigade to keep an eye on Howe's army. Intimate with the terrain, Wayne posted his men in a hidden camp only four miles from the British. He advised Washington, "For God's sake, Push on as fast as possible." Washington declined the invitation to launch a full-scale battle. He sent Wayne more ammunition but warned him to "take care of Ambuscades."[9] Wayne planned an attack on the British rear guard for the morning of September 21. He failed to take care of ambuscades.

While Wayne's men huddled in makeshift huts or gathered around campfires near the Paoli Tavern, a British force, alerted by local loyalists, was marching toward them through the darkness. British general Charles Grey gave orders for the soldiers of his battalion to unload their muskets or remove the flints. They were to rely on their bayonets rather than risk shooting their comrades in the dark.

At midnight they came stampeding into the American camp and attacked the men they could see silhouetted against the fires. Wayne galloped among the tents to alert his men, but British soldiers were able to mingle with his troops before they could form a line or run. The violence became ugly. The British drove the points of their bayonets into human flesh and slashed opponents with swords. An officer described it as a "dreadful scene of Havock."[10]

Wayne was able to muster his troops and save his field guns as he organized a hasty retreat. Civilians found fifty-three bodies on the battlefield in the morning and buried the fallen in a common grave.

"No-Flint" Grey acquired a reputation as a butcher. Stories of the merciless bayoneting of men trying to surrender gained wide currency. But giving quarter in the heat of battle was always discretionary, and the wholesale slaughter of prisoners was belied by the fact that Grey led away seventy of Wayne's men as captives. Yet the battle lived in history as the "Paoli Massacre."

Wayne would be acquitted with "highest honor" by a court-martial investigating his conduct in the battle. But the misadventure remained for him a keen embarrassment, one he was determined to avenge.

———•—•———

Howe feinted an attack on Washington, then marched into Philadelphia unopposed on September 26. He stationed some of his men in the city and encamped most in the northern suburb of Germantown, a row of one hundred houses and shops along the north-south road out of town.

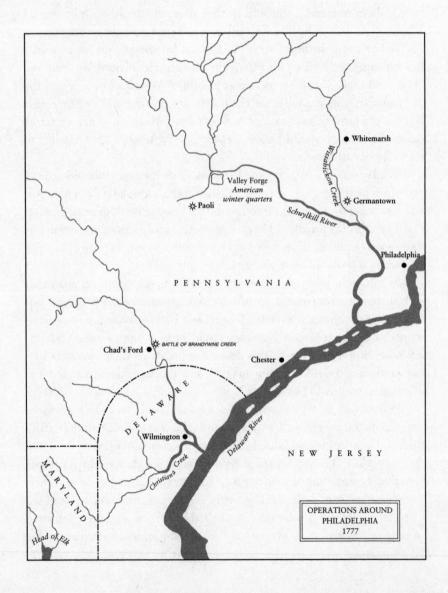

Washington gathered his army about twenty miles north of this village, hoping to pull off a repeat of the raid on Trenton. He wanted to hit Howe one more time before cold weather brought an end to the campaign.

Although Wayne and his wife had drifted apart emotionally, he and Polly continued to correspond. "Every Artery beats in unison," he wrote to her as he prepared for the attack, "and I feel unusual Ardour."[11]

The night of October 3, the Continental Army marched sixteen miles along four separate roads to carry out Washington's typically complicated battle plan. Around eight in the morning, the troops under Wayne and Sullivan ran into the popping fire of British pickets. The enemy gave way. Wayne led forward his panting, cheering men. The sight of retreating redcoats thrilled them. For the first time in the war, an entire British army was fleeing before an American attack. For more than a mile, Wayne's Continentals drove the enemy. Sullivan's brigade pushed ahead on the other side of the road.

Wayne's men had not forgotten the Paoli battle and "took Ample Vengeance for the Night's work," Wayne later wrote to his wife. "The Rage and fury of the Soldiers, were not to be Restrained." [12]

Then fog, smoke, confusion, lack of ammunition, tangled communications, and friendly fire combined to cancel the victory. Suddenly, it was the Americans who were retreating.

Critical mistakes let the chance slip. Some British infantrymen had taken refuge in the stone house of Benjamin Chew on the north end of Germantown. Henry Knox, ill served on this occasion by his voluminous military reading, remembered that a commander should never leave a castle manned in his rear. The pointless fighting around the Chew house delayed the reserves needed for the actual battle up front.

General Adam Stephen, marching with Greene's division, heard the commotion at the Chew House and veered off without orders. Coming on Wayne's brigade in "thickest fog known in the memory of man," his troops opened fire on their own men. The clash broke the cohesion of both groups and accelerated the retreat. Stephen was blamed for the debacle and cashiered, although he was not, as accused, drunk during the battle. His military career had begun fighting beside Washington at Jumonville Glen. It ended at Germantown.

"A *windmill* attack was made upon a house," Wayne later stated, referring to the futile assault that wasted time at the Chew mansion. "Confusion ensued and we ran away from the arms of victory open to receive us."[13]

Yet for all their mistakes, the Americans remained upbeat. The thrill of watching the best army in Europe run before them in a pitched battle softened the regret of having to "leave the ground to a conquered foe."

Thomas Paine, who breakfasted with Washington the day after the battle, correctly observed that the Americans could only acquire the art of war "by practice and by degrees." They could "feel themselves more important," he said, as they trudged into winter quarters.[14]

The Continentals had not pulled off another Trenton, but Washington's audacious plan had come breathtakingly close to succeeding. His soldiers, Washington reported to Congress, had "gained what all young troops gain by being in actions."[15] They were learning.

TWELVE

SOMETHING MORE
AT STAKE

1777

Facing increasing dangers as he edged southward, British general John Burgoyne would have preferred General Howe to have come up the Hudson to bring him aid rather than travel south to attack Philadelphia. But the flamboyant Burgoyne remained confident of reaching Albany. "Britons never retreat," he told his men.[1] He still thought of his army as an irresistible force.

Horatio Gates hardly gave the impression of an immovable object. His receding chin, thin gray hair, and spectacles suggested a counting house clerk rather than a military hero. But following the fall of Ticonderoga, Congress had had enough of General Philip Schuyler. They wanted a man who could inspire militia and who knew how to fight. They gave Gates, the former British major, his long-sought independent command.

Under Schuyler, the American troops had fallen back all the way to the juncture of the Mohawk and Hudson Rivers, barely ten miles north of Albany. Gates arrived there on August 19. He scorned advice from a disappointed Schuyler, who wrote, "I have done all that could be done . . . it is left to you, General, to reap the fruits of my labors."[2] In fact, neither general had played a role in the serious check that John Stark's men had delivered Burgoyne's forces at Bennington three days earlier.

The new commander sent Schuyler to Albany to attend to the army's supply problems. In camp, Gates found troops who had endured nothing but defeat and backward movement. His arrival, a soldier said, "raised us, as if by magic. We began to hope and then to act."[3]

More help came. Daniel Morgan, released from captivity, had rejoined the army in January 1777, and Congress had promoted him to colonel. Washington, impressed with Morgan's grit, wanted him to lead an entire regiment of mobile fighters. His men would dress in hunting shirts, carry rifles, and intimidate their enemies by "screaming and yelling as the Indians do." Residents of northern New York wanted these hardy soldiers in particular to help neutralize the scourge of Burgoyne's Indians. "Oh for some Virginia rifle-men!" cried a citizen of Albany. Washington hurried Morgan north. "I know of no Corps so likely to check their progress," he wrote to Morgan, "as the one you Command. I have great dependence on you, your Officers and Men."[4]

Another, more problematic, fighter came to Gates's aid as well. During the summer, Benedict Arnold had rushed westward to help stop a second arm of the enemy invasion force. British general Barry St. Leger had brought a force of regulars, loyalists, and Indians down the Mohawk Valley from Lake Ontario to reinforce Burgoyne. A bloody battle with local militiamen at Oriskany and a ruse cooked up by Arnold had prompted the Indians to depart and forced St. Leger's retreat.

Gates quickly ordered Arnold to rejoin the main army. The two had worked together the year before, but even then Gates had recognized "the warmth of General Arnold's temper." Now Arnold was on edge because Congressional politicians had refused to make him a major general in the February round of promotions, during which they had also passed over John Stark. Although they got around to raising Arnold in May, seniority left him suffocated under less experienced officers. He had gone so far as to tender his resignation, then suspended the action to attend to the current crisis. Arnold's friendship with Schuyler made Gates wary. Arnold found himself welcomed at headquarters "with the greatest coolness" and quickly took offense. His prickly, presumptuous personality rubbed his commander the wrong way. Trouble was brewing.

Gates put Arnold in charge of the army's left wing, giving him Morgan's elite corps. Additional Continentals arrived from the south. New York and New England militiamen responded to Gates's call. He took advantage of events like the Jenny McCrea murder to boost recruitment. He tightened discipline and improved conditions in camp. On September 8, Gates ordered his troops to advance rather than retreat for the first time that summer. A sense of exhilaration shot through the men as they stepped off to march twelve miles to the north.

At the village of Stillwater, Gates found the river plain too wide for easy defense. He decided to proceed a bit farther to a mostly wooded plateau known as Bemis Heights. From there he could train guns on the river road, along which Burgoyne's force would have to pass. The men spent the next week digging. The Polish volunteer Tadeusz Kosciuszko, a genius of engineering, directed the construction of fortifications stretching west more than a mile up the slope from the riverbank and across the plateau. Having attended military academies in both Poland and France, "Kos," as American officers called him, designed as effective a defense as was possible to throw up in a short time.

Gates reinforced Morgan's regiment with three hundred fighters chosen for their ability and under the command of Major Henry Dearborn. The muskets and bayonets of these troops would add another lethal weapon to Morgan's arsenal. Morgan's riflemen ranged in front of the works, gathering intelligence and keeping Burgoyne's scouts from discovering the Americans' intentions. They terrorized the Indians, until none of the braves could be "brought within the sound of a rifle shot."

———•—•———

Fellow officers knew Horatio Gates as a worldly, convivial soldier, fond of jokes that went "beyond the nice limits of dignity," and given to swearing in a way that made "a New Englandman's hair almost stand on end." He was, a biographer wrote, "a good hand at cards, a jolly drinking partner."[5]

Gates's primary talent was for organization, for staff work rather than battlefield command. After being seriously wounded at Braddock's Monongahela disaster, Gates had seen little additional action in the Seven Years' War. His career, like those of many officers, had stalled with the peace. In 1773, he sold his commission and retired to a small Virginia estate, bringing with him his wife, Elizabeth, and teenage son Robert. Enamored of the republican ideals percolating in America, he embraced the cause of independence early.

Gates scrupulously looked after his men's welfare. Samuel Adams, a Gates booster, noted that his men loved him because "he always shares with them in fatigue and danger."[6] Gates was careful not to squander lives for glory. Militiamen responded to his call because they knew he would promptly send them home when they were no longer needed.

Having taken his stand, Gates waited to see what Burgoyne would do. The enemy army had camped ten miles to the north, on the east side of the river opposite the village of Saratoga. Burgoyne's hope of supplies from Bennington and of reinforcements down the Mohawk had been dashed. But his army was still dangerous. He commanded six thousand professional killers and more than fifty field cannon.

Dangerous and desperate. British food supplies would run out in less than a month. Burgoyne's two options were clear. He could prudently pull back to Fort Ticonderoga before winter and hope to complete his mission the following year. Or he could push toward Albany. To get there he would have to follow the road across the river and fight his way past the rebels.

On September 13, American scouts reported British activity. Burgoyne marched his army across the Hudson on a pontoon bridge in a showy manner "reminding one of a grand parade in the midst of peace." Once over, his men dismantled the bridge, severing their supply line back to Canada. Five days later, the British army was camped along the river four miles north of the American position. The men from both armies could hear the drums of the enemy pounding signals within their camps. A violent confrontation was now imminent.

<hr>

Increasingly at odds with each other, Horatio Gates and Benedict Arnold disagreed about whether the Americans should adopt a strategy of defense or offense. Gates was content to wait inside his fortifications and let Burgoyne attack him. Arnold yearned to go out and fall on the British before they reached the American lines.

Personality dictated their positions: Gates cautious, Arnold impetuous. Each had reason on his side. Why waste men and risk his army in a pitched battle, Gates figured. Far better to remain behind breastworks against which Burgoyne would wear out his troops. From long experience, Gates respected British fighting ability. So far, he had read Burgoyne's intentions perfectly. His opponent, he knew, was an "Old Gamester." He observed that it was clear "the General's Design is to Risque all upon one Rash Stroke."[7]

Arnold argued that it was in the woods that American fighters excelled. If the British overpowered them there, they would still have the option of pulling back to their fortifications. If they waited, the enemy might drag up heavy guns and demolish their hasty earthworks.

Gates, wearied of the paperwork of staff positions, had fixed his sights on fame and honor. Arnold, already a blazing comet in the American firmament, was determined to show an ungrateful Congress its error in denying him the laurels he deserved. Each man saw the pending battle as an opportunity to fulfill his deepest need. Meanwhile, the "awful expectation and suspense" mounted.

The tension peaked on the dank morning of September 19. American scouts reported redcoats moving out of their camp and mounting Bemis Heights. By eleven, the sun had burned off the early fog. The boom of a British signal cannon broke the silence. The American soldiers, still inside their fortified line, nervously gripped their weapons.

Gates held to his defensive plan. His only concession was to allow Arnold to send Morgan and his regiment to the north and west to see what the enemy was up to. The riflemen hurried forward through the woods. They took up a position on a farm once owned by a man named Freeman, one of the few areas of cleared fields on the heights. A British picket force came into view on the north side of the clearing. Morgan's men fired. So accurate was their aim that all the British officers but one fell dead in an instant. The rest of the advance party fled in panic.

The Americans, their blood up, sprinted after them. They collided squarely with a heavy force of British infantry. A ripping volley stopped the patriot riflemen cold and scattered them. Morgan lost touch with his men during the charge and assumed the worst. He was reported to have wept with frustration at the setback. But his turkey call signal soon drew the men back into formation.

With a fight on, Arnold ordered the rest of his regiments into action to support Morgan. The battle concentrated on the farm clearing. General Enoch Poor's brigade of nine hundred New Hampshire Continentals, backed by additional militia, came into line with Morgan's men. The explosion of their fire echoed for miles through woods that had never known such a roar. The British fell back, the Americans rushed ahead to capture enemy guns. Burgoyne ordered his grenadiers to charge with bayonets.

Here the patriots had no trenches or breastworks to protect them. A flat-out slugging match raged in the open field. The Continentals, now with two years of experience behind them, faced the cold steel of Britain's largest and fiercest soldiers. The rebels did not break. They leveled their muskets and fired. Their volley stunned the grenadiers and made them recoil.

Poor, a forty-three-year-old merchant, later remembered that "the blaze from the artillery and small arms was incessant and sounded like the roll of the drum. By turns the British and Americans drove each other, taking and retaking the fieldpieces . . . often mingling in a hand to hand wrestle and fight."[8]

The brawl became a scene of utter mayhem, a wild confusion of fire and smoke. "Senior officers who had witnessed the hardest fighting of the Seven Years' War declared that they had never experienced so long and hot a fire."[9] The death of many British officers was "attributed to the great execution of the riflemen, who directed their fire against them in particular."[10]

Arnold tried frantically to coordinate the action. One of Dearborn's men remembered Arnold "riding in front of the lines, his eyes flashing." It was a sight that "electrified the line."[11]

The battle went on and on. Late in the afternoon, it seemed the Americans were on the verge of defeating what was clearly Burgoyne's effort to smash the rebel army. The fighting had reduced the British regiment at the center from 350 men to a mere 60 still firing. Morgan's riflemen had picked off two-thirds of the enemy gunners. Arnold, who "seemed inspired with the fury of a demon," galloped back to headquarters, two miles from the action, where Gates had remained throughout the day.[12] He begged for more troops to finish off Burgoyne then and there. Gates "deemed it prudent not to weaken" his lines.[13] Prudence prevailed.

As day slipped toward evening, the Americans heard a noise on their right. A cannon blasted their ranks from barely a hundred yards. Fresh troops, the Brunswick forces of General Friedrich von Riedesel, came rushing straight at the Americans, drums beating, German throats howling. The surprise took the wind out of the American attack. Arnold pulled his troops back. The British occupied the farm clearing, now strewn with dead and wounded men. The fight was over.

Burgoyne tried to put a positive face on the battle, calling it "a smart and very honorable action," a victory even.[14] Although he occupied the field, the rebels looming in the dark made it too dangerous even to gather his wounded. The screams of fallen men cut through the chill night. Six hundred British soldiers had been killed or injured or taken prisoner. The Americans had lost three hundred. The rebels had gotten the better of the best army in the world.

"They are not that contemptible enemy we had hitherto imagined them," a British officer admitted of the Americans. The reason, Henry Dearborn suggested, was that in contrast to the enemy "we . . . had Something more at Stake than fighting for six Pence Pr Day."[15]

The fight at Freeman's farm, which had involved only a portion of the troops on each side, did not decide the matter. The British army was still potent. The Americans had run desperately low on ammunition. But

Burgoyne had received a stunning blow. He ordered his men to dig in. They quickly built breastworks behind Freeman's farm and two substantial redoubts of logs and earth to protect their right flank and rear.

British general Henry Clinton, who was commanding in New York while General Howe sparred with Washington's army around Philadelphia, had gotten word through to Burgoyne that he would soon "make a push" up the Hudson and attack the forts guarding the Highlands. If he was successful, he might force Gates to send part of his army south. If that happened, Burgoyne might break through to Albany. If . . .

An avid gambler, Burgoyne thought the chance was worth the wait. As it happened, Clinton outsmarted Israel Putnam, captured an American fort and sailed a short distance up the Hudson. But thinking of the action as a diversion only, he soon returned to New York. Burgoyne waited in vain.

The interlude was no pleasant respite for Burgoyne's troops. Morgan's riflemen ranged the woods, taking aim at every redcoat they encountered. "Not a night passed without firing," Burgoyne would later remember. British and German soldiers slept in their clothes for weeks, ready for a surprise attack. Flour and salt pork were running out.

Gates, elated that his men had severely punished the cream of the British army, smelled victory. From the militiamen streaming into camp he formed a comforting reserve for his Continentals. General Schuyler dutifully procured gunpowder and ammunition to restore the army's fire power. A rare mood of exhilaration swept the rebel force.

At this critical juncture, the smoldering rivalry at headquarters burst into flame. Perhaps Gates felt Arnold's shadow creeping over the glory he was now all but certain of attaining. In his report to Congress about the battle at Freeman's farm, he failed to mention Arnold's name or to acknowledge the troops under Arnold's command, informing the world that the engagement had involved only "a detachment of the army."[16]

To add injury to insult, he weakened Arnold's left wing by reassigning Morgan's elite regiment to his own command. Washington, hard pressed around Philadelphia, had asked him to send Morgan's corps back to Pennsylvania, but Gates had declined. "Your Excellency," he wrote, "would not wish me to part with the corps the army of General Burgoyne are most afraid of."[17]

By the evening of September 22, three days after battle, Arnold had had enough. He stormed into Gates's tent "in great warmth" and loudly protested his treatment. Gates became "rather passionate and very assuming." He fired back that, since Arnold had resigned his commission, he really held no rank in the army. Because General Lincoln would soon return to camp, Arnold was not needed—Gates relieved him of all duty. "High words and gross language ensued," a witness reported, "and Arnold retired in a rage."[18]

With a still-powerful enemy camped on their front, the American high command was thrown into turmoil. Arnold asked for and received a pass to travel to Philadelphia, where he would join Washington's army and plead his case. But the situation on Bemis Heights was far too precarious to lose a warrior of Arnold's caliber. Every general officer in camp signed a petition "requesting him not to quit the service at this critical moment." Arnold agreed to stay.[19]

He continued to browbeat Gates, pushing for an immediate attack. "The army are clamoring for action," he wrote. Gates stopped inviting him to his staff meetings. Arnold wrote angry notes to Gates complaining of treatment that would mortify "a person with less pride than I have." Gates refused to placate him.[20]

The relentless, urgent demands of war certainly contributed to this clash of personalities. Both Gates and Arnold had oversized egos, but both were also under extraordinary pressure. "The Fatigue of Body & mind, Which I continually undergo," Gates wrote to his wife the day of his worst altercation with Arnold, "is too much for my Age and Constitution."[21] Arnold had been active in the cause almost continuously for two-and-a-half years. His personal fortune had evaporated, his wife had died, and he had been seriously wounded. He had just finished fighting his third pivotal battle of the war.

From the battlefield at night, the men heard animals howl. Packs of wolves had come down from the mountains. They were digging up shallow graves, feeding on the decaying flesh of dead men.

———————

Morgan continued to lead the men of his regiment out to scout and harass the enemy. On October 6, he took eight hundred men through the woods into the enemy's rear. They grabbed seven prisoners. A heavy rain and oncoming night forced Morgan's men to hunker down where they were rather than risk stumbling into the enemy in the dark.

With daylight, the rangers returned to the American camp. They gathered around fires to dry off, eat, and rest. About midday, Gates's aide, James Wilkinson, brought word that British troops had begun to move forward. Gates laconically replied, "Well then, order on Morgan to begin the game."[22]

Having been over the ground repeatedly, Morgan suggested that his men filter through the woods and appear on the British right just as a regiment of Continentals slammed into their left flank. Gates agreed. He sent Enoch Poor's experienced New Hampshire men to attack Burgoyne directly, while Morgan looped to the west.

Half an hour later, Poor's men encountered the British. A reconnaissance force, which included a substantial part of the British army backed by ten field guns, was making a thrust toward the American left. Burgoyne, who led the operation himself, sought clarity. He wanted to see how the enemy forces were aligned, still hoping he could dislodge them from their fortifications. As Poor's infantrymen climbed a slope toward the enemy, the British grenadiers fired. Their musket and canister shot lacerated the air over the heads of the Americans. The redcoats extended their bayonets in the sun and charged down the hill, bellowing hoarse war cries. Poor's men let loose a searing volley of musketry. Then they too charged.

At almost the same moment, Morgan's men, who had reached high ground slightly behind the British right, "poured down like a torrent from the hill." Major Dearborn's musket men slammed into the enemy from the other side, running and shouting as loudly as they could. The British "Retreated with great Precipitation & Confusion."[23] They tried once to form a line, but could not withstand the onrushing Americans. They sprinted for the closest fortification, a redoubt guarding the west end of the British position.

Soon afterward, Wilkinson came to the spot where Poor's men had attacked and beaten the grenadiers. The ground, he later remembered, "presented a scene of complicated horror and exultation." Lying at his feet were "eighteen grenadiers in the agonies of death," and three wounded officers. Colonel Joseph Cilley, a forty-three-year-old New Hampshire farmer, had climbed atop the largest of the British field guns to celebrate its capture. The British commander, Major Acland, lay wounded in both legs. Wilkinson rescued him from a thirteen-year-old rebel who was about to fire a musket ball into his head.[24]

The first phase of the battle had lasted less than an hour. The reconnaissance had told Burgoyne all he needed to know. Hope of a breakthrough was an illusion. He sent his secretary with a message to the other commanders to call off the probe and pull back, but the fortunes of war intervened. The aide was shot and captured. The battle would continue.

———•◦•———

With growing impatience, Benedict Arnold had been listening to the sounds of the pitched fight. "I am afraid to trust you, Arnold," Gates had told him.[25] Although he held no official position in Gates's army, Arnold could no longer restrain himself. He jumped astride his horse and galloped out of the American fortifications. Gates sent an officer to recall him. Arnold spurred his horse onward, and "behaved more like a madman than a cool and discreet officer."[26]

With Morgan routing the light infantry on the British right and Poor decimating the grenadiers on their left, the Brunswick troops who formed the enemy center were exposed. General Ebenezer Learned's Massachusetts Continentals were forming to attack them when Arnold arrived on the scene. Arnold rode to the head of the advancing troops. In a joint command with Learned, he led three regiments against the German line. They failed to break through, but kept up a steady fire that drove the enemy back.

On the other side of the field, General Simon Fraser, the most gifted of Burgoyne's lieutenants, tried to rally his troops to stop the British collapse. He rode up and down the lines, giving orders and shouting encouragement. Squinting through the smoke, Daniel Morgan recognized that Fraser was stiffening the resistance in front of his riflemen. According to an often repeated story, he ordered an illiterate young Pennsylvania sergeant named Timothy Murphy to kill the scarlet-clad general. An expert marksman, Murphy climbed a tree and took aim at the officer from several hundred yards away. He fired a ball into Fraser's stomach. As the general slumped, the British position began to crumble. The loss of Fraser "helped to turn the fate of the day," a British officer later admitted.[27]

Arnold, meanwhile, "rushed into the thickest of the fight with his usual recklessness."[28] As the Germans and British maneuvered back toward their fortifications, Arnold, in his blue and buff uniform, rode headlong across the field, through fire from both sides, to again take charge of Learned's brigade. He led them toward a British redoubt. When that fortification proved too solid, he charged on. Along with Morgan and Dearborn, he attacked another, larger fort blocking access to the British rear.

Brunswicker colonel Heinrich von Breymann, whose men Seth Warner's Green Mountain Boys had roughed up at Bennington, commanded the troops who defended this fortified rise. The Americans came on from all sides. Arnold, intoxicated by the fighting, spurred his horse through an opening into the midst of the redoubt. The Americans followed him. All through the fighting, Arnold had possessed a charm that had protected him from flying lead. Now a musket ball tore through his leg and smashed his thigh bone. His horse collapsed. Arnold was out of the fight.

If he had not been wounded, Arnold might have rallied the Americans to rush into the British rear, capture their supplies, and end the campaign in an hour. As it was, the enemy mounted an unsuccessful attempt to retake the Breymann redoubt before darkness brought the curtain down on the day's fighting.

———•◦•———

Burgoyne, his army battered and exposed, saw that his options had run out. Britons must now retreat. In the middle of the night, the army pulled back from Bemis Heights and assumed a defensive position near the river. He had lost almost 900 men killed, wounded, or captured. American casualties were less than 150. The guns that Burgoyne had dragged onto the field had been lost. The next day, he continued his withdrawal, leaving behind a hospital crowded with men too badly injured to travel. They did not include General Fraser, who sighed, "Oh, fatal ambition!" and died at eight o'clock on the morning after the battle.

It was not only the British who were dismayed. American artillery captain John Henry, the twenty-year-old son of Virginia governor Patrick Henry, had distinguished himself in the battle. After the cataclysm died down, he wandered the field, staring at the faces, the blue lips, dead staring eyes, and glistening teeth, of men he had known. The sight unhinged him. He broke his sword in half and went "raving mad." He disappeared for months and never fought again.[29]

The British commander still imagined he could make a stand to the north at Fort Edward. Harassed by Morgan's riflemen, his army limped the few miles back to the village of Saratoga, which would give the whole bloody affair its name. The next day, it rained.

Burgoyne, the dashing cosmopolitan who had mocked the rebels and plotted their demise, who had given stretch to murderous Indians, who had slogged through the wilderness with wagons loaded down by his glad rags and intoxicants, now grew rattled and indecisive. He still hoped that General Clinton would appear to distract the Continental Army that was moving in for the kill. He still hoped he could move his own army, even his remaining artillery, out of harm's way.

He hoped against hope. Among those who tightened the noose was John Stark. The hero of Bennington led a thousand fresh New Hampshire recruits across the Hudson into the enemy's rear and blocked the road with field guns. John Burgoyne had run out of options.

———•◦•———

On a sunny, chilly Friday, October 17, 1777, British soldiers marched out of their camp and laid their arms down in a meadow. General Gates, wary of the sudden appearance of Clinton in his rear, had offered generous terms. To spare British feelings, the surrender would be termed a "convention," as if it were the conclusion of a business deal. The Americans were to allow Burgoyne's troops to return home under a promise not to fight again. Congress would find plenty of excuses to avoid ever doing so.

Burgoyne donned his best dress uniform and rode with his generals and staff to meet Gates. The man in scarlet and gold braid cut a fine figure compared to the smaller American, who wore a plain blue coat, no wig, and wire-rimmed spectacles. The men dined in Gates's quarters, hardly more than a shack.

The British troops marched into captivity along a road lined on either side by American soldiers. The ragged, motley victors observed strict silence. Their discipline impressed the men they had defeated. An American band struck up "Yankee Doodle Dandy," a tune that a British surgeon had written during the French and Indian War to mock the pretension of the provincials.

Happy explosions of cannon greeted the news of the surrender all over New England. When word reached the American soldiers near Philadelphia, still licking their wounds after the battle at Germantown, they erupted in jubilation. Neither Tories nor enemy soldiers, hearing the joyful firing, could believe that an entire British army had surrendered to the rebels.

Gates, relieved from a tremendous strain, issued a magnanimous report of the battle, generously lauding "the gallant Major General Arnold." He informed Congress that "too much praise cannot be given the Corps commanded by Col. Morgan." After the battle he embraced the "Old Wagoner" and said, "Morgan, you have done wonders."[30]

During the nineteenth century it became customary to call the victory at Saratoga the turning point of the Revolutionary War. The battle did more than neutralize the long-threatened invasion from Canada. Soon after the surrender, the Foreign Affairs Committee of the Continental Congress sent word of the event to France, hoping that it would result in the "public acknowledgment of the Independence of these United States."[31] It did. The French committed themselves to war with Britain in December and signed a treaty with the United States in February 1778.

But for the Americans, Saratoga was only a bright spot in a back-and-forth contest whose end no one could yet predict. The British ministry sent additional reinforcements across the Atlantic. The war continued. The patriots' darkest moments still lay before them, as George Washington would soon learn. He was about to lead his army into winter quarters in an area outside Philadelphia called Valley Forge.

THIRTEEN

THE DISCIPLINE
OF THE LEGGS

1778

"You might have tracked the army from White Marsh to Valley Forge by the blood of their feet," George Washington wrote.[1] A private who endured the march to winter quarters remembered the trail of "blood upon the rough frozen ground" left by his shoeless companions.

The image is iconic—the reality of walking barefoot in the snow was excruciating, humiliating, and disheartening. News of the defeat of General Burgoyne's army proved a brief solace. An autumn of unsuccessful fighting had culminated in the enemy occupation of the new nation's capital, a disintegrating Continental Army, and a dispirited populace. Rather than pull back to more comfortable lodgings in inland cities, Washington installed the army in a makeshift camp at Valley Forge, twenty miles northwest of Philadelphia. Protected by the Schuylkill River, the troops would be far enough from the British for safety but close enough for vigilance.

While Howe and his officers savored the comforts of town, danced at balls, gambled in taverns, and fraternized with the city's many loyalists, Washington's ragged soldiers chopped down trees, notched logs, and plastered the chinks with mud to create their primitive, dirt-floor huts. The men compared them to dungeon cells.

Their suffering in the midst of one of the most productive areas of the country baffled the soldiers. One explanation was that they were fighting a war during a revolution. The break with Britain had brought an upheaval of public administration and order. Congress, a flimsy deliberative body, was guided by no traditions and few formal structures. The inexperienced state governments were often inept. The notion of paying taxes repelled many inhabitants, and the largely agricultural colonies lacked a surplus of wealth.

But the administrative tangle was only part of the explanation. The meanness, indecision, delay, and general contrariness of citizens in each of the thirteen states amplified the army's burden. The citizen soldiers who had rushed to fight early in the war were mostly gone from the army now. The Valley Forge soldiers, many of whom had signed on for three years or the duration of the war, were drawn largely from the young, the landless, the footloose, the poor. The people, as much as their representatives in Congress, had lost interest in the troops, whom they could look down on as the dregs of society.

The ongoing supply problems drove Washington to distraction. Pushing through brush and brambles, men quickly wore their clothing to rags. The garments continued to disintegrate until some men were literally naked, unable to emerge from their huts. Thousands lacked blankets. Three thousand were barefoot—frost-blackened toes required amputation. Hunger gripped bellies. "No meat! No meat!" the soldiers chanted, imitating crows. Receiving no meat, they cried: "No bread, no soldier!" They survived on a flour-and-water mixture baked into "fire cake" on hot rocks. Blanketless men sat shivering and coughing around smoldering green wood. They gagged on the smell of dead horses that lay decomposing in camp. They drew water from turbid, infected creeks. They fell to disease: putrid fever, pneumonia, and dysentery. In the hospital, they were thrown together with those still agonizing from battle wounds. Even there, blankets were scarce. More than two thousand men would die over the winter, twice as many Americans as had fallen in the battles around Philadelphia.

Pennsylvania farms had yielded a bumper crop in 1777. But the opposing armies had devoured the surplus food and forage. The British had captured a number of rebel supply depots. Ensconced in Philadelphia, they offered local farmers payment in silver coinage rather than the steadily deteriorating paper currency of the rebels.

The bungling of Congress amplified the supply crisis. The representatives—they were now meeting in York, Pennsylvania—neglected the army's needs until prodded by Washington and other officers. General Enoch Poor wrote angrily to officials back home in New Hampshire: "If any of them desert how can I punish them when they plead in their justification that on your part the Contract is broken?" The men needed supplies immediately or it would be "impracticable to keep them much longer in the field."[2]

"Poor food—," a camp physician summed up in his diary, "hard lodging—Cold Weather—fatigue—Nasty cloaths—nasty Cookery—Vomit half my time—smoak'd out my senses—the Devil's in't—I can't Endure it."[3]

Before Christmas, Washington wrote a blistering letter to Congress, laying out the army's difficulties in the starkest of terms. Unless supplies started flowing immediately, he said, "this Army must inevitably be reduced to one or other of these three things. Starve, dissolve, or disperse." He added, "Rest assured Sir this is not an exaggerated picture." He concluded with a biting sentence: "I can assure those Gentlemen that it is a much easier and less distressing thing to draw remonstrances in a comfortable room by a good fire side than to occupy a cold bleak hill and sleep under frost and Snow without Cloaths or Blankets."[4]

Their fellow citizens offered the Continental soldiers scant respect and little sympathy. Washington, however, wrote, "I feel superabundantly for them."[5]

———·—·———

Congress slowly creaked into motion. The commander in chief turned to his most trusted lieutenant to take the matter in hand. Nathanael Greene, a businessman before the war, organized foraging parties to scour the surrounding countryside. Both Washington and Greene loathed the confiscation of civilian property, but no other choice remained. "Inhabitants cry out and beset me from all quarters," Greene wrote to Washington, "but like Pharoh I harden my heart." He was determined to "forage the Country naked." He had civilians whipped for transporting produce to the British.[6]

Washington persuaded Greene to give up his field command and to assume the position of quartermaster general. Craving martial glory, the Rhode Island general bitterly resented the assignment. "Nobody ever heard of a quarter master in history," he complained to Washington. To his friend Henry Knox he bemoaned being "taken out of the line of splendor."[7]

Greene, who found the position "humiliating to my Military pride," spent the two years following the Valley Forge winter of 1778 laboring over accounting books, contracts, and shipping problems as he tried to keep the Continental Army in shoes, axes, blankets, and the thousand other supplies needed to wage war. Overseeing a battalion of three thousand clerks, buyers, and haulers, he was continually chagrined by inadequate finances and lack of cooperation. "The Growing avarice, and a declining currency," he observed, "are poor materials to build our Independence on."[8]

He hated the job and he was good at it. He brought discipline to the department, insisting that foragers display "proper deportment." He set up grain depots and improved logistics by sending men to repair bridges, improve roads, and commandeer wagons. Greene, like Washington, knew that keeping an army supplied in the field was just as crucial as winning battles. His business skills and common sense saved the army from dissolution. By the spring of 1778, conditions at Valley Forge had begun to inch toward improvement, but problems of supply would vex commanders until the very end of the war.

The army's senior officers lived in houses in the area surrounding the Valley Forge camp. Some were joined by their wives. Martha Washington came in time for her husband's forty-sixth birthday in February. She boosted the commander's spirits. The soldiers loved her. She was "busy from early morning until late at night" knitting stockings and sewing shirts for the troops. Martha was no stranger to death, having lost her first husband, three of her four children, and five younger siblings, including her dear sister Fanny, who had died in December. She organized a band of women who delivered food to soldiers and cared for the sick and wounded. Just the sight of the women heartened the troops.

Lord Stirling's wife came, as did his daughter, Lady Kitty, a favorite of Washington. Lucy Knox, with her baby daughter, arrived, escorted by a limping Benedict Arnold, for whom she had acted as go-between with an eligible young lady. An inveterate card player, Lucy loved the social life of camp. Nathanael Greene observed that she was mortified by her obesity, but that Henry was just as fat. The couple lacked a permanent home during the entire course of the war. When they were together, they slept in an iron bed that could hold their combined weight. They were, Greene thought, the ideal of marital bliss.

Greene's own young wife, Caty, had left her children with relatives to journey to camp. "The lady of General Greene," a soldier recorded, "is a handsome, elegant, and accomplished woman."[9] She conversed with French officers in their own tongue and flirted quite brazenly. Washington was not immune to her charms. He would, during one winter ball, dance with Caty for three hours straight. Anthony Wayne was another of her admirers. His own marriage had become a cinder—Polly declined to visit him, though she lived only a few miles away. Caty's loose behavior might have rankled Greene, as Lucy Knox reported that "all was not well with Greene [and] his lady."[10]

Modest dinner parties and communal songfests helped pass the winter days for the generals and their families. Some junior officers put on a performance of Washington's favorite play, Joseph Addison's *Cato*. The Enlightenment drama about Cato the Younger's resistance to Julius Caesar's tyranny, written in 1712, had already contributed to the rhetoric of the revolution. The lines rang out that winter:

> *What pity is it*
> *That we can die but once to serve our country.*
>
> *It is not now a time to talk of aught*
> *But chains or conquest, liberty or death.*

Help arrived from abroad. Benjamin Franklin and Silas Deane, American envoys in Paris, had recruited the most talented officers from among those who volunteered. In addition to engineer Tadeusz Kosciuszko, they sent over the Polish cavalry expert Casimir Pulaski and the experienced German officer Johann de Kalb. The veterans provided the army the experience, military insight, and leadership it was sorely lacking. Some came because they needed work, but many were inspired by a cause they saw as the embodiment of Enlightenment ideals. One European recruit would prove to be the most luminous of all the Revolutionary fighters. He was the nineteen-year-old French nobleman Gilbert de Motier, known as the Marquis de Lafayette.

Portraits from that time show Lafayette a slender, homely, effeminate, and impossibly youthful soldier. Possessed of enormous inherited wealth, he came to America at his own expense. He instantly charmed Washington and the entire high command with his affability, modesty, and sheer brilliance. Congress named him a major general but did not intend him to lead troops. Washington loved him and recognized his preternatural ability. Nathanael Greene found him irresistible due to "an inexplicable charm."

In September 1777, Lafayette had seen his first action at Brandywine Creek, where he had been shot in the leg. "Take care of him as if he were my son," Washington admonished those attending him.[11] By December the youth had assumed a role as one of Washington's most trusted confidants and was in command of an entire army division.

Given the defeats the army had endured, it was not surprising that grumbling about Washington's leadership rustled through the ranks and ignited whispers in Congress. He'd been outgeneraled, then outgeneraled again. By contrast, Horatio Gates had bagged an entire British army. Some thought Gates might be the man to take charge. A Congressional committee accused Washington of "Want of Genius & Activity." Even Anthony Wayne, a Washington supporter, detected in the commander "an over stretched caution, which is oftentimes attended with as fatal Consequences, as too much rashness."[12]

Congress formed a Board of War to look over Washington's shoulder, with Gates at its head. They sent a committee to Valley Forge to investigate the condition of the army. They appointed Thomas Conway, an Irish volunteer and critic of Washington, to the new post of inspector general, putting him in charge of training the troops.

To Washington and his close supporters, including Greene, Knox, Lafayette, and aide-de-camp Alexander Hamilton, these actions amounted to a "cabal" aimed at deposing the commander. Washington feared that Gates would "be exalted, on the ruin of my reputation and influence."[13] Showing his aptitude for political infighting, Washington deftly outmaneuvered his opponents. By spring, Congress had accepted Conway's resignation and Washington was again firmly in charge.

As winter began to relent, a foreign officer arrived in camp who would transform the beleaguered army almost overnight. At first glance, Baron Friedrich von Steuben appeared to be the most experienced and prestigious officer of any to join the American cause. In Europe, he held the exalted rank of lieutenant general. He had served as aide-de-camp to Frederick the Great, the Prussian king widely considered the military mastermind of the century. He traveled with an entourage of handsome young French officers, as befitted a personage of great stature. He bragged about his European estates.

It was a show. Yes, Steuben was a baron—a Germanic prince had made him a knight in the Order of Fidelity and given him the title *Freiherr.* He wore a large star on his breast to prove his nobility. Yes, he had served under Frederick the Great—he had been wounded twice during the Seven Years' War. But the highest rank Steuben had gained in Frederick's army was captain. After the war ended, he had been dismissed from the service.

He owned no estates. He had filled the past fourteen years managing the household of a prince in a minuscule German dominion. His prospects had been marred by a rumor that he had once "taken familiarities with young boys."[14]

Desperate for work, Steuben came to the attention of playwright Pierre-Augustin Caron de Beaumarchais, a former watchmaker who had transformed himself into a brilliant courtier at Versailles. The author of the satires *The Barber of Seville* and *The Marriage of Figaro*, Beaumarchais was an idealist and an intriguer. He had been helping to funnel French money and gunpowder to the Americans through the West Indies. Steuben might win a position in America, Beaumarchais told him, if he was willing to play a role. Steuben loved theater and agreed to assume the part his French friends created for him. They supplied him with the entourage and with travel expenses.

Steuben's sparkling credentials impressed Congress. His modesty and sincerity made their mark on Washington, who probably suspected that he was less than what he claimed to be. A gallant knight at heart, Steuben used his charm and refined social skills to win over the top American officers.

When he arrived in Valley Forge in late winter, 1778, he found that he was desperately needed. Order in the camp was missing, sentries not always posted, sanitation deficient, drunkenness common, marching sloppy. The Americans were novices, as a young patriot captain admitted, who "had everything to learn, and no one to instruct us who knew any better than ourselves."[15]

Washington had already been planning to put the army on a more professional footing. Greene's efforts as quartermaster were part of it. Someone had to oversee the rigorous training in a uniform method of drill that would shape the troops into a more efficient fighting force. That was Steuben's job.

In March, the baron began the daunting and urgent task of imparting military basics to ten thousand men in two months. Starting with a "model company" of a hundred men drawn from Washington's personal guard, Steuben began to train those who would in turn serve as trainers in their own regiments. He taught them how to stand at attention, their heads turned to a precise angle so that each man's left eye lined up with his coat buttons. He drilled them in uniform march: seventy-five paces a minute, each step twenty-eight inches long. Then he imparted more complicated maneuvers like wheeling, advancing obliquely, and deploying from a column of march into a line of battle. This last was an exercise that could easily descend into chaos. He taught them to wield the bayonet.

Steuben wandered the camp, asking questions through an interpreter and listening carefully to the answers. He came to empathize with the American soldiers, to admire them, and to understand the way that pride could mesh with patriotism in a republic. He strictly forbade officers to abuse their men, insisting that "their faults are to be pointed out with patience."[16]

He slowly turned the troops into a semblance of the disciplined, agile, and lethal infantry that had given Prussia its edge in European fighting. He understood that American soldiers responded more readily when they were told *why* to do something, not just given an order. He admired the men's perseverance. "No European army could have been kept together under such dreadful deprivations."[17]

The Prussian, who had put on a show to get his job, understood that spectacle was a critical part of military affairs. His alleged rank, his spruce uniform, and the shining star on his chest inspired awe. "Never before, or since, have I had such an impression of the ancient fabled God of War as when I looked on the baron," a private wrote.[18]

When necessary, Steuben swore. "Goddamn!" was one of his few English words. The French and German oaths he spouted amused the troops, who, like all soldiers, were connoisseurs of profanity. His rants prompted them to try and try again. Steuben made a show of his anger, and when it reached the point of absurdity, joined in the laughter.

Drilling the troops by day and feverishly writing out new instructions to be shared with the army by night, Steuben impressed his system on the forces. The men learned what Horatio Gates called "the Discipline of the Leggs."[19] They learned to respond instantly to an order or to the compelling tattoo of a drum. The Baron trained majors, captains, and lieutenants as if they were privates and insisted that officers participate in drilling their men, not leave the duty to sergeants. "My task," he wrote later, "has not been an easy one." He embraced it as a passion, not a job. "He is exerting himself like a Lieutenant anxious for promotion," an officer reported.[20]

———

At the end of April, word arrived that Benjamin Franklin had secured a treaty of alliance with France. The news gave Washington "the most sensible pleasure." Patriots were ecstatic. The alliance "puts our Independence beyond a doubt," one gloated.[21]

On a green day in May, Washington's entire army turned out on the grand parade ground at Valley Forge to celebrate the alliance. Knox's gunners fired off salutes from thirteen cannon. Baron von Steuben choreographed a rolling volley, with the ten thousand men firing their muskets in quick succession. The sound went twice around the lines like an earsplitting drumroll. *Vive la France!* The men were given extra rations of whiskey. Officers and guests feasted at an outdoor buffet. Through the whole affair, Washington "wore a countenance of uncommon delight." He even joined in a cricket game with some younger officers.[22]

More good news arrived. The British were planning to depart from Philadelphia. The taciturn Henry Clinton had replaced William Howe as commander. The threat of a French fleet coming up the Delaware to trap his army in the city made Clinton nervous. He understood that Howe had been wrong to think that capturing the rebel capital would strike a fatal blow. This was not Europe, where capital cities were the nerve centers of nations. America had no nerve center. Clinton decided to consolidate his army in the more defensible bastion of New York City.

Just as many of Boston's loyalists had fled with the evacuation of that city, the Philadelphians who had enthusiastically collaborated with the British were struck with "Horror & melancholy" at the prospect of being abandoned. Thousands demanded to be shipped to safety in New York. The civilian cargo would leave little room on the ships for Clinton's army, baggage, or horses. These he would have to transport to New York by trekking the ninety miles across New Jersey.

When word of this impending hegira reached Washington, he saw a ripe opportunity to test his newly trained army. Each side had about twelve thousand troops. Washington could additionally count on several thousand New Jersey militiamen to harass Clinton as he crossed their state.

During the early weeks of June, Washington held several councils of war to listen to the opinions of his generals. They split into two factions on the advisability of an attack. Leading one was General Charles Lee, the distinguished, crotchety former British officer who had helped Washington in the early days of the war, and who had resisted his orders during the retreat from New York in 1776. Washington had warmly welcomed Lee when he finally returned to the American camp in April following a prisoner exchange. The story circulated that Lee, who initially occupied a room in the quarters Washington shared with Martha, appeared late and disheveled at breakfast on his first morning back, having snuck "a miserable dirty hussy" into his bed.[23]

Washington did not know—no one knew until a document turned up in Henry Clinton's papers many decades later—that Lee, while held by the British, had suggested to them a plan by which their forces could most effectively defeat the rebels. Had Lee turned his coat out of fear for his neck? Was his scheme a ploy to trick the British into a doomed strategy? The questions remain unanswered to this day.

What's certain is that Lee, having been away from the American camp for more than two years, was out of tune with the sentiment of the army and the country. He scoffed at Steuben's efforts and broadcasted his conviction that the British military was unbeatable, that the Americans' only hope was to stay on the defensive and wait for French help. Privately, he continued to regard Washington as a hopeless provincial, "not fit to command a sergeant's guard."[24] Yet Lee's counsel of caution won the support of the majority of generals. Even Steuben did not feel an all-out attack was advisable.

Leading the side for a more aggressive strategy was Anthony Wayne. The logic of attack was clear, the glory of the fight beckoned. Fall on Clinton's creeping, burdened army? Of course.

To reoccupy Philadelphia, now abandoned by the British, Washington sent a small force headed by Benedict Arnold. His Saratoga wound still kept the enterprising general from a field command. With the rest of the army, his Excellency ferried across the Delaware north of Trenton and marched on a route parallel to Clinton's. The British and Hessians, who were dragging a twelve-mile-long, thousand-wagon baggage train, made an inviting target.

At a final council of war a week later, Lee and some other officers advised Washington to take the army to safety in the Hudson Highlands and wait. Washington instead decided to send out 1,500 men to shadow the British rear and look for a chance to mount an attack. The generals judged this a measured response, all except Wayne, who refused to sign the compromise plan. When Washington asked his opinion, Wayne said, "Fight, sir."[25]

The next day, Generals Greene and Lafayette reconsidered and joined Wayne in begging Washington to deploy a larger force. "People expect something from us," Greene insisted. Persuaded, Washington ordered out more than four thousand men to attack the British rear. He would follow with the rest of the army, ready to join in a full-scale battle if the opportunity arose.

Charles Lee, by rank still second in command of the army, had refused to lead the detachment when the force was small. Washington handed the duty to Lafayette, an indication of his confidence in the boy general. But now the thought of the twenty-year-old Frenchman gaining glory in a major battle galled Lee, who demanded to take over the expanded division. Washington compromised, leaving Lafayette in charge of the initial march, with Lee to assume command when contact with the enemy became imminent. Was it wise to assign a plan to a man who disagreed with it? Time would tell.

An early summer heat wave, with temperatures in the high nineties, made the chill of Valley Forge seem a distant memory to the Americans. The suffocating humidity and frequent rain storms turned marching into a nightmare for Clinton's men, who were dressed in wool coats and carrying eighty-pound packs. Hordes of biting insects and sporadic firing by hidden militiamen tormented them. Even at a pace of seven miles a day, the journey was wearing them out. They spent June 27 resting near Monmouth Courthouse, thirty miles from Sandy Hook, where British ships would ferry them up the bay to New York.

That same Saturday, Washington gave Charles Lee a specific order to attack the British rear guard on the morrow. Although Steuben had been out scouting the British position, Lee remained unfamiliar with the terrain. He decided that the situation was too fluid to make detailed plans.

Hessian general Knyphausen led the British baggage train and part of the army out of camp at four o'clock on the morning of June 28, 1778. Clinton planned to take the main body of the army a little way down the road until he determined the rebels' intentions. Lord Cornwallis would stay at Monmouth with the two-thousand-man rear guard.

Lee assigned Wayne's brigade, two Pennsylvania regiments, to lead the attack. Wayne's men marched out and crashed into the British near the courthouse. The Americans deployed into a line of battle and began shooting. Lee sent brigades to the right and left, forming a pincer to envelope Cornwallis's men with two times their number. "The rear guard of the enemy is ours," Lee boasted in a message to Washington. Hot firing pounded a staccato along Wayne's front and he found himself pressured by charging British cavalry. He called for reinforcements.

In the growing heat, confusion hampered the American deployments. Some officers did not receive orders, some acted without orders. Wayne wanted to push ahead. Lafayette pulled his men back to reposition them. Other officers did the same, thinking the line was retreating. Daniel Morgan and his riflemen never reached the field, which had become a "great anthill" of moving men. "The dust and smoke . . . sometimes so shut out the view that one could form no idea of what was going on," one officer lamented.[26]

The gist of what was going on soon became clear. Clinton had countermarched his main force and sent an additional five thousand men into the fray to back up Cornwallis. The all-out battle that the American officers had feared was now unavoidable.

Sensing that the attack had gone very wrong and worried about losing his whole detachment, Lee called a retreat. Wayne protested, but the danger was very real. It was no time for bravado. Pulling off an orderly retreat in the face of an enemy attack is one of the most difficult of military operations. Lee managed to disengage and maneuver his men back through terrain broken by ravines and wetlands.

Meanwhile, George Washington was moving toward the sound of the guns with the rest of the army. He heard rumors of a retreat and refused to believe them. Lee would have informed him. But as he approached the edge of a ravine, he encountered a steady stream of men moving in the opposite direction.

General Lee himself came up. His intention, probably, was to form his men near that very spot, where the oncoming British would have to attack uphill. Washington reined in his lathered horse and confronted the man who had disobeyed his orders, had defied him. In a blistering passion, he demanded "What is this? What is this unaccountable retreat?" Lafayette said Washington cursed Lee as "a damned poltroon," others that he swore "till the leaves shook on the trees." By one report, Lee, ordinarily so voluble, was dumbfounded at the reprimand and could only stammer, "Sir. Sir."[27]

With the enemy advancing and musket fire mounting, the two red-faced generals had time for only a brief horseback confrontation. Washington's aides credited his personal charisma with stopping the retreat and forming a line of battle. An observer attributed "the orderly manner in which the Americans retreated" to the discipline Steuben had instilled in them.[28]

The British came on fast. The second phase of the daylong battle was about to begin. The task of stopping the enemy until units could be sorted out and order restored went to Anthony Wayne. He took three regiments and two field guns more than a half mile east toward the enemy and arrayed them in the face of the Hessian grenadiers, British infantrymen, and mounted dragoons.

Wayne's men let loose a volley that brought the advancing troops to their knees. The British reformed and again came on. Another volley. Wayne's men beat back three charges before they were overwhelmed and had to give way. Wayne marched them rearward and inserted them into the solid line that Washington had formed at the top of the ravine. Nathanael Greene took command of the American right, Lord Stirling of the left. Steuben, thrilled to be breathing gun smoke in battle for the first time in twenty years, rallied men and returned them to the fight. Henry Knox directed the firing of the artillery.

This second fight would last all afternoon. As summer pressed its hot palm onto the field, the British struggled forward and were repulsed. Men on both sides fired, reloaded, fired again. The air, Private Joseph Plumb Martin noted, was like "the mouth of a heated oven," making it "almost impossible to breathe."[29] Many grew disoriented with the heat. Men's minds disappeared down echoing tunnels. Dozens on both sides dropped dead with heatstroke.

Knox, sweating profusely, set up a battery and directed his gunners in holding off British advances with accurate shots. The thundering guns licked out blasts of flame and smoke that turned the hot air thick and sour. For a while, the gut-punching boom of artillery dominated the action. The stunning noise was louder than ears could hear. It was "the severest cannonade," a newspaper correspondent observed, "that it is thought ever happened in America."[30]

Around six in the evening, Clinton saw that he could neither break through nor outmaneuver his enemy. He decided to end the engagement. Wayne urged a counterattack, but Washington realized that his men were "beat out with heat and fatigue." The troops slumped to the ground in their sweat-salted clothes, still in line of battle and muskets at the ready. Dead bodies lay where they had fallen.

Washington himself stretched out under a large oak tree just behind the lines. Lafayette shared his cloak. When the sky brightened, there was no one to attack. Clinton had kept his campfires burning as he slipped quietly toward safety in New York.

After Monmouth, Anthony Wayne found himself famous. Washington reported to Congress that all his officers had performed superbly, but singled out Wayne, "whose good conduct and bravery thro' the whole action, deserves particular commendation."[31] Having dreamed of military glory since his days on the schoolyard, Anthony Wayne had finally achieved it.

Lee had led his men poorly, but having saved his command from destruction, he felt that he hardly deserved an ignominious dressing down from the commander in chief. He waited for Washington's apology. When it did not come, he wrote a series of ill-considered, vituperative letters to his superior, labeling his Excellency's most trusted advisers "dirty earwigs" and referring to Washington's "tinsel dignity." He demanded a court-martial to clear his name. Washington gave it to him. Lee's fellow officers convicted him of disobeying orders, instigating a disorderly retreat, and disrespecting the commander. His punishment was a one-year suspension from the service. He would continue to hector Congress until the members dismissed him from the army altogether.

The Battle of Monmouth Courthouse, militarily a draw, had demonstrated the pride and discipline that Steuben's drills had instilled into the American soldiers. They had stood in the open field against Britain's best and acquitted themselves favorably. The winter's ordeal had prompted Washington to trust, even to love, the ordinary soldiers who served under him. They had shown "incomparable patience and fidelity," he wrote.[32] His generals had also proven their growing capability. Washington had gathered around him a cadre of loyal and effective senior officers: Greene, Knox, Stirling, Steuben, Lafayette.

Now, after two long years of fighting, both armies had returned to almost the identical positions they had held in the autumn of 1776: the British fortified in New York City, the Americans hovering around them in the Hudson Highlands and New Jersey. Although none knew it at the time, Monmouth, the longest battle of the entire war, was to be the last major clash in the north. As Washington waited in a "disagreeable state of suspence," the strategic axis of the conflict was about to shift.

FOURTEEN

THE BOLDEST CONDUCT

1779

While forces in New Jersey battled at Monmouth Courthouse, George Rogers Clark led two hundred men recruited from isolated settlements in the West on one of the most quixotic and consequential expeditions of the war. It was a plan so audacious, so ambitious, that before they set off down the Ohio River in May 1778, Clark refused to reveal their objective. When they had gone as far as the Falls of the Ohio, present-day Louisville, he informed the men of their goal. He had already struggled to find volunteers intrepid enough to accompany him, and when he disclosed the objective, some of his men refused to continue on what seemed like a fool's errand. Clark and about a hundred of the toughest pioneers, whom he named the "Big Knives," plunged ahead into the wilderness. They were intent on nothing less than winning for the American cause the immense interior of the continent, from Pittsburgh to the Mississippi River.

The war to this point had been fought near the Atlantic seaboard and along the Hudson-Champlain waterway. But Americans had long been gazing west. If the conflict on the coast was about the past, the inland war was about the future. One fight was over issues of political supremacy that had festered for a generation, the other about dreams of settlement in a boundless promised land.

Although related to two prominent Virginia planter families, Clark was a natural frontiersman. Keen of intellect but too restless to sit long in a schoolroom, he had, like Anthony Wayne and George Washington, learned the craft of the surveyor. In 1772, at the age of nineteen, he picked up a copy of Euclid's *Elements* and a rifle and headed west.

He joined pioneers like Daniel Boone, who were drawn to the wondrously fertile lands of Kentucky, then a western county of Virginia. These trailblazers had established some of the early settlements west of the Appalachians. The land, Clark felt, was "more Beautiful than any Idea I could have formed of a Country."[1] In 1775, Clark, tall and stocky, loud and pugnacious, took the news of Lexington and Concord to the frontier. He became the political leader of the scattered patriots who populated the region.

While the war in the East raged, the Kentucky frontier at first remained calm. But Shawnee Indians resented the encroachment on their vast hunting territory and saw the Revolution as an opportunity for redress. In 1777, they began to raid frontier settlements, endangering the Americans' fragile hold on the region. The British encouraged the natives' bellicosity. Clark advocated a forceful response. Virginia authorities made him a lieutenant colonel of militia and authorized him to cross the territory along its rivers to two distant outposts. The fort at Kaskaskia, which looked across the Mississippi toward Spanish territory just south of St. Louis, was the westernmost British bastion in North America. The stockade at Vincennes lay further east on the Wabash River. Capturing these lightly defended posts would position Clark to attack Detroit, the heart of British power in the region.

Having traveled down the Ohio River and across the Mississippi, Clark's men surprised Kaskaskia on July 4, 1778. A master of plain, eloquent speaking, Clark convinced the local Indians and the mostly French population of whites to support him. Knowing that Indians respected only strength, he bluffed and blustered, explaining to them that the Revolution had shifted power from the British to the Americans.

The reputation of the Big Knives persuaded the inhabitants of Vincennes, a trading post on the Wabash River 180 miles east of Kaskaskia, to ally with the Americans as well. Clark sent a small force to occupy the old French fort there.

The British could not countenance these rebel toeholds in the future states of Illinois and Indiana. At Detroit, Lieutenant Colonel Henry Hamilton, a career soldier known as "Hair-buyer" for his encouragement of Indian raids on Kentucky and Ohio settlements, gathered a force of about five hundred regulars, militia, and Indians. In October, these men tramped and floated 450 miles to Vincennes and took the decrepit fort from Clark's force without firing a shot. When spring came, Hamilton planned to lead his Indian allies to retake Kaskaskia as well.

What to do? Clark had little hope of reinforcements. His options were unclear. Bluff and audacity had so far served the twenty-six-year-old well. He decided, in the dead of winter, to attack. "I considered the Inclemency of the season, the badness of the Roads, &c. as an advantage to us, as they would be more off their Guard."[2]

He set out with 130 men and twelve pack horses on the fourth day of February 1779. They would walk almost two hundred miles. Another forty-six men, with two small cannon, ammunition, and supplies, headed down the Mississippi on a keelboat. These troops would work up the Ohio, then up the Wabash to rendezvous with Clark at Vincennes.

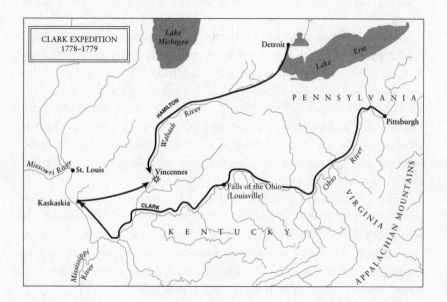

For February, the weather was mild and rainy. Clark's men lacked tents. They spent much of their time wading ankle-deep through drowned flatlands. They fought fatigue, hunger, cold, and wet all the way. Each night, Clark encouraged one company to host a "feast" for the others, serving what game had been killed that day. The men told stories, sang songs, performed war dances, and laughed. On the march, Clark cantered up and down the line, encouraging them. Like Arnold's trek over the Maine Mountains, the Vincennes expedition tested the men's capacity to face and overcome unrelenting hardship.

Clark led by example. "I myself and my principal officers conducted ourselves like woodsmen, shouting now and then and running through the mud and water the same as the men themselves."[3] At times, an observer would have seen only a row of heads and arms, hands gripping rifles, wading through frigid water.

At one flooded river, they made rafts for their supplies, swam the horses, and struggled across the channel, singing comic songs as they went. The sight of a drummer boy floating on his drum elicited laughter. When they reached the Wabash, they found it swollen five miles across. The men waited two days without provisions, hoping in vain for the keelboat carrying the remaining men and supplies to appear. They managed to corral two drifting dugout canoes. The next day they waded into the icy, armpit-deep water. When they reached the land they had seen in the distance, they found that it was an island surrounded by yet more flood water.

Discouragement set in. Clark took some dampened gunpowder, blackened his face with it, and screamed a war whoop. Ordering his men to follow, he plunged onward. Finally, they came onto land a few miles south of Vincennes, where the British had just finished rebuilding the fort. Clark knew that his small force was vulnerable. They could not penetrate the stockade walls without cannon, and they did not know when British reinforcements might arrive. Ever resourceful, Clark again fell back on pretense and flagrant courage. "Nothing but the boldest conduct," he declared, "would ensure success."[4]

First, he issued a proclamation to the town's French inhabitants, promising that "friends of liberty may depend on being well treated." It was a tour de force of bravado. He marched his men toward the town, staying behind hillocks and waving many banners on long poles to give the appearance of a force of hundreds. "I cannot account for it," he later wrote, "but I still had inward assurance of success."[5]

By the time the patriots reached the village at dusk, the British were secure in their fort and the inhabitants had chosen to side with Clark. They provided his men with food and ammunition.

Clark urged his men to be "as Darring as possible." He aligned the riflemen on three sides of the fort and ordered them to keep up a steady fire. The frontier marksmen managed to pick off some of the enemy through cannon embrasures. Rotating shifts maintained a steady loud crackling. They accompanied the rifle blasts with a stream of catcalls, insults, and laughter, unnerving the British troops and Canadian militiamen inside.

During a truce, Clark demanded that Hamilton surrender unconditionally. If forced to storm the fort, he declared, his men would have no mercy. The British commander refused. More bullets tore into the walls. A white flag rose over the fort. The British would surrender, Hamilton declared, if given the honors of war and allowed to return to Detroit. Clark refused. Surrender must be unconditional.

Just then, a dozen Indians appeared on the horizon, a war party returning from raiding American settlements. They led two prisoners. Clark ordered a company of his men to walk out and greet them, hoping to gull them into a trap. The ruse worked. Whooping and yelling a welcome, the Virginians managed to come close enough to the warriors to fire on them point blank, killing half of them. Some escaped; six were brought to a clearing in front of the fort.

Indian bands like this one, encouraged by the British, had murdered friends and family members of the Americans—even now they carried fresh scalps. Clark's men were not inclined toward mercy. With the British looking on, Clark ordered the Indians to sit in a circle. Knowing what was coming, the braves began to sing their death songs. Someone, perhaps Clark himself, systematically crashed a tomahawk into the head of each man. Like the Half King's act at Jumonville Glen, the butchery was a gesture, a piece of theater. The immediate audience was Hamilton and his men, but Clark was also sending a message to the Indians who might continue to oppose him.

The spectacle rattled Hamilton. He knew the Indians personally and had sent them on their mission. He later claimed that when he came out to negotiate, he found a vision of savagery: a wild-eyed Clark, his hands and face "still reeking" with human blood. The ploy worked. "After such a scene we had little hope of being very secure in capitulation," Hamilton later wrote.[6] Nevertheless, he had no choice but to turn over the fort to the Americans. The British prisoners were sent marching under guard to Virginia. George Rogers Clark, a master of stratagem and show, had become the hero of the West. "Great things," he wrote, "have been effected by a few Men well Conducted."[7]

Although none of his repeated attempts to attack Detroit succeeded, Clark later claimed with some justification, "I have given the United States half the territory they possess," referring to the vast tracts which Britain would cede to the new nation.[8] After the war, Clark was considered for an exploratory mission farther west, but that duty fell to his younger brother William, who would join Meriwether Lewis on the groundbreaking Lewis and Clark Expedition of 1804.

———————

In the East, the war had bogged down. With the British fortified inside New York City, Washington did not feel he could do much more during 1779 than hold his position and wait. He did not have the force to take the city without the help of a French fleet. In July, British general Henry Clinton sent troops to raid the Connecticut coastal towns of New Haven, Fairfield, and Norwalk, hoping to lure Washington away from his strong positions in the Hudson Highlands and New Jersey. The American commander did not take the bait.

With the British in his front, Washington began to feel increasingly pressed by the loyalists and Indians in his rear. The six tribes of the Iroquois federation, whose territory abutted the settlements of the Americans, had played a complicated political game since before Washington's alliance with the Half King. Now the confederacy was splitting. Four of the tribes, including the powerful Seneca at the western end of Iroquoia and the Mohawks at the eastern end, had sided with the British. Only the Oneida and Tuscarora had allied themselves with the patriot cause.

Beginning in the spring of 1778, raids against frontier villages in Pennsylvania and New York grew increasingly frequent. In June, Colonel John Butler led a force of four hundred loyalists and five hundred Seneca Indians from the British base at Fort Niagara on the western end of Lake Ontario down to the Wyoming Valley. This fertile bottomland lay along the Susquehanna River between two ridges of hills in northeastern Pennsylvania, near the site of present day Wilkes-Barre. The settlers there had built a series of small forts where they could seek refuge.

Butler's war party surprised and captured several of these forts. Three hundred patriot militiamen gathered to march against Butler. In a hot firefight, the Indians got the best of the settlers and set on them with tomahawks and knives. Blood flowed—all but sixty of the patriots were killed or captured. Those taken prisoner had ample opportunity to envy the dead as the Seneca braves inflicted on them slow and imaginative tortures. Having taken 227 scalps, Butler ran the rest of the civilians out and burned more than a thousand houses, leaving the Wyoming Valley a wasteland.

The massacre terrified settlers across the backlands of New York and Pennsylvania. In October 1778, Walter Butler, John's son, joined with Joseph Brant, a gifted Mohawk leader, to mount an assault on Cherry Valley, just south of the Mohawk River in New York State. The 200 rangers and 500 Indians approached the prosperous settlement, where New York officials had posted 250 Continental Army infantrymen for protection. The patriot colonel ignored warnings. The raiders descended, slaughtered him and his officers, killed thirty civilians, took forty prisoners, and put the town to the torch. Women and children were among the dead. "The bloody scene," a white trader reported, "is almost past description."[9]

Given the tense standoff around New York City, Washington had doubts about diverting part of his army to deal with the elusive natives.

But by February 1779, Congressional representatives from New York and Pennsylvania were screaming for action. Congress passed orders to Washington, who began to plan an expedition for the "chastisement of the savages."

This was not to be a raid but a major military operation carried out by experienced Continental soldiers and backed by artillery. The men would plunge into the largely unexplored territory with two objectives. One was to replicate the ruin the Indians and loyalists had visited on patriot settlers. The country was to be not "merely *overrun* but *destroyed*," Washington ordered.[10] The other was to abduct a large number of prisoners and hold them as hostages for the natives' good behavior. As a bonus, Washington hoped his soldiers could capture the fort at Niagara, cutting the Indians' source of supplies and putting an end to British incitement. Military protocol dictated that Washington offer this important command to Horatio Gates, his highest ranking subordinate. Gates begged off, claiming he lacked the "youth and strength" for a wilderness venture. John Sullivan was next in line. His assignment, Washington informed him, was to terrorize the Indians and "to carry the war vigorously into their own country."[11]

Sullivan had the qualifications that might have made him an effective officer. Intelligent, educated, and principled, the thirty-nine-year-old New Hampshire lawyer had dedicated four years of his life to the American cause, all at the highest level of command. Nathanael Greene had once called him "sensible, active, ambitious, brave, and persevering in his temper."[12]

Yet the knack of leadership eluded Sullivan. Lapses in judgment combined with sheer bad luck to plague him at nearly every step. He had failed in his effort to reinforce the wavering American army in Canada. Commanding the line on Long Island, he had allowed the enemy to rout his men and take him prisoner. At Brandywine Creek outside Philadelphia, he had again fallen short as the British turned his flank and nearly destroyed the Continental Army.

At the end of 1778, Sullivan had commanded an effort to retake Newport, Rhode Island, the nation's fifth-largest city, which had been snapped up by the British two years earlier. He was to cooperate with French general Charles d'Estaing, who commanded a powerful fleet and an army of 4,500 men. This was the first French-American joint operation. But when a British armada was spotted nearby, d'Estaing hurried away to give battle. An intervening tempest scattered both fleets and d'Estaing did not return. Sullivan's men, abandoned by their allies, were forced to retreat. Then, to the annoyance of George Washington and Congress, Sullivan lambasted the French and insulted d'Estaing in a manner that threatened to overturn the alliance entirely.

As a young man, Sullivan, whose parents had come from Ireland as indentured servants, had purchased mortgages at a discount and dunned the debtors for payments. He had so enraged his neighbors that they fired musket balls into his home. His manner of defending himself during the controversy over the Newport campaign prompted Nathanael Greene to comment, "General Sullivan I find has turnd Lawyer again."[13] The qualities of a lawyer—exacting, contentious, and blameful—may have worked to Sullivan's advantage at times, but they cramped his mind and kept him from coming into his own as a warrior.

Ten months after the Rhode Island disappointment, he found himself in command of fully one third of the Continental Army. He was about to set off on one of the most extensive offensive operations of the war. The responsibility would rest entirely on him. Once he trekked into the wilderness, he would pass beyond the possibility of advice, reinforcement, or resupply.

Washington and his staff had grown increasingly skilled at intelligence and planning. They gathered facts about the terrain and the forces Sullivan might encounter. To keep the enemy off balance, American forces would approach Indian territory from three directions. Sullivan would lead the main force up the Wyoming Valley from the south. General James Clinton would bring a smaller corps from the Mohawk Valley down the Susquehanna to meet him. Another war party, under Colonel Daniel Brodhead, would venture from Pittsburgh and ascend the Allegheny River.

Washington needed to be sure that the British would not withdraw Canadian troops to counter Sullivan. He ordered Colonel Moses Hazen to begin building a military road through Vermont for an invasion of Canada. Even Hazen did not know that this effort was a stratagem—no invasion was planned. But the road had the intended effect, and British troops in Canada stayed put.

Sullivan's expedition entailed plenty of risks. If he were to be ambushed deep in the wilderness, the whole of the frontier would become vulnerable and Washington could lose some of his best troops. By detaching such a large force, the commander was leaving his remaining troops vulnerable if British general Henry Clinton decided to seize the Hudson Highlands. Washington sweated over the preparations, then placed his faith in the luckless John Sullivan.

Sullivan studied the intelligence and the plans. The commander in chief had assigned him reliable Continental regiments under seasoned officers like Saratoga veterans Enoch Poor and Henry Dearborn. As the forces gathered, Washington gave Sullivan detailed instructions: travel light; move fast; do not listen to peace proposals from the Indians until you've destroyed their villages; if the opportunity arises, drive the British from Fort Niagara.

Weeks passed—Sullivan remained at his base in Easton, Pennsylvania. He was, Alexander Hamilton wrote, "in his usual pother."[14] Finally, his main force marched to the Wyoming Valley, the edge of Indian territory. Again they waited—for boats, supplies, arms, more men. Washington knew firsthand how baggage could slow a wilderness expedition and was impatient for Sullivan to get moving. Nathanael Greene thought that Sullivan was oversupplied. "I hope his success," he noted, "will be equal to the preparation."[15]

For another month, the force marked time at Wyoming. To pass the midsummer hours, Sullivan debated theology with his officers. A deist and even an atheist earlier his life, the general had become a believer "by fair and impartial reasoning." He was inspired to write a lawyerly thirty-page treatise "to prove the existence of a Supreme Being."[16] Meanwhile, his troops consumed the provisions intended to sustain them in the wilderness and time slipped by.

———————

While Sullivan prepared, British general Henry Clinton saw an opportunity. He sent troops sailing up the Hudson, where they captured two posts on opposite sides of the river. Stony Point and Verplank's Point, barely a thousand yards apart, were the terminals of King's Ferry, an important link between New England and the rest of the colonies. Loss of the ferry required a five-day detour to cross the river. The seizure deflated patriot morale and added to Washington's anxiety.

With a large portion of his army committed to the Sullivan venture, the American commander worried that Clinton might be preparing for an attack on the key fortress at West Point, fifteen miles north of King's Ferry. He was not about to let the move stand. To lead the counterattack, he turned to Anthony Wayne, a national hero for his performance at Monmouth Courthouse the year before.

A revamping of military command had created a conflict between two of Washington's most aggressive natural warriors, Wayne and Daniel Morgan. Washington had decided to phase out Morgan's original rifle corps and establish an elite light infantry brigade of sixteen rifle companies manned by veterans picked from across the army. Morgan wanted to lead this unit and was a natural for the position. But because of its size, it required a brigadier general and Morgan was still only a colonel. Given the politics of rank, a promotion was not possible.

Anthony Wayne, already a general, also wanted command of the new unit. Washington handed him the assignment. Morgan, who had fought superbly for four years, could not accept being passed over. The Old Wagoner resigned his commission and returned to his farm in Virginia.

After two weeks of intense drills, General Wayne declared his 1,400 men ready. His plan was to surprise the enemy with a night attack. On the afternoon of July 15, Wayne's men began a march through the rugged Highlands, circling well west of the river. By eight o'clock, they gathered a little over a mile from their objective.

Stony Point was aptly named, a rocky prominence separated from the mainland by a tidal marsh, with access along a narrow causeway. The British had labored to make the position impervious to an attack. They had constructed two rows of abatis—stacks of felled trees, their sharpened branches pointing outward. They had also built three strongpoints armed with cannon. They felt safe.

To emphasize the audacity of his assault, Wayne forbade his men to load their muskets. They would attack with bayonets only, just as British general Grey's troops had swarmed Wayne's men at Paoli two years earlier. Wayne was serious—when a nervous infantryman stopped and insisted on loading his musket, his officer killed him with a sword thrust. The only exception was a detachment of North Carolina troops who would advance up the causeway, shooting noisily to draw the defenders' attention.

Wayne himself led the main advance to the south of the peninsula, wading waist-deep through the marsh. In the early hours of July 16, the North Carolina troops fired their muskets. Wayne and his men were able to get around the end of the first abatis. They charged through the dark, and scrambled up the steep, rocky slope, taking the British by surprise.

American axemen slashed an opening through the second abatis. A musket ball struck Anthony Wayne in the forehead. He dropped down bleeding. Witnessing his fall, his men surged vehemently into the ranks of British. In less than half an hour, the patriots had overrun the enemy, and the British soldiers had called for quarter. Wayne recovered quickly from what proved to be a blow by a spent bullet. The attack on Stony Point had been a brilliant coup. The troops had fought, Wayne declared, "like men who are determined to be free."[17]

The Americans had no hope of holding onto the position in the face of British naval power. They demolished the fort, removed the guns, and left. Two days later, George Washington appeared to shake hands with every man who had joined the assault and survived—one hundred Americans had fallen.

"Our streets . . . rang with nothing but the name of General Wayne," a Philadelphian reported.[18] Patriot morale soared. Officers praised Wayne's operation as a military classic. The child in him exulted.

———•·•———

John Sullivan continued to delay. July came and went. The first week in August, he proceeded to the rendezvous point at Tioga, just below the border between New York and Pennsylvania. While he waited for James Clinton's force to come down the Susquehanna, his own men marched a few miles up the Chemung River to an Indian village of thirty homes and turned it into a "glorious bonfire," killing fifty of the enemy. A lieutenant went looking for dead Indians and "skinned two of them from their hips down for boot legs."[19]

When Clinton arrived, the combined force of 3,600 men finally headed into the unknown. They took eleven large cannon and twenty-seven days' provisions. Three days later, several hundred Indians and loyalists made a stand along Sullivan's route. They erected log breastworks and enticed his men forward so that a group hidden on a hill could descend on the Americans' flank. The ambush failed and the Indians fled. To lighten his load, Sullivan sent most of his artillery back. With his men, he plunged onward.

Most of the Americans viewed Indians as savage barbarians. They were blind to the complex culture of America's native tribes, knew nothing of their deep spirituality, and gave them little credit for their innate honesty, generosity, and courage. They imagined that the Iroquois lived a primitive life within a primeval forest. What they saw as they invaded the Iroquois homeland startled them.

In the century and a half since making contact with Europeans, the material lives of Indians had changed dramatically. They had grown accustomed to a steady stream of manufactured goods—pots, muskets, cloth, and rum. Their homes, as the invaders soon found, were not traditional bark-covered long houses but "were larger than common, and built of square & round logs & frame work," some with brick chimneys and glass windows.[20] They were as fine as or finer than the homes of most whites.

And situated in finer lands. The territory beyond the mountains was blessed with wonderfully fertile loam. Iroquois women planted vast fields of corn, which in places grew sixteen feet high. They raised squash and beans and cultivated ancient orchards that yielded apples, plums, and peaches. The lush crops astounded the inhabitants of the rocky, hardscrabble hills of New England.

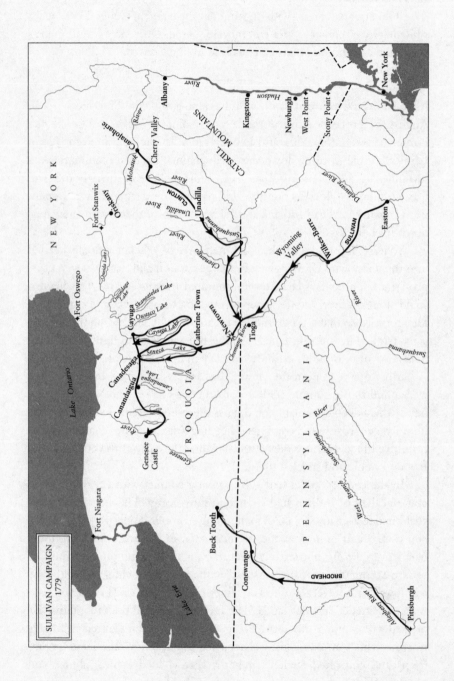

Sullivan's men first admired, then destroyed. All of it—the houses, the fields of grain, the stands of fruit trees—they hacked down and set aflame. The Indians, acutely aware of the invaders' progress but unable to match their strength, kept melting into the forests.

Through the Finger Lakes and ever westward, the expedition carried out its mission. Sullivan was wary of ambush, but none came. By early September, he arrived at his final objective, the town known as Genesee Castle on the opposite side of the Genesee River south of present-day Rochester. After destroying the town, Sullivan turned back. The lateness of the season that resulted from his long delay, along with his personal lack of initiative, kept him from ever coming near the British stronghold at Fort Niagara.

By the end of September, all his men had returned to their base at Tioga. They had leveled forty villages and destroyed 160,000 bushels of corn. Only three dozen soldiers had been killed in the operation. To the west, Colonel Brodhead had managed to destroy Seneca settlements along the Allegheny, also with few losses.

Had the expedition been a success? On the surface, yes. "I flatter myself that the orders with which I was entrusted are fully executed," Sullivan boasted.[21] Deprived of food and shelter, the Iroquois were forced to congregate along the Niagara River by the hundreds, hoping for British handouts. Many died during the ensuing bitter winter.

But Sullivan, with a third of the Continental Army at his disposal, had managed to capture almost no prisoners. He brought back no hostages who could be held pending the cessation of Indian raids. The hostile Iroquois were now even more dependent on British gifts and trade goods, but they were not vanquished by the destruction of their property. "We do not look upon ourselves as defeated," a sachem proclaimed, "for we have never fought."[22] New war parties ventured east as early as February 1780. Raids continued for two more years, as Indians and loyalists inflicted the same destruction on the homes, barns, and mills of patriots that Sullivan had visited on the Iroquois towns. An American officer put it succinctly: "The nests are destroyed, but the birds are still on the wing."[23]

Sullivan's expedition loomed over the future. His men spread the word about a new and tantalizing territory in western New York. Some of them settled there after the war, pushing the dispirited Iroquois west. The tenor of the campaign—the wanton destruction of civilian homes, the girdling of peach trees—presaged the increasingly toxic relations between Native Americans and European settlers that would dominate the next century and beyond.

The expedition did not nullify Iroquois power—the Indians would not be broken until their British allies sold them out in the peace treaty four years later. But for Sullivan, the campaign of 1779 was the end. He had carped and complained and criticized too often. Congress dismissed him from the service.

———•••———

Americans would remember the winter of 1779–80 as the coldest they had ever experienced. Indian refugees suffered at Niagara—patriots shivered in New Jersey. Snow fell every few days and winds whipped drifts twelve feet high. American soldiers, undersupplied as always, huddled in log cabins outside Morristown. "Poor fellows, my heart bleeds for them," an American officer noted, "while I Damn my country as void of gratitude."[24] By comparison, the Valley Forge winter had been balmy.

On Christmas Day 1779, General Henry Clinton and his staff boarded a warship in New York Harbor. A large portion of his redcoats were already crowded onto transports. They sailed out and disappeared across the gray, snow-flecked ocean. Even the captains of the ships did not know their destination until they opened sealed orders on the high seas.

For George Washington and the patriots, the worst year of the war was about to begin.

FIFTEEN

THE FATE OF BATTLE

1780

In the early months of 1780, George Washington found out where British general Henry Clinton was headed. Charleston, the South's major port and the nation's fourth-largest city, was suddenly in peril. Still camped north of New York City, his Excellency could do nothing to counter the threat. He had few troops to spare. He had to depend on his commander in the South, General Benjamin Lincoln.

According to the quasiscientific humoral theory widely accepted in the eighteenth century, Lincoln's personality was of the phlegmatic type: affable and steadfast, but potentially slow and diffident. Contemporaries described the forty-seven-year-old Lincoln as "judicious," "very gracious," and "exceedingly popular" with his militiamen. Friends referred to his "composure and self-possession."[1]

The "uncommonly broad" Lincoln dressed plainly. "His speech was with apparent difficulty" due to an impediment.[2] All his life he suffered from the condition we now know as narcolepsy, which left him liable to drop off to sleep "in the midst of conversation, at table, and when driving himself in a chaise."[3]

A phlegmatic type might make a good farmer, which was Lincoln's profession before the war, but he was perhaps too easy-going to be a stellar general. He certainly did not lack the will. The very day that violence broke out at Lexington, Lincoln marched his corps of volunteers the fifteen miles to Cambridge from his home in Hingham, Massachusetts. A year later, the state made him a general of militia. He commanded troops at White Plains during Washington's 1776 retreat from New York.

During the controversial promotions of February 1777, Congress vaulted Lincoln over generals like Benedict Arnold and John Stark, raising him to major general in the Continental Army in spite of his limited experience. Sent north to help stop Burgoyne, he cooperated with the resentful Stark during the maneuvering before the Battle of Bennington. Afterward, he commanded the fortifications at Saratoga. He saw no action there except during a patrol, when he was shot in the ankle.

On recovering from his wound in the autumn of 1778, he took command in the South just as the British shifted their attention in that direction. Washington warned that the region suffered from "internal weakness, disaffection, the want of energy." South Carolina authorities were stingy with supplies and tried to dictate Lincoln's every move. He hoped he would not be driven to "altercating with the civil power."[4] Altercation was not Lincoln's style.

The British had attacked Charleston twice before 1780. In 1776, Colonel William Moultrie, with some help from General Charles Lee, had prevented a British fleet from entering Charleston Harbor. Three years later, the enemy, having captured Savannah, made another attempt on Charleston. Lincoln was able to fend off this raid, in spite of civilian leaders' impulse to capitulate.

In September of 1779, French admiral Charles d'Estaing arrived at the port with a powerful fleet, six thousand soldiers, and a plan to cooperate with Lincoln to retake Savannah. The joint operation collapsed during a brutal hand-to-hand melee in the trench before the town. The allies lost one of their bloodiest fights since Bunker Hill. A discouraged Lincoln returned to Charleston.

———————

By the end of 1779, Henry Clinton had decided to shift even more of the focus of the war to the South. He hoped to spark a loyalist uprising, the perpetual British panacea for curing the rebellion. In the South he would not face the bulk of Washington's annoying Continental Army. He would also be closer to Britain's valuable West Indies territories should the French launch an attack there. In preparation, he had withdrawn the men who had been idling in Rhode Island since Clinton had captured Newport in 1776. Then he embarked 8,700 soldiers and sailed away, leaving New York under the command of General von Knyphausen.

After a rough passage, Clinton and his men landed just south of Charleston. The city lay on a peninsula between two rivers, the Ashley to the west and the Cooper to the east. Fort Moultrie, whose guns had thwarted Clinton's first attack back in 1776, still protected the mouth of the harbor.

The city's location offered opportunities for a spirited defense. Lincoln had sufficient time to complete its fortifications as Clinton crept forward, his men's minds haunted by tales of wolves, venomous snakes, and sixteen-foot "Crocodiles." It was not until March 29 that British troops crossed the Ashley and began to fortify the neck that joined the city to the mainland, preparing for a slow strangulation.

The amiable, round-faced Lincoln had no use for military affectation—he wore his gray hair unpowdered and lived the frugal, pious life of a New England Puritan. In spite of his rank, he wielded a shovel on the earthworks to set an example. The state had pressed six hundred slaves into the effort, but white citizens remained reluctant to perform manual labor. Nor would they listen to proposals to enlist blacks into the army in exchange for freedom. Moreover, the coastal planters' chronic conflict with poorer inland residents prompted the backlanders to ignore state requests for aid and militia service.

Lincoln's defenses included a stone "citadel" housing sixty-six cannon, a water-filled canal across the neck, and a fleet of three frigates and numerous gunboats to protect the harbor. He drew more troops into the city until 2,600 Continentals and more than 2,500 militiamen manned the works. Then it dawned on him that he had made a mistake.

On April 10, Clinton sealed the neck, trained his guns on the American fortifications and demanded that Lincoln surrender. Two days earlier, British ships had run past Fort Moultrie virtually unscathed to enter the harbor. Lincoln could feel the noose tightening.

His hope was that, like Washington at Brooklyn Heights, he could still escape. His small fleet kept British ships from the Cooper River. If he ferried his men and supplies across, he could preserve a formidable army in the South at the price of relinquishing the city.

Lincoln knew that he was in over his head. He had written to Washington about his "insufficiency and want of experience," asking to be relieved.[5] What was he to do? His honor would not allow him to surrender. Any hope of reinforcements arriving in time was a pipe dream. On April 13, 1780, the British guns opened up. Bombs rained on the houses and fortifications. Fires raged through the town. British sappers kept digging, preparing gun emplacements ever closer to American lines.

The time for escape was now. When Lincoln called a war council, he unwisely included representatives from the civilian government. They would not hear of a retreat. They told him that if he tried to abandon the city they would burn his boats, throw open the town gates, and aid the British in destroying his army.

The chance to break out faded as the British established themselves east of the Cooper River. By May 8, Clinton had fourteen thousand men working on the siege. His guns kept pounding the American defenses. Lincoln saw that all hope had evaporated. He asked for a cease-fire to discuss terms. A blessed spell of quiet settled on the town, but Lincoln was in no position to bargain. Unconditional surrender was Clinton's only offer. The American commander could not accept.

The next day, hostilities resumed. A tremendous cannonade erupted from both sides, two hundred guns firing at once. "It appeared as if the stars were tumbling down," an observer reported.[6] The apocalyptic fury pointlessly destroyed houses and killed more citizens and soldiers.

Now the residents of Charleston, anxious to save their town from utter ruin, petitioned Lincoln to surrender. On May 11, an American soldier ran up a white flag. Clinton would not let the defeated army march out of the city with the honors of war, their flags flying and the troops released on parole, as was the custom. More than 5,500 ragged and humiliated American troops headed for British prisons, where inhuman conditions killed almost half of them. Their sad departure from the city was known derisively as the "Lincolnade."[7]

The loss at Charleston staggered patriots in all the colonies. An entire army captured: irreplaceable troops, four hundred cannon, thousands of muskets, valuable stores of gunpowder, three frigates. Across the Atlantic, joyful Britons greeted the news as an indicator that "a speedy and happy termination of the American war" was imminent.[8]

———•—•—•———

While celebrating his victory, General Clinton received word that a force of about 350 Virginia Continental soldiers under the command of Colonel Abraham Buford had come south to reinforce Lincoln. Forty miles from the city, they learned of Charleston's fate and turned back north. Although the rebels had a hundred-mile lead, Clinton sent Lieutenant Colonel Banastre Tarleton to chase them down. The twenty-six-year-old Tarleton had cemented his reputation as a daring cavalry leader by capturing American general Charles Lee during the 1776 debacle in New Jersey. A natural warrior, Tarleton was praised for his "velocity." Now he set out with his mounted 130-man British Legion, composed mostly of loyalists. Forty regular army dragoons rode with him. They galloped north at a punishing pace, commandeering fresh horses as their animals dropped under them.

They caught up with Buford at a settlement called Waxhaws on the North Carolina border.

Claiming he had more men than he did, the young cavalryman sent Buford a surrender demand under a white flag. Buford refused. The British horsemen and infantry swept toward Buford's men on open ground. The American commander decided to stop them with a single volley of musketry. His men held their fire until the stampeding attackers were only ten yards away. The muskets exploded in unison. The shock of fire met the shock of hurtling horseflesh. The momentum of the cavalry prevailed. In an instant, the dragoons were in the midst of the rebels, slashing with razor-sharp sabers.

Without time to reload, the Americans were helpless. Blades cut into men's arms, tore their necks, sliced open their faces. Blood gushed. Buford tied a white handkerchief to his sword and ordered his men to ground their muskets. Tarleton's troopers hacked those who stood and ran down those who fled.

"I have cut 170 Off'rs and Men to pieces," Tarleton bragged afterward.[9] As at the bloody battle at Paoli, it was not firearms but the more intimate edge weapons that decided the matter at Waxhaws. Patriots loudly proclaimed it a massacre.

They had a point. More than a quarter of Buford's men were killed "on the spot." Another 150 were wounded too badly to walk away. Buford himself escaped with about ninety others. Tarleton said his men acted with "vindictive asperity not easily restrained." A British officer later wrote that "the virtue of humanity was totally forgotten."[10]

Like the murder of Jane McCrea, the Waxhaws Massacre became a centerpiece of American propaganda. The British scored a tactical victory but enraged their enemies. For the rest of the war, the image of "Bloody Tarleton" fueled the patriot fighting spirit, and "Tarleton's quarter," meaning no quarter, remained the bitter catchphrase that excited American vengeance.

But the immediate outcome disheartened patriots: British control of South Carolina was now complete.

————•·•————

Washington had to respond to the Charleston catastrophe. In addition to Buford's small contingent, he had already sent a corps of his best Continentals marching south. In Virginia they learned of the fall of Charleston. Leading these crack Delaware and Maryland troops was Baron Johann de Kalb. The son of Bavarian peasants, the fifty-nine-year-old de Kalb was, like Steuben, a soldier of fortune and a dissembler. Not really a baron, he was something better: a hardened and expert warrior. Having come over with Lafayette in 1777, the tall, graying, broad-shouldered de Kalb had become one of the Americans' most valuable foreign officers.

Hearing of Lincoln's fate, de Kalb encamped his men in North Carolina. His regiments of Continentals were now the only obstacle preventing the British from charging all the way to Virginia. He formed a base at Hillsdale, near present-day Raleigh, and waited.

Congress turned to Horatio Gates, the "Victor of Saratoga," to redeem patriot hopes. The former British officer had served as head of the War Board and had commanded in New England during the previous two years of relative quiet. He yearned for action.

Gates was still popular among New England congressmen, but his alleged plotting against Washington during the Valley Forge winter had left him out of favor with the commander's allies. His friend Charles Lee, who had come a cropper at Monmouth Courthouse, warned him, "Take care lest your Northern laurels turn to Southern willows."[11]

Gates arrived in de Kalb's camp on July 26, 1780. The force Gates called his "grand army" was far from grand: 1,400 Continentals, six field guns, and a tiny remnant of cavalry. Gates had to depend on a North Carolina militia brigade already in the field and the hope that other militiamen would turn out. He admitted to "an army without strength—a military chest without money."[12] Food was scarce—the countryside had little to offer, and Tory farmers refused to supply rebels.

Administration and logistics were Horatio Gates's strong suit. He might have spent time consolidating and rebuilding his army and prying supplies from Virginia and North Carolina authorities. But he knew that British general Cornwallis, whom Clinton had left in South Carolina with a substantial force of redcoats, presented a grave danger to the southern states. Intelligence reports suggested that if Gates rushed his men south within two weeks, he could manhandle the advance corps of the British at Camden, South Carolina, and capture a tempting supply depot as well. The time seemed right to strike.

Gates was an optimist. He had always believed in the ability of militia to carry the fight. "There is every Reason to Hope," he told his men, "that this Campaign will decide the War."[13] The day after he arrived, he announced that the army would march toward the enemy—tomorrow.

His officers expressed "blank amazement." Not only were they to be on the march at three in the morning, but they would be taking a route that de Kalb had already ruled out. It was the most direct path to Camden, but it passed through barren territory thinly populated by loyalists. De

Kalb's plan had been to circle west through an area of patriot farms, where they might scrape together provisions. A few officers protested the new route, but Gates was decided.

Off they went through sandy pine barrens. Nothing to eat—Gates's promises that food would catch up with them were empty. Already foot-weary after their six-hundred-mile trek from New Jersey, the Continentals soldiered on, punished by the South Carolina heat, electrified by mosquitoes, sand flies, and ticks. They marched another 150 miles, "living on green apples and peaches, which rendered our situation truly miserable."[14]

Gates's men overtook and merged with the force of North Carolina militiamen on August 7. Twelve miles from Camden, Gates received reports of about two thousand British troops standing guard north of the city. In spite of his superior numbers, he ruled out a frontal assault. From long experience, he knew that the outcome of any battle is uncertain. No general could control all the unforeseen factors that dictated victory or defeat. He preferred a chess match, a war of maneuvers in which calculation and stratagem could shift the odds in his favor.

He continued his march, seeking a strong defensive position. He finally encamped, after seventeen hungry days on the road, at a place called Rugeley's Mills. The British fell back toward their main camp just north of Camden. Encouraged by the enemy's timidity, Gates remained confident. Seven hundred Virginia militiamen under General Edward Stevens arrived to swell his grand army. Because Rugeley's Mills did not offer the solid defensive position Gates wanted, he decided to move to a more favorable spot along Sanders Creek, seven miles closer to Camden. He ordered his officers to have their men on the road at ten o'clock that night. Again they were dumbfounded. A march through the dark was a challenge for the most disciplined troops. Raw militiamen could easily fall into confusion and lose all cohesion. Gates asked no advice and would listen to no dissent.

Before they left, an aide informed Gates that a count of his effective rank and file stood at three thousand, not the six thousand that, with the influx of militiamen, he had assumed were under his command. The general stated simply, "These are enough for our purpose."[15]

Under a sky of silver-rimmed clouds, the men headed off. Fingers of moonlight illuminated the carpet of pine needles under their feet. At two in the morning, the troops had only a mile to go before they reached the ridge where they could dig in. Suddenly, a startled shout broke the lukewarm stillness. A rifle crack. A rumble of horses' hooves. Men's hearts bounded.

They had collided with the enemy in the dark. Danger crackled around them. British cavalrymen thundered ahead. Gates's outnumbered horsemen gave way. American riflemen opened up. The five-minute firefight ended almost as suddenly as it had begun. Both groups of startled soldiers fell back.

Told that he faced a substantial force commanded by Cornwallis himself, Gates's "astonishment could not be concealed." One of the most experienced of all American commanders was suddenly rattled.

Gates could only guess what had happened. Cornwallis, hearing of the Americans' approach, had galloped north from Charleston to join his men. Figuring he would substitute surprise for numbers, he had put his force on the road that night at the exact moment Gates's troops were stepping out. He planned to assault the American camp at dawn. The extraordinary coincidence brought the cavalry of the two ignorant armies together in the dark at a spot where neither commander had planned to fight.

Gates's men hunkered down six hundred yards from the enemy. Calling a quick council of war, Gates at last asked his officers for advice. None wanted to risk his honor by advocating a retreat. Militia general Stevens suggested they fight—it was too late for anything else. In retreat the army would be vulnerable, especially to Tarleton's dragoons. No one objected. Gates affirmed the decision. They would fight.

In spite of their numbing fatigue, few of the Americans slept. Sporadic gunfire punctuated the unholy hours. Before light, the men moved into position on the rolling ground under a cathedral of longleaf pines. The Continentals formed on the right under de Kalb. The North Carolina men stood in the center behind eight cannon. The Virginia militia, exhausted after their punishing forced march, held the left. Swamps protected both flanks. Two Maryland Continental regiments waited behind the lines as reserves.

As light leaked into a nervous sky, Cornwallis ordered his men ahead in columns, regulars on the right, Tory militia to the left. The arrangement of the armies put two of the best regiments of redcoats directly opposite the Virginians, many of whom had never seen an enemy soldier before that morning. General Stevens hurried back to Gates and excitedly suggested that his men could attack the British before they fully deployed into a line of battle. Gates said, "Let it be done."[16]

The patriot artillery opened up. The guns' detonations took the men's breath away. The Virginians moved forward with timid steps. The well-drilled British regulars formed quickly. Their glistening bayonets floated toward the militiamen as if disembodied. From behind the imperious prongs of steel roared the confident chant: "Hus-SAH! Hus-SAH! Hus-SAH!"

The Virginians stood awestruck. "We have bayonets, too!"[17] Stevens screamed at them. The redcoats halted, shouldered their muskets, and fired a crashing volley. Some militiamen fell. The rest panicked. Most dropped their weapons without ever firing. They turned toward the reassuring rear. They ran faster than they had ever run, officers as well as men. The panic, one observer remembered, was "like electricity"—it operated instantly and was "irresistible where it touched."[18]

The terror spread to the battalions of North Carolina militiamen. The troops of every regiment but one turned and sprinted away. One soldier ran because "everyone I saw was about to do the same. It was instantaneous."[19] Men tripped, fell, got up, ran on. By this time, the battlefield had become an inferno: the cannon pulverized the silence; great clouds of smoke clogged the motionless air; visibility shrank to a few yards; ears were assaulted by screams, shots, the tramp of feet and hooves, incomprehensible shouting, wails of pain, whizzing balls, and the otherworldly braying of gutted horses.

Gates ranged behind the lines, trying to gain control of his troops. To no avail. He cantered away from the lethal melee and continued to marshal the stampeding soldiers behind the line. The men, caught up in a fever dream, ignored him. The chaos brought to mind the scene on the Monongahela a quarter of a century earlier, where a young Horatio Gates had felt a sickening thud tear his chest amid a similar disaster.

"They ran like a Torrent," Gates later reported, "and bore all before them."[20] He decided to ride on ahead of the soldiers and rally them at the camp they'd left the night before. Even there, with the sound of the guns a distant rumble, the men would not cohere into a fighting force.

Gates now knew that the worst had happened. Soon the British cavalry would come charging along the road to scoop up the fleeing rebels. If they could capture a general of Gates's stature, the blow to the American cause might be fatal. He must pull together a new army. To do that, he must survive. To survive, he must put distance between himself and the scene of the cataclysm. Gates and a small group of aides took off. By nightfall they had covered the distance to Charlotte, sixty miles from the scene of the action. Cold military logic dictated Gates's decision, but leaving a battlefield where his men were still hotly engaged would indelibly stain his reputation.

After Gates fled, the fight continued. De Kalb actually believed he was winning. The smoke and disorder kept him from perceiving the collapse of the militia. His Maryland and Delaware men had rushed at the

Tories opposite. They attacked "with great alacrity and uncommon bravery, making great havock" among the enemy.[21] They took fifty prisoners. The reserve battalions stepped forward to try to cover the yawning gap on the left.

But de Kalb's six hundred could not stand against two thousand. His horse collapsed bleeding. A saber stroke opened his scalp. He fought on. The battle grew elemental: men looked each other in the eye, grappled, swung muskets as clubs. De Kalb mounted one last bayonet charge. He and his troops surged ahead, stepping over heaps of dead men. He fell, mortally wounded. "After that last effort of the continentals," Tarleton reported, "rout and slaughter ensued in every quarter."

Defeated armies of the day often managed a more or less orderly retreat. Sometimes they surrendered. Only rarely was an armed force utterly obliterated. This was the fate of Gates's grand army. By noon that hot day, 650 Americans had been killed or wounded, 300 captured. The rest had scattered to the winds.

Having failed to designate a fallback position for his men, having established no base in Charlotte, Gates felt his only option was to continue all the way back to Hillsborough. He was desperate to start rebuilding a force that could keep the enemy from sweeping through that state and into Virginia. "I proceeded," he wrote, "with all possible Dispatch."[22] He covered the two hundred miles in three days.

Horatio Gates was no coward, but in the wake of Camden he was both reviled and ridiculed. "Was there ever an instance of a general running away, as Gates has done, from his whole army?" young Alexander Hamilton sneered.[23] The unfortunate general was berated for his "military absurdity." The loss of another entire army barely twelve weeks after the disaster at Charleston brought the hopes of patriots crashing down.

In November, Gates learned that his beloved twenty-two-year-old son Robert, young Bob, his only child, had died of illness a month before. His aides had not dared add to his suffering by telling him earlier. He was devastated. "None but an unfortunate soldier, and a father left childless," an officer wrote, "could assimilate his feelings."[24] In December, amid the weeping willows, a stricken Gates turned over the southern army to Nathanael Greene and headed home to his Virginia farm. All hope of glory was gone. He made no excuses, simply stated an eternal truth of war: "The fate of battle is uncontrollable."[25]

Prospects had not looked so bleak for Washington since the dark days at the end of 1776. Now, well into 1780, he was struggling just to hold his meager army together. Even during the summer, his troops were forced to survive on short rations. Except for Anthony Wayne's stroke at Stony Point, the commander in chief had no recent victories to boast off. He had not commanded troops in battle since Monmouth, two years earlier. The interim he had spent waiting, worrying, and frantically working to keep his army intact. His hope that the entry of France into the war would bring a quick resolution had faded. The grinding stalemate frustrated him beyond measure.

The state of civilian society was even more depressing. An officer spoke of "the dreadful gloom which now overspreads the United States."[26] Continental currency was "fit for nothing But Bum Fodder." A hat cost $400, a horse $20,000. Lacking buying power, the army was forced into outright confiscation of civilian property. But confiscation crippled the people's morale. Unable to sell crops for cash, farmers had no incentive to produce a surplus.

A taste for luxury on the part of many patriots had become a sickness. "Speculations, peculation, and an insatiable thirst for riches seem to have got the better of every other consideration and almost of every order of men," Washington lamented. He called profiteers and hoarders "pests of society and the greatest enemies we have to the happiness of America."[27] In Philadelphia, leading citizens enjoyed expensive feasts while fighting men went hungry.

Congress had exacerbated supply problems by unwisely turning the responsibility over to the states. Nathanael Greene protested that the representatives were simply multiplying problems. They responded by removing him as quartermaster general. Fortunately for the American cause, they did not dismiss him from the army altogether.

The country, Greene said, was allowing "an Army employed for the defense of every thing that is dear and valuable, to perish for want of food." Writing to Steuben, Washington lamented, "The prospect, my dear Baron, is gloomy and the storm thickens."[28]

One glimmer of hope. On July 15, 1780, a French fleet sailed into the harbor at Newport, Rhode Island, and disembarked 6,500 soldiers. With these professional troops under his command, Washington was determined finally to attack Clinton and regain New York. He would endeavor "by one great exertion to put an end to the war."[29]

Henry Knox suggested besieging the city. Lafayette favored a direct assault. The French commander, the Comte de Rochambeau, remained wary. A large British fleet had just arrived to protect New York. Washington's small army and shaky finances appalled the Frenchman. "Do not trust these people," the Comte wrote back to Versailles.

Direct talks between the allies were essential. In mid-September 1780, Washington traveled with Knox, Lafayette, and a guard of twenty horsemen to the small village of Hartford, Connecticut, to meet Rochambeau. Washington was reluctant to leave his own army, partly for security reasons—he remembered Charles Lee's capture in 1776—and partly because his presence kept the beleaguered force from succumbing to desertion and discouragement. But now he entrusted the troops to Nathanael Greene and rode off. Crossing the Hudson, he lunched with Benedict Arnold, who had for the past month commanded the Hudson Highlands and the army's important fort at West Point.

The American officers could not convince Rochambeau to cooperate in an attack on New York. The tough, mistrustful French soldier had more military experience than all of them combined. The meeting established some rapport between the two commanders, but it was clear that Rochambeau, nominally under Washington's authority, was not to be commanded. The meeting left Washington discouraged. "I see nothing before us but accumulating distress."[30]

Ever wary, Washington led his entourage back by a roundabout route that brought him to Fishkill, a village and supply depot along the Hudson. The next day, he would ride south to dine with Arnold and his wife at their mansion on the east side of the river and to inspect the crucial fortifications at West Point.

The group rose early on Monday, September 25, and trotted their mounts through a pristine late-summer morning. Stopping to look over some defensive positions along the way, Washington sent two aides ahead to let Arnold know they would be late for breakfast. He noted Lafayette's impatience—his young colleagues were all in love with Mrs. Arnold, Washington joked. He was referring to Peggy Shippen, the lovely twenty-year-old daughter of a Philadelphia loyalist. Arnold, while commander there, had played Othello to her Desdemona, wooing the petite, clever blonde with his gallantry and tales of military exploits. They had married against her father's wishes, and she had recently borne him a son.

On arrival, the group learned that General Arnold had already crossed to West Point. After breakfast, Washington and his aides were rowed across the river themselves to examine the complex of forts that protected the crucial narrows of the river. No salute or welcoming party greeted them, only a handful of surprised guards. Arnold was not there. Washington later noted that, "the impropriety of his conduct, when he knew I was to be there, struck me very forcibly."[31]

Washington's puzzlement turned to alarm as he toured the site. Arnold had assured him that he was restoring West Point from its weakened state. Yet the undermanned fortifications were clearly vulnerable to attack.

Disconcerted, Washington and the others went back across the river. If the British were to take the Highlands, cutting the link between New England and the southern colonies, it was unlikely the Revolution could survive. It would be the crowning disaster in a year of sinking fortunes.

Arnold had not returned to his headquarters. Washington went up-stairs to rest before dinner. His aide Alexander Hamilton brought him a packet of dispatches. One was a message from a Colonel Jameson, in charge of an outpost near the American lines to the south. A man calling himself Anderson, possibly a spy, had been taken there with suspicious documents hidden in his sock. Washington glanced through these papers. They contained detailed information about West Point and its defenses as well as minutes of a council of war that Washington had entrusted to the fort's commander. The papers made clear that this "Anderson" was involved in a plot instigated by Benedict Arnold himself.

He sent Hamilton to bring Lafayette to him.

"Arnold has betrayed us!" a stunned George Washington told him. "Whom can we trust now?"[32]

The very notion that the most accomplished general on the American side, the hero of Quebec, Valcour, and Saratoga, could turn traitor made the brain reel. Washington's question hung in the air. If Arnold could go over to the enemy, which other wavering or disgruntled officers might follow?

The commander in chief ordered Hamilton and another aide to chase after Arnold, who they learned had headed down the river by boat. In the surreal atmosphere, an even more bizarre scene was unfolding. Peggy Arnold had gone mad. One of Arnold's aides had found her wandering the hallways, naked but for her morning gown, raving and hysterical. Wash-ington went in to see her. He was not Washington, she said, but a demon come to murder her child. Arnold had gone, gone through the ceiling toward heaven.

Learning that Arnold had received dispatches just before Washing-ton's initial arrival and had spoken with Peggy before hurrying away, the men were convinced that the sudden news of his treachery had driven his wife insane. The truth—that the delicate Mrs. Arnold had plotted with her husband from the beginning, had aided his treason, and was putting on a mad act to cover his escape—would not be accepted until much later.

Still wary, Washington ordered the house sealed while he and his en-tourage ate dinner. "Gloom and distrust seemed to pervade every mind," Lafayette wrote about that curious meal, "and I have never seen General Washington so affected by any circumstance."[33]

When Hamilton returned, he reported that Arnold had escaped to the British warship *Vulture*. Hamilton had advised Nathanael Greene to put the Continental Army under marching orders. Anthony Wayne's brigade set out for West Point at once. Washington was afraid the British fleet might arrive at that vulnerable place at any moment. A hasty letter delivered from Arnold aboard the *Vulture* admitted that he was changing sides. Peggy calmed down. No fleet appeared. Washington knew that pure chance or "the interposition of providence" had prevented 1780 from ending in utter ruin.

The story came out piecemeal. In June 1779, two months after his marriage, Arnold had sent "a tender of his services to Sir Henry Clinton."[34] He had asked Washington for the West Point command to further his treachery. After a year and a half of intrigue, the British commander had insisted on a face-to-face meeting with the turncoat. He sent his close aide and spy master, John André, up the river on the *Vulture* to meet with Arnold. André had come ashore to discuss the plan to turn over West Point and the money the American general was to receive in exchange.

Arnold's haggling prevented André from returning to the ship. Instead, he set out with a loyalist guide to cross the river and proceeded back through no-man's-land on horseback, disguised and under an assumed name. Before reaching British territory near New York, he was accosted by a group of motley militiamen. André, equipped with a pass signed by Arnold, might have bluffed his way through and kept the plot alive. Instead, he lost his composure and said to the gunmen, "Gentlemen, I hope you belong to our party."

Both loyalist and patriot bands, irregular militiamen and bandits, roamed the area.

"What party is that?" the wary man with the rifle asked.

With the outcome of the war perhaps riding on his answer, André guessed, "The lower party," meaning the British.

"Get down," the man said. "We are Americans." He and his companions searched the stranger, found the papers, and refused a bribe to set André free. Their actions pulled the thread that caused the whole scheme to unravel. A panel of American officers tried André the following Friday and condemned him on Saturday. The elegant young man was hanged by his neck at noon on Monday.

————————

What had prompted Arnold's astounding reversal? During his three and a half years of service since leaving for Quebec, he had not once been paid. When the time came for a well-deserved promotion, he had been snubbed by Congress. The corruption that permeated the land both appalled and tempted him. He enjoyed the friendship of wealthy Philadelphia

Tories. Having engaged in some shady business transactions, he had been hounded by the civil authorities in Pennsylvania, a "set of artful, unprincipled men," he called them. A court-martial for some missteps had ended in a gentle reprimand from Washington, who deeply admired his enterprising subordinate. But the cause had turned septic for Arnold, and he was convinced it was as good as lost.

"I daily discover so much baseness and ingratitude among mankind," he wrote to his wife, "that I almost blush at being of the same species."[35]

That Arnold would be resentful was understandable. Many officers were frustrated by an inept Congress and a greedy populace. But Arnold had plotted to hand three thousand American soldiers over to death or imprisonment. He had casually betrayed the comrades who had followed him to Quebec and fought at his side. He had done it for money. No explanation or excuse could encompass such treachery.

Some patriots saw Arnold's perfidy as a symptom of the pervasive malaise. The love of money had replaced the love of country, had sapped the will of the friends of liberty. Arnold, "freedom's champion," had become "mammon's sordid slave."

"Never since the fall of Lucifer has a fall equaled his," Nathanael Greene said. Even loyalists were repelled by Arnold's "horrid unnatural barbarity."

Arnold possessed the cold heart of a man of action. The quality had served him well through much of his life. Finally it led him astray. A British general who knew him commented, "Arnold does nothing by halves."[36] His words summed up the inner dynamic of the most heroic of battlefield generals and the most odious of traitors.

If that awful year needed a gloomy and dangerous cap, it came on January 1, 1781. Officers of Anthony Wayne's Pennsylvania Line were celebrating at a meager New Year's dinner in their camp in central New Jersey. They heard strange sounds and ran outside to find that their men had left their quarters, guns in hand. The soldiers refused orders to stand down. A skyrocket went up. The men "began to huzza." When superiors imposed on them, they shot one officer dead, mortally wounded two, and beat others. They seized the unit's artillery and fired the pieces as an alarm. Wayne, who had been afraid to leave his sullen troops, as he usually did in winter, appeared on horseback. He could not calm them. "With inexpressible pain," he reported to Washington that a "general mutiny and defection" had occurred. He alerted members of Congress to prepare to flee Philadelphia.[37]

It was not the first mutiny in the Continental Army. The previous May, Connecticut soldiers had demonstrated against the intolerable neglect of enlisted men. Washington and some of the other officers sympathized. "The men have borne their distress with a firmness and patience never exceeded," their commander had noted.[38]

"Our soldiers are not devoid of reasoning faculties," wrote Wayne. "They have served their country with fidelity for near five years, poorly clothed, badly fed and worse paid."[39] Slow recruitment and rapid inflation had compelled Congress and the states to offer bounties of $200, $300, even $1,000 to the new men who now stepped forward to join the army. The veterans, who had enlisted for the duration, resented the newcomers appearing in camp flush with cash.

Now the Pennsylvania men had had enough. Fifteen hundred soldiers marched out of camp fully armed. They would, if necessary, proceed to Philadelphia and confront Congress. They observed the strictest military discipline on the march. They insisted they were not deserting. "We are not Arnolds."[40] They were only demanding what their country owed them.

Apprised of the mutiny, something he had "long dreaded," Washington worried that it could spread. He imagined that his troops would, like Arnold, join the enemy. Or they might ravage the land, taking what had not been provided for them. Or they might simply go home.

The mutineers stopped at Princeton, New Jersey. Joseph Reed, now the president of Pennsylvania, rode out to negotiate with the sergeants. They reached an agreement that covered the payment of bonuses to those who reenlisted and the release of those who wanted no more soldiering. Many experienced fighters left the already undermanned army.

The unrest did not end there. Before the end of January, troops of the New Jersey Line, with similar grievances, left their camp and marched toward Trenton. Learning along the way that their demands had been addressed, they likewise returned to their camp. Marching back, they still grumbled loudly against their officers. Washington could not let the epidemic go any further. He worried about an "end to all subordination in the Army, and indeed to the Army itself."[41]

The New Jersey men awoke in their camp to find loyal Continental troops surrounding them. They were ordered to come out of their huts, instantly, without their arms. From a list of the worst offenders, three were chosen at random and told to kneel. Twelve of the mutineers were handed muskets and ordered to execute them. Two of these ringleaders were shot dead, the third pardoned.

The British, when they heard about the mutinies, were ecstatic.

Washington was dismayed. He sent Henry Knox on an urgent tour of New England to beg for funds and supplies from what Knox called "vile water-gruel governments."[42] The results were paltry. The erosion of the army continued.

"We began a contest for liberty and independence ill provided with the means for war," Washington wrote after the mutinies, "relying on our own patriotism to supply the deficiency."[43] The downward trajectory of the American cause suggested that patriotism might not be enough.

But already, in this blackest of nights, flickers of light were beginning to appear in the most unexpected of places.

SIXTEEN

DOWNRIGHT FIGHTING

1780

Over-mountain men, they were called. Backwater men. Shirt men. Barbarians. Savages. They were mostly Scots-Irish, mostly poor, latecomers to America, forced to search for affordable homesteads in the remote uplands of the Appalachian Mountains. They had spread south and west along the Great Wagon Road until they populated the interior of Virginia, the Carolinas, and Georgia. They had drifted to the far side of the mountains, into what would become Tennessee and Kentucky.

"A race of hardy men, who were familiar with the use of the horse and rifle," American cavalryman Henry Lee called them, "stout, active, patient under privation, and brave."[1] Clannish, suspicious, resentful of arbitrary authority, dissenters in religion, Whigs in politics, crack shots, survivors. They distrusted outsiders, danced reels and jigs, drank knockdown liquor, married young for love. They had until now avoided an all-out struggle with the British. Scratching a living in remote valleys and hollows, they eyed the Cherokee to the west warily and kept to themselves. Most had not gone off to war, but the war was about to come to them.

Having blasted the rebel army at Camden, General Cornwallis saw an open road before him. First, he would roll across North Carolina. Then he would topple the lukewarm rebels in Virginia, who would soon be enduring raids led by the newest British general, Benedict Arnold. After that, Maryland and Pennsylvania would fall and Cornwallis would bring an end to the rebellion in a glorious stroke. He had not taken into account the men from the backwoods.

As his army entered North Carolina, Cornwallis assigned a body of loyalists, recruited and trained by Major Patrick Ferguson, to skirt the Appalachians and protect his left flank. The slender, athletic Ferguson was the perfect choice for the role. Now thirty-six, he had fought as a dragoon in Europe, the West Indies, and Nova Scotia. At the Battle of Brandywine in 1777, a musket ball had smashed his right elbow, forcing him afterward to swing his sword with his left hand.

Nicknamed "Bull Dog" by his men, Ferguson had a special rapport with the country loyalists, whom other officers scorned as "crackers." He gathered several thousand of them near a South Carolina outpost called Ninety Six and rigorously drilled them in European-style tactics. He ordered them to whittle the handles of long knives so they could plug them into the barrels of their rifles and shotguns when they charged the enemy. He believed that only a "war of desolation" that was "shocking to Humanity" could subdue the southern patriots.[2]

In September 1780, he marched north with a thousand loyalists. Because of previous raids by cohorts of over-mountain men, Ferguson decided to shake his fist at the ignorant rebels who might threaten his force from the west. He sent a prisoner on parole with a message to those who thought the mountains would protect them. He ordered them to "desist from their opposition to British arms" or he would "march over the mountains, hang their leaders, and lay their country to waste with fire and sword."[3] He hoped his words would cow the Whigs and encourage those still loyal to the king.

To the contrary, Ferguson's threat woke up the backcountry. Word spread. The settlers took the menace seriously. Isaac Shelby, a tall, muscular, reserved man from the sparsely populated region beyond the Appalachians, had already led two hundred mounted riflemen into the North Carolina foothills that spring to fight bands of Tories. He gathered his men again. John Sevier brought another 250 fighters. Short and thick, Sevier was a hard-drinking Huguenot, as loud and brash as Shelby was quiet. William Campbell came down from the Virginia hills with 400 men. At six foot six, with his family broadsword strapped across his back, he made an impressive figure. A fourth contingent of 350 brawlers accompanied Benjamin Cleveland, a three-hundred-pound hunter, gambler, and fighter of Indians.

On September 25, the men met at Sycamore Shoals in what is now eastern Tennessee. Many brought their families. The congregation was the largest and most exciting gathering any of them had ever attended. As campfires dotted the hills, the rough, mostly uneducated men talked about what to do.

The decision did not take long. The next day they headed out, an army without tents or uniforms, without a hierarchy or a supply system. Armed with knives, tomahawks, and their deadly accurate rifles, they waded through snow over mountain passes and descended into the foothills of North Carolina.

His men outnumbered by this troop of backwoodsmen, Ferguson decided to retreat rather than risk a battle. At first, he headed straight south, then veered east to bring his force closer to the main British army camped at Charlotte. He asked Cornwallis to send him reinforcements.

Continuing to exhibit a tin ear, Ferguson issued a proclamation intended to rouse the loyalists of the region. Warning of "an inundation of barbarians," he advised them to hurry to his camp unless they wanted to be robbed and murdered and see their wives and daughters "abused by the dregs of mankind." Fail to respond and they would be "pissed upon forever and ever by a set of mongrels."[4] Tories were largely indifferent to the appeal, but the over-mountain men took the insult personally.

They were, like the Green Mountain Boys of Vermont, fiercely independent. Their Presbyterian religion, overseen by elected elders, predisposed them to democracy. Like their Gaelic ancestors, they followed war chiefs whom they chose for their physical prowess rather than their education or social standing. Having long sparred with natives, they had learned the tricks of wilderness fighting. A British officer called them "more savage than the Indians."

On the east side of the mountains, they elected the towering William Campbell as their commander. Waiting out a day of rain, the leaders gave the irresolute their last chance to back out. No one did. If a battle ensued, they were to fight Indian style. "Don't wait for the word of command," Shelby told them. "Let each one of you be your own officer and do the very best you can."[5]

They worried that Ferguson's force might elude them and find safety with Cornwallis, so they detached a flying corps of nine hundred men riding the unit's best horses. This mobile army rode out to run Ferguson down. They rested that evening at an open field in South Carolina called the Cowpens, a ranch where local herdsmen grazed and traded cattle. After consuming some hastily roasted beef, the mountain men took to their saddles again and rode nonstop through the rain-soaked dark.

About noon the next day, October 7, 1780, the rain finally abated. Sensing they were closing in on Ferguson's trail, they questioned the inhabitants of a farmhouse. The men there, preferring neutrality, pretended ignorance. But a girl followed the patriots outside and whispered to them that the enemy were camped on a hill about a mile away.

Kings Mountain, two miles inside South Carolina, rose only about sixty feet above the surrounding country. The hill slanted a half mile from southwest to northeast. Its sides were forested and rocky, its flat top cleared of trees. Ferguson was confident his corps of one hundred provincial veterans and a thousand trained militiamen could hold the high ground against the "barbarians." He had formed his wagons into a semicircle at the broader northeast end of the hill as a makeshift fortification.

He reportedly "defied God Almighty and all the rebels out of Hell" to conquer him, swearing he would "never surrender to such banditti." He wrote to Cornwallis: "I arrived this day at Kings Mountain & have taken a post where I do not think I can be forced by a stronger enemy than that against us."[6] He requested the British commander to send him several hundred dragoons to help his men rout his enemies and quench the rebels' fervor for good.

The over-mountain men formed the simplest of plans: to mount the hill from all directions. "The orders were," a soldier noted, "at the firing of the first gun, for every man to raise a whoop, rush forward, and fight his way best he could." Campbell simply told them to "shout like Hell and fight like devils!" If pushed back, they should retreat but immediately regroup and attack, using the trees and rough ground for cover.[7]

Units took up position around the hill and waited for the bellowing that would signal the advance. Ferguson's pickets around the bottom of the slopes suspected nothing as the stealthy mountain men crept into position. Then a shot rang out and an eerie ululation sounded from all directions.

Ferguson's second in command was Abraham DePeyster, member of a wealthy New York loyalist family. "Things are ominous. Those are the same yelling devils I fought at Musgrove Mill," he said, referring to Shelby's earlier raid.[8] Ferguson, the only Briton on the field that day, had aligned his Tory militia down the center of the hilltop. Commanding from horseback, he led his provincial veterans to the southwest end to meet the rebel advance. Just as they had been trained, his men delivered a stinging volley, fixed bayonets, and charged. The rebel riflemen fired, but without time to reload, they had to flee down the hill. Ferguson blew a silver whistle to recall his men. His plan was working.

But a wounded Tory lying among the rocks nervously watched the over-mountain men come climbing back. They looked "like devils from the infernal regions . . . tall, raw-boned, sinewy, with long matted hair."[9] Like devils.

Ferguson now had to wheel around and confront enemy soldiers coming up the sides and northeast end of the hill. Deadly rifle fire was crackling from all directions. Two more bayonet charges failed to stop the onslaught.

"The mountain was covered with flame and smoke and seemed to thunder," a witness said. Another declared that the mountain "appeared volcanic; there flashed along its summit and around its base and up its sides, one long sulphurous blaze."[10]

The groans and screams of wounded Tories began to mix with the relentless bawling and yipping of the attackers. They drove Ferguson's troops back until they occupied a tiny perimeter near the wagons. At that point, Ferguson saw no hope except to attempt a breakout. He found few volunteers to accompany him. As he spurred his horse in a desperate lunge, a dozen riflemen took aim and drilled him with seven balls, including one through his face. He fell and was dragged down the hillside by his panicked mount.

Left in command, DePeyster thrust up a white flag. Confusion and passionate hatred kept the firing from dying out immediately. Some mountain men continued to shoot into the mass of Tories, but Shelby rode in between the forces, ordering the enemy soldiers to sit. More than 150 Tories had been killed and nearly 700 prisoners taken.

"The dead lay in heaps on all sides, while the groans of the wounded were heard in every direction," remembered a teenage patriot. "I could not help turning away from the scene before me, with horror, and though exalting in the victory, could not refrain from shedding tears."[11]

The victors ceased firing but continued to seethe. Remembering Ferguson's edict meant to inflame neighbor against neighbor, they gathered around the dead commander's body, stripped off his scarlet uniform, and pissed on him.

Still worried that Cornwallis might send Tarleton chasing after them as he had after Buford, the over-mountain men marched quickly away, taking their prisoners with them. They left the dead and some of the wounded for their kin from surrounding loyalist families, who converged on Kings Mountain to locate loved ones. Wolves also converged. And feral hogs.

A week later, the patriots further satisfied their thirst for vengeance by trying and condemning thirty-six of the most notorious of their Tory prisoners. By torch light, they hanged nine of the men from the limbs of oak trees before officers thought better of the action and halted the execution. The backwoods army soon dispersed, the men trudging back over the mountains to protect their families.

The patriot victory at Kings Mountain drove a nail through the British hope for a Tory uprising. No organized force of loyalists would ever match in numbers or training the group that Ferguson had commanded. A short two months after the glorious British victory at Camden, a chill ran through the hot blood of the loyalists.

Kings Mountain also discouraged Cornwallis. He decided to delay his invasion of North Carolina. Just as Burgoyne, descending from Canada, had felt the thundercloud of John Stark's militia on his left after the battle of Bennington, Cornwallis now feared an attack on his own left by the ghostly army of shirt men. Before October ended, he was retreating from Charlotte toward winter quarters in Winnsboro, South Carolina, seventy miles to the south. His thinking had turned defensive.

The small but decisive Kings Mountain victory could not be attributed to the American high command nor to any one leader. No general rode at the head of the army that accomplished it. Congress did not order or pay for it. It was, like the rout of the redcoats at Concord five years earlier, a people's victory, an amateurs' victory. The crude, spirited, hardy, determined volunteers who crossed the mountains served, Washington said, as "proof of the spirit and resources of the country."[12]

Virginia governor Thomas Jefferson later called Kings Mountain a "turn in the tide of success" that the British had enjoyed since their capture of Charleston. British commander Henry Clinton wrote in his memoirs that the battle "unhappily proved the first Link of a Chain of Evils that followed each other in regular Succession until they at last ended in the total loss of America."[13]

A turning of the tide is not always immediately apparent. Patriots in the North remained shaken by the stunning, disheartening news of Arnold's betrayal. Washington's main army was still inactive, suffering from lack of men and money. "We have lived upon expedients until we can live no longer," Washington wrote late in October.[14]

During the summer of 1780, Horatio Gates and Daniel Morgan, both of them inactive, both vexed at Congress, had sat on the porch of Gates's Virginia estate, drinking and smoking and discussing the progress of the war. Gates mentioned that he hoped to be rewarded for his Saratoga victory with a major independent command in the South. If he received the assignment, he wanted Morgan with him.

Nearing forty-five, Morgan was afflicted by recurring "ciatick pain," the wear and tear of a rough life. He had sat on the sidelines since 1779, when Washington had passed over him when choosing a leader for the corps of light infantry. Eager to get back into action, he agreed to help his friend if his health permitted. Gates received his southern command, but by the time Morgan recovered and set out to join him, Gates's army had been blasted at Camden. Morgan was needed more than ever.

The rifleman's arrival cheered the shattered army. Gates, gathering the remnants of his command at Hillsborough, asked the Old Wagoner to take charge of a fast-moving "flying army" of infantry and horse. With this mobile force, Morgan could respond to contingencies in that chaotic and dangerous theater of war. Gates assigned him two key lieutenants: The quiet, level-headed John Eager Howard led a reliable contingent of Maryland and Delaware Continentals. Pudgy, round-faced Colonel William Washington was a cavalry commander with a reputation for ferocity in battle.

Before the year was out, Nathanael Greene had arrived to relieve Gates. The southern command was now seen as the graveyard of honor. Although it meant a return to a battlefield command, Greene had been reluctant to take charge of the bleak situation. He reportedly told Washington that his friend Henry Knox was the man for the job: "All obstacles vanish before him; his resources are infinite."

"True," Washington replied, "and therefore I cannot part with him."[15]

Congress had at last recognized Morgan's ability by promoting him to brigadier general. Greene was eager for him to lead his flying army into the field. He added several hundred Continentals to the force, all he could spare. Supply and manpower remained crippling problems. Greene found his army "rather a shadow than a substance, having only an imaginary existence," with barely 1,500 men fit for duty at Charlotte.[16] The new commander kept a nervous eye on Cornwallis, camped ninety miles to the south.

Although the military textbooks argued against it, Greene decided to divide his army in the face of a superior enemy. In the depleted land, feeding a concentrated mass of hungry men was next to impossible. Splitting his force would increase forage opportunities and threaten Cornwallis from two directions, perhaps holding him in place while the Americans rebuilt their capability. Spreading out would also hearten patriots in the countryside.

Just before Christmas 1780, Greene sent Morgan, with about six hundred men, to the northwest corner of South Carolina. He led the rest of the army east across the border of that same state to the town of Cheraw. The two wings, separated by 140 miles, would be unable to come quickly to the aid of each other if Cornwallis attacked.

Morgan camped in an area laced by streams and tributaries flowing into the Broad River, which angled southeast toward the ocean. He sent William Washington and eighty horsemen out to expand his presence in

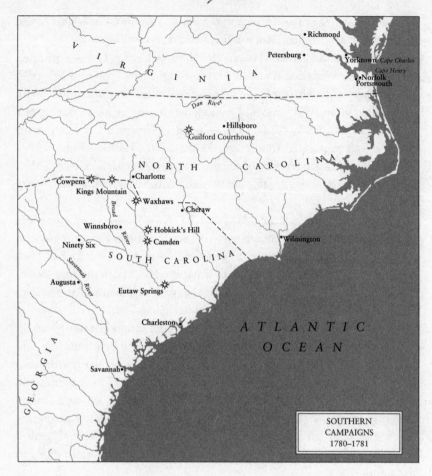

SOUTHERN
CAMPAIGNS
1780–1781

the country. Unlike his distant cousin George, Washington, then twenty-eight, was no good at administrative details. Six feet tall and stocky to the point of obesity, he loved action.

British cavalry master Tarleton went out with a battalion of the best British troops to parry the rebels in the area. Of Morgan, Cornwallis told Tarleton that if he came "within your reach, I should wish you to push him to the utmost."[17] Tarleton found that Morgan was very much within his reach. During the first days of 1781, he began to chase the rebels' flying army.

Tarleton sent a message to his superior: the divided enemy force presented an opportunity for a master stroke. Cornwallis agreed. He would march the main British army up the east bank of the Broad River. Tarleton would pursue Morgan along the west side, hopping tributaries as he went.

One of them would trap and destroy Morgan's smaller corps while Greene remained impotent to the east.

Tarleton's force was, like Morgan's, an independent command designed to move quickly. In addition to his British Legion of horse and foot soldiers, he had with him two crack contingents of British regulars, including the lethal 71st Highlander Regiment, hard-eyed Scotsmen with fight in their blood.

On the surface, Tarleton and Morgan were opposites. The British colonel had been raised in privilege, attended Oxford, and studied law. He was young, debonair, a celebrated womanizer. Morgan knew little of either the classroom or the drawing room. He was still the Old Wagoner, like his men, a rustic backwoodsman. Yet both officers were fighters. Tarleton had forged a reputation with his saber, Morgan with his rifle. Now they were rushing toward a confrontation.

On hearing of Tarleton's approach, Morgan began to scurry north, his troops wading icy river fords. The idea was to draw Tarleton further from his supplies and further from Cornwallis. By January 16, Morgan was camped on the far bank of the Pacolet River, the most northern tributary. Beyond him, the Broad River itself curved westward to form an obstacle. He had left riflemen behind to oppose Tarleton at the fords and to give warning of his approach.

Daniel Morgan's name, like John Stark's, inspired militiamen eager to serve under a man they considered one of their own. A body of South Carolina militia had arrived in camp under Andrew Pickens. The tall brigadier was a man who "would first take the words out of his mouth, between his fingers, and examine them before he uttered them."[18] A devout Presbyterian of the same Scots-Irish heritage as those who had fought at Kings Mountain—some of them were with him now—Pickens had seen his farm burned by Tories. He and his men were eager for action.

They would soon have it. While they ate breakfast that frigid January morning, a messenger arrived with alarming news. Tarleton had pulled the old trick of leaving campfires burning on the far side of the Pacolet while he hurried his men through the night to an unguarded ford and crossed over. His force was now bearing down on Morgan.

Pots were left bubbling on fires as Morgan immediately put his men on the march. He sent word to militia units camped nearby and to those still on their way to join him. If he could not escape across the Broad River, a battle might be imminent.

His men marched all day. As darkness fell, they found themselves at the same cattle ranch, the Cowpens, where the over-mountain men had rested on their way to Kings Mountain the previous October. Morgan decided to camp there, five miles south of the Broad. He could not take the chance of Tarleton catching him while he was fleeing. Surveying the terrain, he judged this an acceptable place to fight, if it came to that. And the cattle wandering the fields offered his men full stomachs.

Morgan also knew that his South Carolina militiamen were unlikely to follow him over the state line, only a few miles away. If he abandoned their state, they would abandon him. And because Cowpens was a well-known crossroads, it would serve as a convenient rendezvous spot for militiamen. Indeed, additional fighters kept arriving in camp all night.

The open ground favored Tarleton's horsemen. The Broad River to the north would block Morgan's escape if events went against them. "As to retreat," Morgan said later, "it was the very thing I wished to cut off all hope of." He knew what had happened at Camden. He wanted his troops to understand that if they gave way, there was no haven in sight. "When men are forced to fight, they will sell their lives dearly." He was preparing a desperate gamble.[19]

In the dark, around the campfires, Morgan planned what he would do if Tarleton should appear. He did not ask his officers' advice—the ideas were all his own. But he communicated his thinking to men of every rank. It was a simple plan, and he knew how to explain it in language that the men could understand. Each body of troops would have a specific task in the fight, he said, and each task would fit into the bigger scheme.

Morgan had very little military training. He had not read books about the art. He based everything on his own experience as a bare-knuckle fighter and a veteran of Quebec, Saratoga, and other battles. He saw with a remarkably clear vision, uncluttered by social furniture and learned biases. The story was told of him that he was once riding past a couple of soldiers trying to clear a boulder from a roadway. A lieutenant was watching them. "Why," Morgan asked him, "don't you help?" "Colonel Morgan, I am an officer," the man replied. "Oh, I didn't think of that," Morgan said, climbing down and adding his own formidable strength to the privates' effort.

All that night, he walked through camp, boosting his men's spirits, telling tales, calming fears. He called Tarleton, the Oxford gentleman, "Benny," as if he were another backwoods bully. "He went among the volunteers," a private remembered, "helped them fix their swords, joked with them about their sweet-hearts."[20] "My friends in arms," he called them, "my dear boys."

All night, Morgan talked. "I don't believe he slept a wink that night," one of his men noted. When morning came, his troops were well fed and rested. Like John Stark, who ordered his men to walk rather than run to

Bunker Hill, Morgan knew that rested troops could fight with far more vigor than those who had spent their energy getting to the battle.

Early on the morning of January 17, 1781, while the winter sky was still black, word arrived from scouts. Tarleton had appeared. He was barely five miles away and was coming "like a thunder storm."[21] Morgan roused his men. "Boys, get up, Benny's coming!" he told them. They had time for a quick breakfast before their officers positioned them for battle. The field Morgan had selected was about a quarter mile long. Largely free of brush and dotted with a few trees, it undulated over knolls and hollows, gently rising from south to north. Morgan positioned his men facing south, their flanks ending at low, wet areas that would discourage the movement of horsemen.

All were in position before dawn. Their officers allowed the men to sit or squat as they waited, blowing on their hands in the bitter, clammy morning. Morgan climbed onto his horse and rode the lines, pounding his fist into his hand as he spoke, haranguing his men "in a popular and forcible style of elocution."[22]

As the sky began to lighten, the men's ears picked up the crackle of distant gunfire. Scouts were sounding the alarm. Men and horses appeared in the trees at the far end of the field. Men in green coats faced with black. Men in scarlet and white. Drums. The sour skirl of bagpipes.

"We look'd at each other for a considerable time," a private remembered.[23] Time was growing elastic, stretching and compressing.

Morgan had sent 150 North Carolina riflemen to the forward edge of the field as skirmishers. Hiding behind trees, they fired to halt the British and make them form their line. "Pick off the epaulets!" Morgan told them. Aim for the officers.

Tarleton was in a hurry. He saw a line of enemy opposing him three hundred yards beyond the skirmishers. Was this the main body of Morgan's force, or a rear guard left to delay him while Morgan escaped across the river? He had to find out quickly. He had to attack.

He sent fifty dragoons charging toward the enemy. The rifle shots from the North Carolina men became a rapid staccato, a "galling fire." Fifteen of the horsemen fell from their saddles. The rest heaved on their reins and retreated.

The British battle line now began to tromp forward, drums pounding. The rebel riflemen scurried toward their own lines. With "the Discharge of two pieces of Cannon and three Huizzas," the attack began. The British came on, one militiaman remembered, "rapidly as if certain of victory."[24]

"They give us the British halloo, boys," Morgan shouted, "give *them* the Indian halloo!" The howl of the wilderness arose from raw American throats. Morgan "galloped along the lines, cheering the men."

What the British regulars saw ahead of them was a line of militiamen, armed only with rifles and shotguns, no bayonets; amateur troops, certain to break. Tarleton's men came on at "a sort of trot." The enemy "Raised a prodigious yell," Morgan would report, "and came Running at us as if they Intended to eat us up."[25]

"Don't fire!" was the word from the American officers directing Pickens's South Carolina militiamen. Let the enemy approach. Closer, closer. At thirty-five yards, faces became recognizable. Now the patriots let loose a volley. The sound was like heavy canvas ripping. The militiamen saw "something like a recoil" in the enemy line.

But the disciplined regulars immediately "rent the air with their shouts and quickened their advance." The British fired and charged. It took them twenty seconds to reach the American line. Unable to reload fast enough, staring at oncoming bayonets, the militiamen turned and ran, desperate to avoid the sharp steel.

It was another Camden. The sight of enemy soldiers' backs delighted the British infantrymen, inspired them. Victory! Yelling redcoats pounded forward, thrusting their lethal bayonets.

Passing over a low ridge, the British caught sight of another line of soldiers ahead of them. Not so many men as in the militia ranks, but these were American Continentals, uniformed in blue and white, their own bayonets glittering in the cold morning light. The militiamen were slipping through gaps in their line and disappearing to the rear.

British officers screamed orders. The men slowed, halted to dress their ranks. The battlefield narrowed here. The British now stood shoulder to shoulder. Their line, longer than that of the rebels, extended beyond Howard's Maryland and Delaware Continentals on the American right.

The British presented their muskets and fired. When the last of the militiamen had cleared their front, the Continentals answered, one corps, then another delivering a disciplined fire. "It seemed like one sheet of flame from right to left," an officer said. Morgan later wrote to Greene, "When the enemy advanced on our lines they received a well directed and incessant fire."[26] Incessant—the field was now a cauldron of hammering, ear-numbing noise, the deep roar of muskets, the crackle of rifles, an all-out contest of fire against fire.

A Delaware private recalled Morgan's "powerful & trumpet like voice" that "drove fear from every bosom, and gave new energies to every man."[27] It was the "awful voice" that had heartened soldiers during the snowy struggle at Quebec.

Men tasted gunpowder, tasted waxed paper as they bit cartridge after cartridge. They sweated. Their faces turned black with scorched powder. Bullets tore the air with a hoarse hum or a singing crescendo. Wounded men screamed. Officers bellowed. Prime and load! Fire! The intensity of the action lifted men's minds from their bodies and let them view the confusion from on high.

Tarleton ordered the powerful Highlanders, supported by fifty dragoons, to sweep past the Americans' right and crash into their rear. The horsemen burst through a small group of the North Carolina riflemen shielding the American flank, hacking shoulders and heads with sabers, trampling men. The Highlanders screamed Gaelic curses and came on at a run.

Howard directed the unit on the end of his line to wheel backward to take the charge from their front. The order was misunderstood, they retreated instead. Then, spontaneously, the next unit fell back, and the next.

Morgan had been busy behind the line rallying the militia. "Form, form my brave fellows! Give them one more fire and the day is ours. Old Morgan was never beaten." His plan was for the militiamen to find safety behind the bayonets of the Continentals, sort themselves out, and form a reserve force.

Now he galloped to the collapsing Continental line. The repositioning of troops was a mistake, Howard told him. But they could see that the retreating men were still under the control of their officers. They were reloading as they marched. Let them retreat, Morgan said, then form again on a new line. He rode back a hundred yards and chose the spot. Here.

The Highlanders smelled victory. The enemy was giving way before them. They charged, broke ranks, stumbled ahead, eager for the kill. They came on "like a mob." The Continentals, on order, halted and faced about. The Highlanders were nearly on them, barely fifteen yards away. Fire! Their "close and murderous fire" smashed into the faces of their pursuers.

Many Highlanders fell dead. All were stunned. Howard saw his chance. He told his drummer to sound the charge. His men leveled their bayonets and started forward. Morgan ordered Washington to sweep in with his dragoons. The American horsemen came on, "shouting and charging like madmen." Pickens's militiamen, whom Morgan had helped reorganize, rushed up to help, pouring fire into the mass of scarlet uniforms.

It was too much. The Highlanders, the best troops in the British army, buckled. Then the entire British line broke, reeled backward, turned to the rear, and ran. Many threw down their guns and, a Continental private chortled, "did the prettiest sort of running!"[28]

The Americans surrounded the disorganized Highlanders. Their commander, seeing that all was lost, handed Howard his sword. Continentals rushed forward to grab the British cannon. More and more enemy soldiers were surrendering. Tarleton tried to lead his cavalry reserve into the fray. The horsemen refused to obey their young commander.

"All attempts to restore order, recollection, or courage, proved fruitless," Tarleton later reported.[29] Two hundred dragoons turned and rode away, pursued by Washington's cavalry.

Quiet fell on the field like a heavy weight. The whole thing had lasted barely forty minutes. An exuberant Morgan picked up a nine-year-old drummer boy, who had risked his life amid the din, and kissed him on both cheeks.

Morgan had read the impulsive Tarleton precisely. "I knew my adversary, and was perfectly sure I should have nothing but downright fighting."[30] He had positioned his men in a brilliant, unconventional arrangement—militiamen in front but with permission to fall back behind stronger lines. He had used his charisma and energy to exert his will against the enemy. He had won the most decisive patriot victory of the war, utterly destroying Tarleton's dreaded Legion. He had, he wrote to a friend, given Tarleton "a devil of a whiping."[31] His masterly handling of his men is studied by tacticians to this day.

He had little time to savor his victory. Escaping to the north with his haul of eight hundred prisoners, Morgan needed to keep moving, keep crossing rivers, to avoid Cornwallis. But when Cornwallis sent the news to General Henry Clinton in New York, he wrote that it was "impossible to foresee all the consequences that this unexpected and extraordinary event may produce." To Lord Rawdon, he sighed that "the late affair has almost broke my heart."[32]

Abigail Adams called Morgan "the rising Hero in the South." But Cowpens was to be the Old Wagoner's last battle. During the first week in February 1781, he reunited his troops with Greene's army. Morgan had increasingly been laid low with sciatica, malaria, and fever, and, he told Greene, "Nothing will help me but rest." Reluctantly, Greene let him go. "Great generals are scarce," he lamented. "There are few Morgans to be found."[33]

SEVENTEEN

WAR IS AN INTRICATE BUSINESS

1781

Nathanael Greene, born to the middle class, had never lost the habit of looking over his shoulder. In spite of his exalted position in the Continental Army, he remained nervous about his rank in society. When he wrote to his wife, Caty, about joining him in camp, he suggested that she send a letter to Lucy Knox to ask for new clothes from Boston. "But remember when you write to Mrs. Knox . . . mind and spell well. You are defective in this matter, my love. . . . People are often laught at for not spelling well."[1] Greene's own spelling was shaky, and the memory of being barred from leadership of his militia unit because of his limp still galled him. The rank of major general fueled his pride but brought with it a certain vertigo.

As the army's quartermaster general, Greene had responded to a mild admonition from Washington by complaining, "I can submit very patiently to deserved censure; but it wounds my feelings exceedingly to meet with a rebuke for doing what I conceived to be a proper part of my duty."[2]

Greene could evoke mirth with his dinner table imitations of Dr. Slop, a character in the popular comic novel *Tristram Shandy*, yet he was subject to bouts of gloomy disappointment. "There is so much wickedness and viliany in the World," he wrote Caty in the autumn of 1780, "and so little regard paid to truth, honor and justice that I am almost sick of life."[3]

Now, as commander of all forces in the South, Greene's doubts resurfaced. "How I shall be able to support myself under all these embarrassments God only knows," he wrote to Washington. "Censure and reproach ever follow the unfortunate."[4]

Early in 1781, before Morgan's victory at Cowpens, Greene's situation appeared truly dire. He could not "find a Clue to guide me through the Complicated Scene of Difficulties. I have but a Shadow of an Army." Neither militiamen nor supplies were forthcoming. "I see but little prospect of getting a force to contend with the enemy upon equal grounds." He took Virginia governor Thomas Jefferson to task, explaining that "it is impracticable to preserve Discipline when Troops are in Want of every Thing."[5]

Yet Greene had a valuable ability to grasp the complex geometry of war. He knew how to make and remake calculations about space, time, and movement in a landscape that ranged along the coastal plain from Florida to tidewater Virginia. "Dispassionate and minute research" was his specialty.[6] "Greene is beyond doubt a first-rate military genius," wrote Washington's aide Tench Tilghman, "and one in whose opinions the General places the utmost confidence."[7]

With the eye of a mill owner, Greene quickly mastered the complicated network of rivers and streams that meandered through the Carolinas. How strongly did they flow? How fast did they rise? Where were the fords? Unlike General Gates, the former quartermaster general paid close attention to supply issues. He turned over in his mind intricate equations involving the morale of his troops, the mood of local patriots, the availability of forage, and the intentions of his enemy.

The war in the South differed from the encamped stalemate in the North. Mobility was essential, cavalry a prerequisite, hit-and-run the main tactic. His entire force would become a flying army, always on the march and ever reacting to the moves of the enemy. He would be on his own, too far from Washington to expect help in a crisis. The initiative would be his, but he would also have to deal with southern politicians, placate militia leaders, and channel partisan bands toward effective action.

He was favored with some capable lieutenants. William Washington and Henry Lee both led effective corps of cavalry. Greene called on the capable, thirty-two-year-old Otho Williams to take over the light infantry after Morgan departed. Back in 1776, when Greene had insisted on manning Fort Washington on Manhattan Island, Williams was one of those captured in the doomed fort. After being exchanged, he had emerged as a precise and effective tactician.

Greene especially cultivated Francis Marion, a South Carolina partisan who had been named brigadier general of militia. Marion, though barely literate, had formerly served as a Continental Army officer at Charleston. Luckily, he had left the city with an injured ankle before the British captured the garrison. Despite Marion's reputation as a warrior, General Gates had shown little regard for the slight, homely, knock-kneed partisan leader, or for his band of troops, some white, some black, whose appearance was described as a "burlesque." However, Marion's force of stealthy, dirty, unconventional fighters would prove a constant irritant to the enemy and an inspiration to Greene. "I like your Plan of frequently shifting your Ground," Greene wrote to the austere, pious Huguenot.[8] Banastre Tarleton, who hunted in vain for the partisan band, called Marion, who was forty-eight, a "damned old fox." Marion would live in our national memory as the Swamp Fox.

Also roaming the southern countryside was a battalion led by Thomas Sumter. A country mill owner with experience fighting Cherokees, the pugnacious Sumter hated the British and loyalists who had burned his home to the ground while his invalid wife and young son watched from the yard. Sumter's energy, fierce independence, and fanaticism in battle had earned him the nickname "Carolina Gamecock."

With these allies, about 1,400 Continental soldiers, and a few hundred militiamen, Greene faced the most fraught situation of the war since Burgoyne's threat in 1777. Lord Cornwallis, Britain's most zealous general, was determined to run down and dispose of the exhausted American army of the South. The conflict would begin with a perilous chase.

———

Cornwallis had begun his pursuit of the American flying army immediately after Morgan's stunning victory at Cowpens on January 17. Eight days later, as Morgan hurried north, the British commander ordered his three thousand regulars to shed their baggage in order to pursue the more mobile American forces. Tents, wagons, beds, clothing, rum—all was set aflame. This was a desperate step—"something too like a Tartar move," Henry Clinton said when he heard of it. But Cornwallis was determined to catch and destroy the enemy. "With zeal and with Bayonets only," wrote Brigadier General Charles O'Hara, "it was resolved to follow Greene's army to the end of the World."[9]

Greene could do nothing but retreat to the north and east. He planned to pull back from North Carolina and escape over the Dan River into Virginia. There his men could catch their breath and regroup. His study of the rivers told him he would need boats to get across. He sent a detachment ahead to gather and conceal sufficient vessels. On February 10, the British were approaching at high speed. Greene began the critical four-day retreat that would be known as the Race to the Dan.

He again divided his army. He sent Otho Williams with the light infantry and cavalry, the cream of his troops, to the northwest, as if heading for the upper reaches of the Dan, where the river was fordable. They would lead Cornwallis astray and at the same time screen the movement of the bulk of the army, with whom Greene pushed toward the lower river, where the boats were stashed.

Rain turned the red clay soil to a thick paste that sucked the shoes off the men's marching feet. At night, the mud froze into lacerating ridges. Williams's men had no tents. His infantry started marching at three A.M., stopped in the late morning for their one daily meal, and continued to trudge until dark. Cornwallis's men barked at their heels the whole time. Occasionally the two armies marched within sight of each other as they hurried through the backlands. At night, the Americans rested briefly, but with half the force on guard duty, the men could sleep only six hours every other day. Greene calculated that he slept a total of four hours over four days.

Greene and his main force reached the ferry points and began to cross the Dan. Williams turned his troops to follow. The next day his men, hearing that the main army was across and their mission a success, sent up a cheer. The British were near enough to hear the shouts and guessed what they meant. The race was over.

Williams's men hurried on with new energy. They reached the swollen river that night and boarded the boats. Lee's dripping horses were just clambering up the far bank at dawn when Tarleton's cavalrymen appeared. Cornwallis could no longer keep up the pursuit. Lacking boats, his men could only stare and contemplate how close they had come to capturing Greene and ending organized resistance in the South.

In Virginia, "joy beamed on every face" as desperately needed supplies arrived. Greene had accomplished one of the most intricate strategic retreats of the war without the loss of men or equipment. Since the battle at Cowpens, his army had covered two hundred miles and crossed four major rivers. He had been required, Greene said, to accomplish "by finesse which I dare not attempt by force." Fellow officers marveled at Greene's talent. "A masterpiece of military skill and exertion," Alexander Hamilton wrote.[10]

Having narrowly missed the chance to destroy Greene's army, Cornwallis declared victory. He had restored King George's sovereignty over the southern colonies from Florida to the border of Virginia. But in the process he had lost 250 valuable men to illness and desertion. He now found himself in a barren country, at the end of a precarious supply line. He had to admit that Greene was "as dangerous as Washington. He is vigilant, enterprising, and full of resources."[11]

For his part, Greene had outmaneuvered the enemy and saved his army. Now it was Cornwallis who was falling back. To press him, Greene coordinated his movements with the partisan bands led by Marion, Sumter, and Pickens. He also relied on the creative strategist Henry Lee. The Lee family had been prominent in Virginia since an ancestor began growing tobacco there in the 1640s—Henry was a cousin of Richard Henry Lee, a signer of the Declaration of Independence. Henry had studied law at the College of New Jersey in Princeton. In 1776, he had dropped out and, at the age of twenty, enlisted in the Continental Army. General Charles Lee, no relation, had said the young man "seems to have come out of his mother's womb a soldier."[12] Henry Lee was a man suited to the high-adrenaline sensations of war, when, he wrote, "the mind was always on the stretch."

Like George Washington, Lee loved fine mounts and used his eye for horseflesh to gain an advantage over enemy cavalry. He fought at Brandywine and Germantown, but his forte was the quick, hit-and-run raid. He pulled off a successful coup in 1779, capturing stores and prisoners from the British post at Paulus Hook, New Jersey, across the river from New York City.

In the South, where the coastal plain favored cavalry operations, Lee came into his own. His self-contained unit, known as Lee's Legion, comprised about two hundred light cavalrymen and the same number of mounted infantrymen. He acquired a nickname: Light-Horse Harry Lee.

Greene valued Lee, writing to him after the race to the Dan that "no man in the progress of the Campaign had equal merit with you."[13] George Washington had earlier honored the young officer with an invitation to join his staff as an aide. Lee turned down the prestigious position, averring, "I am wedded to my sword."[14] A slender, agile man of medium height, he combined an aptitude for violence with a precise rationality—he dared carefully.

On February 18, three days after reaching the safety of Virginia, Greene sent Lee back over the Dan to shadow Cornwallis and keep the British off guard. His presence would encourage the patriots of North Carolina, whom Greene had been forced to abandon. A few days after that, Otho Williams brought the light infantry across the Dan for the same purpose.

Cornwallis desperately needed the support of armed loyalists. A local doctor named John Pyle recruited four hundred Tories to join the British. Lee overtook this group and convinced them that he was Banastre Tarleton, come to escort them into camp. The gullible Tories stepped to the side of the road so Lee's horsemen could pass. Lee claimed that he was about to reveal his identity and order Pyle's recruits to disperse when the delicate pretense suddenly shattered. Before the loyalists realized what was happening, Lee's dragoons had wheeled and plunged into their ranks. From their mounts, they slashed jugular veins and fired point-blank with pistols.

Ninety loyalists died and most of the rest were wounded in what came to be known as Pyle's Massacre, Pyle's Hacking Match, or simply Pyle's Defeat. Cries from Lee's men of "Remember Buford!" highlighted the cycles of revenge and retribution that made the conflict in the South so ruinous. Word of the massacre spread. "It has knocked up Toryism altogether in this part," the laconic Andrew Pickens observed.[15]

Baron von Steuben sent Greene four hundred additional trained but untested Continentals from Virginia. Along with new militia recruits, they gave the southern commander a total force of more than five thousand men. Knowing that the militiamen would begin to go home before long if he did not use them, Greene was determined to try his army against the two-thousand-man force of Cornwallis.

He ferried his army back over the Dan to North Carolina and began a period of maneuvering that lasted through early March 1781. At times, barely ten miles separated his men from the British army. Greene feinted, probed, shifted direction, all with the goal of keeping Cornwallis guessing his intentions.

"There are few generals that has run oftener or more lustily than I have done," Greene declared. "But I have taken care not to run far."[16] The stress of perpetual vigilance left him afflicted with a painful inflammation of his eyes.

In the middle of March, Greene's intuition told him that it was time to take a stand. He led his men to Guilford Courthouse in north central North Carolina, now Greensboro. They arrayed for battle. Cornwallis, having chased the rebels fruitlessly for a month, had little choice but to respond to the thrown gauntlet. He had full confidence that his regulars could manhandle Greene's pick-up army in spite of their greater numbers.

Daniel Morgan, in a message to Greene, emphasized the importance of the militia. If they stand, he wrote, "you'l beat Cornwallis if not, he will beat you."[17] Greene heeded the advice and adopted on a larger scale the tactics Morgan had used at Cowpens. Instead of two lines, he established three: first raw militiamen, then an echelon of more experienced Virginia militia, whose ranks included Continental Army veterans. The backbone of the force would be the 1,400 Maryland and Delaware Continentals, posted on a ridge at the rear. Woods covered much of the half mile that separated the first and third lines.

Among those on the field that March 15 was Brigadier General Edward Stevens, who had seen his men flee in panic from the battlefield at Camden. To avoid a repeat of the earlier debacle, he posted marksmen ten yards behind his men with orders to shoot down "the first man who flinched."

Before the British arrived, Greene rode along the lines of militia, encouraging the men and asking for only two volleys from the frontline troops before they fell back. These men looked out from behind a rail fence over plowed fields on either side of the road. A militia major wrote to his wife while waiting: "It is scarcely possible to paint the agitations of my mind."[18]

At eleven-thirty in the morning, the troops caught sight of red uniforms and "gay banners" in the woods beyond the fields. The sky-filling boom of artillery pieces from both sides punctuated a period of further tense waiting. Finally the British and Hessian infantry came marching across the plowed field in precise parade-ground fashion. Rebel riflemen peppered them from the flanks. In the lines, a few jumpy North Carolina militiamen fired their rifles and shotguns ineffectively when the targets were still a hundred yards away, then fled. At fifty yards, the British saw the mass of rebels, and one noted that the "whole force had their arms presented and resting on a rail-fence."[19] The redcoats hesitated.

"At this awful period," a British sergeant recorded, "a general pause took place, both parties surveyed each other a moment with anxious suspense."[20] British colonel James Webster cantered to the front and urged his men forward. Forward they came. Suddenly the thousand muskets along the fence ignited as one, roaring out flame, smoke, and flying lead balls. The punishing gunfire lacerated the British line but did not stop the hardened troops, who unloosed their own volley and charged. The militia had no time to reload. Gleaming British bayonets bore down on them. They ran like "a flock of sheep frightened by dogs."[21]

"Dreadful was the havoc on both sides." And it was only beginning. The real fight began at the second line. There the Americans wavered, fell back before a bayonet charge, regrouped, fired a volley that brought the British to a standstill, and for a while fought a fierce back-and-forth contest. War became work. Principles of country, honor, and patriotism gave way before the grim need to do a job.

With the British attack thrown into confusion by the terrain and the unexpected resistance, an opportunity suddenly opened. Greene could have ordered a charge backed by his cavalry. He might have demolished Cornwallis's force as Morgan had blasted Tarleton's regiments at Cowpens. He might have achieved the decisive triumph he craved. But Greene ranked survival above glory. He could not risk his army and did not.

The British pushed on and began to grapple with the Continentals of the third line. Violence convulsed the American left. Greene finally decided that it was time to retreat. His men broke off the action. The two-hour-long fight was over. Cornwallis held the field, but five hundred of his men, a quarter of his force, had fallen.

Afterward, the British general prudently retreated to Wilmington, on the North Carolina coast, for resupply. He would not take the field again in the Carolinas, admitting that he was "quite tired of marching about the country in quest of adventures."[22] He shifted his sights to Virginia, where he thought glory might be won more easily.

Greene could not keep from bragging to Caty, to whom he wrote the hardly reassuring words that he had come "very near being taken having rode in the heat of the action full tilt directly into the Midst of the enemy."[23] He had been vexed by the long retreat and the complexity of maneuvering. Now his spirits soared. Guilford Courthouse was his Trenton. "The Enemy got the ground," he wrote, "but we the victory."[24] Like his mentor, he had retreated, then turned and delivered the enemy a telling blow.

———

Having boldly faced the British in North Carolina, Greene now made another radical and far-reaching decision. "In this critical and distressing situation," he wrote to Washington, "I am determined to carry the War immediately into South Carolina."[25] There he would face eight thousand British troops stationed in a chain of fortified outposts stretching in an arc from Charleston to Augusta, Georgia. Greene's move away from his own lines of supply and communication risked disaster. Cornwallis could descend on his rear, or British commander Henry Clinton could embark an army from New York to crush the meager American force.

Greene had to take the chance. If he did not, the authorities in South Carolina and Georgia would most likely give up the cause, and the states would remain a permanent part of the British empire no matter how the war turned out.

On April 7, 1781, Greene's men marched south. Two weeks later, they camped near Hobkirk's Hill, just outside of Camden. The town was now a fortified British outpost. Greene contemplated besieging the garrison there. Lord Rawdon, a young man whose bony visage and hammock jaw had earned him a reputation as "the ugliest man in England," commanded the British.[26] He possessed a keen military instinct. Rather than wait inside his lines for Greene to act, he rushed out and attacked the rebels.

His men caught the Americans at breakfast. The British pushed back the enemy pickets and engaged the army in a hot battle. Greene rallied his men. Rawdon called up his reserves. He outflanked the American line. Panic soon caught the patriots by the neck. They began to run. So close was Greene to the action that he pitched in to haul back the American field pieces, preventing their capture.

It was not a major battle. Again British casualties outpaced those of the Americans. Yet the loss cast Greene into a funk. "I am much afraid these States must fall," he wrote.[27] He again worried that his reputation was at risk. He cast blame on his subordinates. He remained downhearted until, three weeks later, word arrived that Rawdon had abandoned Camden and pulled his battered force back to Charleston. The American general breathed new confidence.

Writing to a French envoy following the engagement, Greene stated, "We fight get beat rise and fight again."[28] The succinct description summed up not only Greene's strategy in the southern campaign, but the American experience throughout the war. What had been true at Bunker Hill was true at Hobkirk's Hill. Determination and perseverance were the Americans' most important resources. Get beat. Rise. Fight again.

As spring progressed into summer, Greene reduced the British outposts one by one. Lee's Legion worked with Francis Marion's and Thomas Sumter's partisans to capture isolated forts. The success gave patriots in the state hope. Greene's movements were "critical and dangerous," he recognized, "and our troops exposed to every hardship. But as I share it with them I hope they will bear up under it."[29] To a North Carolina officer, he commented, "Don't be surprised if my movements don't correspond with your Ideas of military propriety. War is an intricate business."[30] Once an avid student of warfare, the general was now a master writing his own rules.

Nathanael Greene was appalled by the viciousness that continued to flare between patriots and their loyalist neighbors. The two sides pursued each other like "beasts of prey." To Caty he wrote, "My dear you can have no Idea of the horrors of the Southern war."[31] He issued proclamations urging restraint. "We have a great reason to hate them," he admitted, but winning loyalists away from the British cause should be done by "gentle means only."[32]

With the arrival of high summer, marching in suffocating heat appealed to neither side. In June, Greene took his men to the High Hills of the Santee, a twenty-four-mile-long plateau north of Charleston and south of Camden where they could rest away from the malarial miasma of the lowlands. During the next six weeks, he rebuilt his depleted force while Lee, Marion, and Sumter continued to harass the enemy. Marion waged a classic guerrilla war, hitting his opponents and dissolving into the swamps, never camping in the same place twice.

By the end of August, having gathered two thousand men, Greene was ready to come down from the hills. British colonel Alexander Stewart had taken over from Rawdon, who had worn himself out and fallen ill chasing after Greene. Stewart came out from Charleston with a force equal to Greene's. The American caught up with him at the hamlet of Eutaw Springs, about fifty miles from Charleston. A battle was inevitable.

When Nathanael Greene had first arrived in the South, barely nine months earlier, the enemy had been ascendant. The British had captured a major city and an entire American army at Charleston and had destroyed another army at Camden. They controlled all the territory south of Virginia. Loyalists were optimistic and under arms.

During week after week of maneuvers, battles, raids, and sieges, the audacious, careful, asthmatic American general had achieved something wonderful. The British now held only Charleston and Savannah. Greene had strangled the substantial garrison forces piecemeal. Patriots could hold up their heads. The South was in American hands.

Greene had outthought Cornwallis, the keenest of the enemy generals. He had applied patience, determination, and common sense to a situation of baffling complexity. "Without an army, without Means, without anything," wrote his old friend Henry Knox, "he has performed wonders."[33]

Greene was not a Morgan, an Arnold, or a Wayne, who might have attempted a brilliant, risky stroke and ended the campaign earlier. He was instead an officer who understood the overriding importance of movement, logistics, and survival. He was a Washington.

Just past nine o'clock on the morning of September 8, 1781, under an incandescent sun, the two armies arrayed for battle outside the British camp at Eutaw Springs, South Carolina. Greene again put his militia, including Francis Marion's Carolina partisans, in the first line. He held back his Continentals. The men gulped down their hearts as the concussion of artillery shook the ground. The air shivered with the painful rattle of musketry. The British attacked. The stalwart militiamen fired. The blasts came like waves breaking on a stormy coast. Some men got off seventeen shots. The redcoats pressed, the militia faltered. The Continentals pushed back, the British buckled. Stewart brought up his reserves. The Americans retreated in disorder. The redcoats charged. Greene sent more Continentals forward. A British volley crippled Lee's cavalry. William Washington's horsemen tried to break into the rear and were cut down. Washington was wounded and captured. The fighting in the center became sheer muscle. Officers clashed "hand to hand and sword to sword." Men slashed with bloody blades. They screamed in their enemies' faces and killed each other with simultaneous bayonet thrusts. The heat grew suffocating. Lips turned black with thirst. Cannon blasts pounded men's skulls. The British line disintegrated. The American light infantry "rushed furiously" ahead. They crashed into the British grenadiers. Bodies lurched out of control, yanked by puppet strings of bellowed orders. The enemy tumbled backward "in utter confusion." Only one British regiment fought stubbornly on. The Americans grabbed two enemy guns, took three hundred prisoners. At last, a decisive victory loomed. Greene ordered up his own cannon to secure the field. In their camp, the British still held a fortified brick house. Artillery could not dislodge them. Greene's militia, even some of his Continentals, paused. The sun blistered them to madness. The men broke open barrels of British rum. They drank. They celebrated. Too soon. Stewart rallied his men. His cavalry came drumming back. The counterattack swept the confused patriots from the camp. The British captured the American guns. Greene ordered a retreat. Again a retreat.

Yet the British held the field only briefly. Badly mauled, they slogged back to Charleston, leaving their wounded for the Americans to succor. The toll for the four-hour battle was agonizing: hundreds dead, hundreds stretched in pain, men mangled, lacerated, prostrated, tormented. It was a "most Obstinate fight," Greene wrote, "by far the hottest action I ever saw."[34]

The battle was technically a British victory, practically a draw. Yet as one British officer observed about Greene, "the more he is beaten, the farther he advances in the end." Greene could not be blamed for calling the fight a "complete victory."[35] He had wiped away more than a third of Stewart's fighting force. He had ruined all British hopes in the South.

It was one of the most violent, bloody, heartbreaking fights of the entire conflict. More than that, Eutaw Springs was the last pitched battle of the Revolutionary War.

EIGHTEEN

AMERICA IS OURS

1781

During the spring of 1781, while Greene was maneuvering in the Carolinas, the Marquis de Lafayette, twenty-two years old, was on his way to Virginia with 1,200 Continental troops. His quarry was Benedict Arnold, who had compounded his betrayal by assuming the rank of brigadier general with the British. Although terrified of being captured and hanged, Arnold had raised a force of loyalists and taken them to Virginia to raid on a large scale. Washington, hurt and enraged by Arnold's disloyalty, had directed a French fleet to cut him off from resupply by sea. He sent Lafayette to bag him.

It didn't work. The fleet was repulsed off Chesapeake Bay by a stronger British armada. British commander Henry Clinton dispatched General William Phillips and an elite force of two thousand redcoats from New York to reinforce Arnold. The combined force was perfuming the Virginia landscape with the smoke of burning tobacco warehouses, destroying one of the colonies' most important sources of hard currency. More crucially, they were capturing and wrecking supplies and armaments intended for Greene's beleaguered force in the Carolinas.

Lafayette's army was weak. Anthony Wayne was still trying to equip a portion of the Pennsylvania Line to join him, but he had yet to come south. Lafayette had purchased hats and boots from his own purse for his ragged and restless troops. Yet desertions continued to erode his force. Lafayette ordered one captured deserter hanged, pardoned another, and told his troops that anyone who wanted to leave would have one chance, and one chance only, to do so. Thus challenged, the men stayed. "From that hour, all desertions ceased."[1]

Steuben had been able to recruit only a few hundred new Continentals to add to Lafayette's force. Virginia militia had not turned out in sufficient numbers, and Governor Thomas Jefferson had done little to help protect the Old Dominion. Lafayette arrived in Richmond at the end of April and saved the city from further destruction, but he could do little to counter the British raiders rampaging through the countryside.

The third week in May, Cornwallis arrived from the south and assumed command of the British force in Virginia. He was still smarting from his blistering encounter with Greene's troops at Guilford Courthouse. Another 1,500 reinforcements from New York brought the total British force in Virginia to 7,200. Even with his militiamen, Lafayette had fewer than half as many troops under his command. He could do nothing but retreat, allow the British their way in the state, and hope for reinforcements of his own. Cornwallis sent Tarleton's Legion galloping west to Charlottesville, intent on capturing rebel legislators who had taken refuge there. All but seven lawmakers managed to flee. Tarleton's dragoons next rode down on Monticello, forcing the author of the Declaration of Independence to scurry out the back door just in time to avoid capture.

Cornwallis grew sanguine about destroying Lafayette's hodgepodge army. "The Boy cannot escape me," he bragged.[2] The Boy was keenly aware of the threat. "To speak plain English," he wrote to Alexander Hamilton, who was almost exactly his own age, "I am devilish afraid of him."[3]

Schooled by Washington, Lafayette knew that his role was that of the fox. He had to slip away and draw Cornwallis's pack of hounds farther from their maritime base. He had to avoid battle to avoid disaster. "Independence has rendered me the more cautious," he told Hamilton, "as I know my warmth."[4] But an abject retreat risked dispiriting the citizens of Virginia. The art of maneuvering, shifting position, and fighting skirmishes without falling into a major battle was a delicate one. To Washington, Lafayette admitted, "I am not Strong enough even to get Beaten."[5] His mentor had confidence in him. Command in Virginia, he wrote "cannot be in better hands than the Marquiss."

Like Washington and Greene, Lafayette was a learner. "I read, I study, I examine, I listen, I think," he explained to his father-in-law.[6] He kept his aggressive nature in check with regular doses of "common sense," an intuition about when to gamble and when to proceed with caution.

Washington understood that the young man was a rare genius. "He is a prodigy for his age," Johann de Kalb had said of the marquis, "full of courage, spirit, judgment, good manners, feelings of generosity and zeal."[7]

Exuberant, guileless, and big-hearted, Lafayette had a singular ability to lead men in battle. "He possesses," Washington declared, "uncommon Military talents."[8]

————•◦•————

Anthony Wayne struggled to bring his Pennsylvania men to the rescue. Following their January mutiny, they remained recalcitrant. They balked at orders to march toward the disease-ridden South. They wanted the pay still owed them. The grumbling, the talk of another mutiny, went too far. One man was heard to say, "God damn the officers, the buggers." To restore discipline, Wayne found him and five others guilty under the Articles of War. Executioners blew the heads off four of the men with close musket fire. Two were pardoned. A few days later, as the troops began their march, twelve more men refused orders, saying they were not "to be trifled with." Furious, Wayne instantly had them court-martialed and executed. He was afraid to give the rest of the troops access to ammunition or bayonets. His eight hundred reluctant men marched southward, "Mute as Fish."[9]

Wayne joined Lafayette on June 10, 1781. A few days later, William Campbell, who had led the attack on Kings Mountain, showed up with six hundred mounted fighters. Lafayette appealed to the ailing Daniel Morgan, who had become his close friend, to raise a force to protect his home state. Morgan rallied once more, appearing with a unit of tough backwoods riflemen. "What a people are these Americans," Lafayette marveled, "they have reinforced me with a band of giants." Helping foil an attack by Tarleton's cavalry, the riflemen "ran the whole day in front of my horse without eating or resting."[10]

Morgan himself, now forty-five, could no longer summon such stamina. Afflicted with "the infirmities of age," he caught a cold, grew steadily sicker, and had to return home a second time. "I am afraid I am broke down," he wrote to his friend Nathanael Greene.[11]

Lafayette now led a force of nearly 4,500 men. Cornwallis, long out of touch with General Clinton in New York, began to pull back toward the sea to receive orders. Lafayette shadowed him at about twenty miles distance, shifting position daily, spreading out his army to make the force appear larger. Still too weak to fight a major battle, he stuck close to Cornwallis "to give his movements the appearance of a retreat."[12]

During the first week in July, Cornwallis led his men southeast from Richmond, down the peninsula formed by the James and York Rivers, both of which drained into Chesapeake Bay. He was following an order from a nervous Clinton to send three thousand of his men to New York to beef up the defenses against a combined French and American army gathering on the outskirts. Cornwallis's men were to embark from Portsmouth, on the south bank of the James.

As the British general ferried his advance guard and baggage across the river, Lafayette thought he saw a chance to catch and rough up the enemy rear guard. He arrayed his force along the swampy coastal plain a few miles from Jamestown, where the British had established their first permanent settlement in the New World in 1607. Lafayette sent Wayne and his Pennsylvanians down a road corduroyed with logs between two morasses to scout the British position.

Cornwallis had outsmarted the Boy. Anticipating Lafayette's maneuver, he was waiting along the river bank with almost his entire force, ready to attack. As Wayne came on, the British commander ordered Tarleton to feign a retreat, drawing the Americans into the trap. At the last minute, Lafayette spotted the massed enemy and realized he had blundered. He had earlier written to Hamilton that he was "afraid of myself as much as of the Enemy" because of his impulsive nature. His duty was to avoid risking too much, and he had risked too much. He galloped forward to try to salvage the situation.

Anthony Wayne, when he saw his five hundred men suddenly outnumbered five to one, faced "a choice of difficulties." Stay and see his troops enveloped on both flanks—or retreat and have them cut down in a swamp. He instantly and instinctively chose another course: he ordered his men to charge.

War is an affair of the spirit as well as the body. Under heavy musket fire and the lacerating spray of grapeshot, Wayne's men fired their own cannon and rushed forward, "making a devil of a noise of firing and huzzaing." They fell into a blistering firefight, hammering the enemy from sixty yards away. Now it was Cornwallis who was brought up short. The unexpected charge made him wonder if Lafayette, now in the center of the maelstrom, commanded a more formidable force than he had imagined. He hesitated. Wayne took advantage of the pause and with the coming of evening extricated his men from the death trap. He had to give up two field guns, but he managed to escape. Lafayette put the best face on the near disaster, praising "the Glory of Genl. Wayne" for attacking the whole British army with "a reconnoitring Party only."[13]

"Madness," one exasperated patriot wrote after hearing of the incident. "Mad A——y, by G— I never knew such a piece of work."[14] Mad Anthony. Sketchy evidence indicates that one of Wayne's neighbors, the eccentric Jimmy the Drover, had earlier referred to the general as mad when Wayne would not intervene to free him from a civilian jail. The anecdote circulated, the nickname gained currency, the wild charge on the James made it stick. Mad Anthony Wayne it was.

Cornwallis completed his crossing. At Portsmouth, new orders awaited him. A dithering Clinton no longer wanted the reinforcements. Cornwallis should stake out a position on the north side of the peninsula and be ready for anything—resupply, reinforcement, or withdrawal. Cornwallis selected a location where the broad York River narrowed to barely half a mile. Lafayette, still hovering near him, was puzzled by the enemy activity. In the oppressive heat of August, the British were constructing fortifications around an out-of-the-way village on a bluff overlooking the river. The village was then called York. History would know it as Yorktown.

George Washington, graying as he approached fifty, had aged during six years of unrelieved responsibility, frustration, and trial. His troops and his wife, Martha, called him the Old Man. To backwoodsmen he was Old Hoss. It had been almost five years since his audacious winter attack on Trenton. Now, in the summer of 1781, Washington had to decide whether he should again stake everything on a single move.

After the disasters of 1780, hope for the American cause, John Adams admitted, "hung upon a Thread." In May, Washington met again with the Comte de Rochambeau to talk over the coming campaign. The French ally afterward observed that "these people here are at the end of their resources."[15]

When Rochambeau finally marched his five thousand men to join Washington's army near White Plains in July, his officers were appalled by the shabby dress and bare feet of the troops there. They chuckled when an amateur American officer, not thinking of soldiering as a permanent profession, asked his French counterpart "what his *trade* was in his own country."[16]

At the same time, the French marveled that these men, "unpaid and rather poorly fed, can march so well and withstand fire so steadfastly." Washington himself seemed to embody a unique spirit. A French chaplain judged that "he never has more resources than when he seems to have no more."[17]

To regain New York had been Washington's dream since his humiliating defeat there in 1776. But the problem had not changed since Charles Lee had first defined it: who commanded the sea commanded the town. Washington needed the French fleet in order to crack open the heavily fortified city. Even then, the chance of success was dubious. Clinton and his fourteen thousand soldiers were so solidly entrenched that the combined French and American army of about ten thousand had scant hope of dislodging them.

The moment of decision came in mid-August. Washington received word that the Comte de Grasse, a battle-tested French admiral, was proceeding from the West Indies not to New York but to Chesapeake Bay. The development offered the possibility of an important victory over Cornwallis's army. But the prospect was a long shot. The French had, again and again, proven themselves unreliable allies. If the operation were to work, it meant marching two armies four hundred miles in summer heat. It meant coordinating that move with the French navy. Two French navies—Admiral Barras, currently in Newport, would need to sail south and rendezvous with de Grasse, bringing with him the French army's siege guns and much of Henry Knox's heavy artillery. It meant that Cornwallis would have to remain motionless at Yorktown rather than brush aside Lafayette's inferior force and depart. It meant that an alerted British fleet would not beat de Grasse to the Chesapeake to reinforce Cornwallis or draw his men off. It meant that Clinton would continue to slumber and not sally out to strike Washington's rear or take possession of the vital Hudson Highlands.

Washington strongly suspected that once his army marched south, it could not return without a victory. The troops had gone unpaid for too long. They were too destitute, too mutinous. Congress was bankrupt, popular sentiment cool. The dissolution of the army that he had warned of during the Valley Forge winter appeared closer than ever.

Was it worth the risk? Through almost the entire war, Washington had bridled under a strategy of retreat and defense. Play it safe, never venture your whole force, make certain the army survived. Now, he decided, it was time to take a chance, time to risk everything. Old Hoss was going south.

———·‹•›·———

War is always dynamic, time its great mediator. Marching at twenty miles a day, it would take the allied armies at least three weeks to reach Yorktown. Would Cornwallis still be there? It was impossible to know. Speed was essential. On August 27, Washington wrote Lafayette, telling him to do all he could to hold Cornwallis's army in place. He asked Virginia governor Thomas Nelson, who had replaced Jefferson, to call out every militiaman armed "with a gun of any sort."

Just crossing the Hudson River at King's Ferry took six days. Leaving behind three thousand men to guard the Highlands, Washington directed the rest of his troops to the area of New Jersey opposite Staten Island. He was at his theatrical best in giving a nervous General Clinton the impression that he intended to attack New York City. He ordered the French troops to build ovens, as if preparing for a long siege; he assembled boats to feign an amphibious attack; he spread rumors of an imminent assault

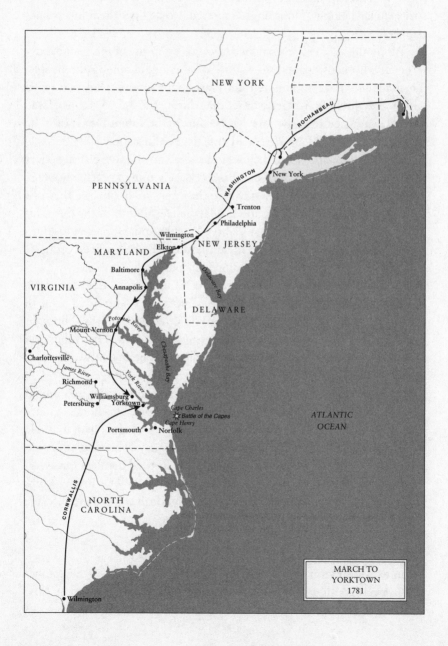

on the city. All the while, he kept his own troops and most of his officers in the dark about the army's actual destination.

At the end of August, the troops turned south. Now they guessed where they were headed, and they didn't like it. By the time they reached Philadelphia, they were grumbling so loudly that Washington borrowed $20,000 from Rochambeau so that his paymaster could hand out a month's wages in half-crown coins. For many of the men, it was their first pay in specie. "Hard money," Washington figured, would "put them in a proper temper."[18]

Along the way, crowds strained to catch a glimpse of the commander in chief, who had attained the stature of a demigod among the people. Their adulation did nothing to calm Washington's mind. He was gripped with nervous agitation as at no other time during the war. "I am distressed beyond expression to know what has become of the Count De Grasse," he wrote to Lafayette. "I am almost all impatience and anxiety."[19]

Rochambeau and his staff chose to proceed down the Delaware River by boat; Washington traveled on horseback. When the French entourage approached the dock in Chester, where they were to disembark, they saw a man on shore waving his hat and handkerchief, shouting at the top of his lungs, practically dancing. It was George Washington. He seemed as if his whole deportment was changed in an instant, a French officer wrote. "I never saw a man so thoroughly and openly delighted."[20]

A dispatch rider from the south had brought word that de Grasse had arrived at the Chesapeake. His fleet included twenty-nine ships of the line, each carrying seventy-four guns on three decks. He had brought additional warships and transports carrying 3,500 men. His troops had already disembarked and were helping Lafayette contain Cornwallis. This time, things might work out.

Now the ebullient commander in chief even allowed himself a brief side trip to Mount Vernon, the first time he had visited his home in more than six years, the first time he had seen his four step-grandchildren. He entertained Rochambeau and his aides for a few days, showing off his estate on the Potomac. As they were leaving, he learned that de Grasse had gathered his fleet and sailed out of Chesapeake Bay. The French ships had all disappeared over the horizon. The American commander became "much agitated" on hearing this discouraging news.

———•◦•———

George Washington arrived at Williamsburg, Virginia, on September 22. Lafayette "caught the General round his body, hugged him as close as was possible, and absolutely kissed him from ear to ear."[21] Cornwallis remained at Yorktown, ten miles further down the peninsula, the marquis told the commander in chief. "We have got him handsomely in a pudding bag," was how Virginia militia general George Weeden put it.[22]

The most important news was that de Grasse had sailed out of the bay in response to an immediate threat. A British fleet under Admiral Samuel Graves had caught him unprepared, with many French sailors and officers assigned to supply duties on land. De Grasse had had no time to recall them. He had hurried his fleet out of the bay to give battle.

Graves had made the inexplicable error of allowing the French ships to assemble in the ocean rather than attack them as they passed between the Chesapeake capes. Two hours of point-blank battering with heavy cannon left both fleets damaged and hundreds of men torn apart. While both admirals jockeyed for position and repaired their vessels, they drifted to the south, allowing Barras's smaller Newport fleet to slip into the bay and deliver the precious siege guns.

"Sentiments upon the Truly Unfortunate Day," was how one of Graves's officers had titled his report of the engagement. Soon Graves had to admit the "impracticability of giving any effectual succour to General Earl Cornwallis."[23] The British fleet would sail back to New York.

Washington and his entourage went out to de Grasse's flagship, the *Ville de Paris*, the largest armed vessel in the world. They met the admiral and thanked him for his crucial effort. De Grasse, "a remarkable man for size, appearance, and plainness of address," taller even than Washington, embraced the American commander jokingly as *"mon cher petit general."*[24] Henry Knox laughed.

Not so amusing was de Grasse's insistence that he would be leaving at the end of October. The possibility of a hurricane and the danger of a British raid on France's valuable and unprotected possessions in the West Indies would not allow him to tarry. The news gave the coming siege of Yorktown a high urgency. "We had holed him," a soldier remarked about Cornwallis, "and nothing remained but to dig him out."[25] They only had six weeks to do it.

Digging an enemy out of a fortified position was an exercise as old as warfare itself. Rochambeau, who had participated in fourteen sieges, assured Washington that it was "reducible to calculation." A siege was a trying and often terrifying slow-motion battle requiring constant vigilance over days and weeks. Boredom alternated with terror as each side sought an advantage in a raid, a sally, an assault, a skirmish, or a stratagem. Time was the key factor. How fast could the attacker dig trenches and bring up guns?

How long could the defender hold out? Would reinforcements show up to relieve the besieged force?

The allied army, in full battle array, marched from Williamsburg to the vicinity of Yorktown on September 25. Washington was surprised that Cornwallis made no effort to oppose him along the road. The enemy's few skirmishers quickly pulled back within their lines, allowing the allies to set up their camp in front of Yorktown, the Americans on the right, the French on the left. Two days later, British soldiers mysteriously abandoned their outer fortifications, tightening their perimeter but allowing the allied armies to begin their operations that much closer.

The British had reinforced their main line, a system of trenches and parapets in a semicircle around the town, with seven strong points and three enclosed redoubts. Cornwallis led about nine thousand men, including those on two warships floating in the river. His works bristled with sixty-five cannon.

The British also held the point of land at Gloucester, half a mile away on the opposite bank of the river. A small army of French cavalry and Virginia militia was assigned to contain them. On October 3, Banastre Tarleton led an armed expedition out of the British fortifications there to forage for food. French horsemen attacked and drove them back. The "pudding bag" was now completely sealed.

During a week of preparation, troops hewed stakes for abatis and stockades and bundled fascines of twigs for filling ditches. On the night of October 5, Washington himself struck the soil with a pick to break ground for the first trench, known as a parallel. The digging began about a half mile from British lines. The works traced an arc from the river edge halfway around the enemy position on the eastern side. Only three weeks now remained before Admiral de Grasse would sail away.

The possibility that the British could move to rescue or reinforce Cornwallis at any time added to the sense of anxious hurry. The goal of a siege was to demolish the enemy's fortifications with large cannon. But since that enemy had cannon of his own already in place, the attacking soldiers first had to excavate trenches and prepare protected batteries from which they could fire. The Marquis de Vauban had formalized the system of parallels and zigzag approaches during the 1670s and his doctrine remained military gospel. But calculations on paper translated on the battlefield into blood and mayhem.

Thousands of sappers had to step into the killing field of British artillery fire and brave enemy sharpshooters in order to excavate ditches four feet deep and ten feet wide. They toiled at the dangerous work in silence and under the cover of darkness. They piled the earth to make a rampart and reinforced it with pointed twelve-foot stakes. The allies could not return the enemy's nerve-rattling cannon fire until their own batteries were in place.

Five and a half years and several lifetimes had passed since the icy days of January 1776, when Henry Knox and his brother William, who

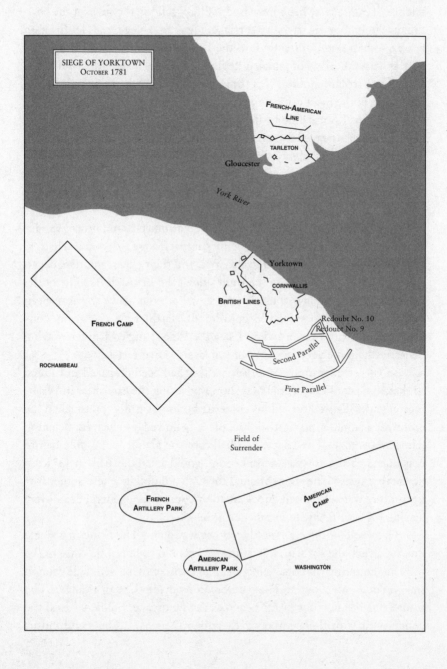

also accompanied him to Yorktown, had manhandled their train of Ticon-deroga artillery through the hills of Massachusetts. In July, the Bostonian had celebrated his thirty-first birthday. During the entire war, he had been in charge of the most exacting facet of the military effort, managing the massive guns and procuring the ammunition on which fighting depended. When not campaigning, he had trained hundreds of men in the intricate science of gunnery at his improvised military school, the first on the con-tinent. He had invented a gun carriage, ideal for a siege, that let his men fire exploding bombs directly into the British breastworks. All the while, as in the mutiny crisis of January, he had served as Washington's principal adviser and troubleshooter. Now the heavyset man with the mangled hand would direct the most critical operation of the war.

The guns Knox would be firing at Yorktown were not the manageable field pieces that heaved 3- and 6-pound iron balls. Siege artillery needed the power to wreck enemy fortifications from long range. These would be 18- and 24-pounders, each gun weighing close to three tons. A great effort was needed to drag the tremendous cannon into position along the swampy, sandy peninsula.

By October 8, six large cannon, as well as mortars and howitzers de-signed to heave bombs over the enemy parapets, were ready in the batter-ies. The French were allowed to fire first, and their expert gunners began to send bombs and balls into the right side of the British lines. The hoist-ing of the national flag would be the signal to commence the American barrage. Connecticut soldier Joseph Plumb Martin, now a sergeant, con-fessed a swelling of pride "when I saw the 'star-spangled banner' waving majestically in the very faces of our implacable adversaries."[26]

An 18-pounder in the American battery had been prepared and aimed so that Knox could set off the first shot. But seeing the eagerness in Wash-ington's eyes, Knox afforded his chief the honor. Washington touched the gun with a smoldering linstock; the piece bellowed and heaved, belching flame and smoke. The heavy iron ball tore the air for half a mile before crashing into the town. An American "could hear the ball strike from house to house." The shot smashed through a building where some Brit-ish officers were at dinner, knocking their commissary general dead while leaving his horrified wife untouched at his side.

The world of the eighteenth century was quiet. The firing of a single musket struck the ear with a startling report. No sound came close to the heaven-shattering roar of a field gun. The thunder of massed siege cannon was of yet another order. Their detonations made the earth quiver. The sound rolled for scores of miles across the landscape. Soldiers heard the concussions with their entrails rather than their ears. The awful music, which went on well into the night, wore on all nerves. At their peak, the allied guns were firing 3,600 rounds a day, one massive blast piled on another.

To be on the receiving end of the barrage was an unrelenting nightmare. Cannonballs crashed into the defenses, blasting the pointed abatis and weakening the breastworks. They tore over the parapets and through the town with ghostly sighs until they took down a brick wall or splintered a house beam or ripped off a human leg.

British and German soldiers who were not manning the lines against an assault hid in basements. Some joined the civilians who sought shelter below the bluffs that lined the river. No cannonball could reach them there, but shells were a different matter. As these iron spheres descended into enemy territory, a charge of gunpowder inside blew them to pieces. The lacerating shards flew in all directions, striking even those cowering behind the earthen banks.

For those not mangled by the projectiles, the bombardment was a stunning sight. "One of the most sublime and magnificent spectacles which can be imagined," American army surgeon James Thacher wrote. He watched the bombs crisscross in the air. "In the night they appear like a fiery meteor with a blazing tail, most beautifully brilliant."[27]

The French were the world's best gunners. Yet a French officer marveled at the intelligence and activity of Henry Knox. "The artillery was always well served, the general incessantly directing it and often himself pointing the mortars. Seldom did he leave the batteries."[28]

At one point in the bombardment, Knox disputed with Alexander Hamilton whether it was honorable for sentries to shout, "A shell!" when an enemy bomb landed, giving those nearby an instant to dive out of the way before it went off. Hamilton deemed such a warning cowardly. Men should stand fire without flinching as a point of honor. While the discussion was going on, the alarm went up: "A shell! A shell!" Knox dove for a shelter, and Hamilton huddled behind Knox's bulky body. Knox tossed the future secretary of the treasury off his back. The bomb exploded.

"Now," Knox reportedly said, "now what do you think, Mr. Hamilton, about crying shell—but let me tell you not to make a breastwork of me again."[29]

The British frigate that floated in the river off Yorktown was called the *Charon*, after the boatman said to ferry souls to Hades. While standing guard over the hell on shore, the ship was hit and set afire by a French cannonball heated red hot in a furnace. As it burned through the night, Doctor Thacher recounted, the vessel was "enwrapped in a torrent of fire," the combustible rigging transformed into a flaming outline of the ship.

By October 11, three days after the bombardment began, few British guns could answer the relentless allied barrage. In the town, a German soldier noted that "many men were badly injured and mortally wounded by the fragments of bombs, their arms and legs severed or themselves struck dead."[30] Americans observed hundreds of dead horses floating in the river. British forage had run out.

Cornwallis was grappling with a fate eerily similar to that of Burgoyne at Saratoga, his hopes pinned on a relief force that Sir Henry Clinton had promised to send from New York. Like Burgoyne, he waited. And waited.

Allied sappers began digging a second ditch, this one only a few hundred yards from the enemy fortifications. To complete this line, on the night of October 14, American and French troops launched assaults against two detached redoubts at the outer end of the British works. Washington gave the eager Alexander Hamilton a chance to lead the four hundred veterans who would storm one of the forts. The men vaulted over the walls and used bayonets, spears, and axes in a fierce hand-to-hand struggle with the British defenders. After ten minutes of brawling, they possessed the redoubt.

Knox hauled his guns even closer to the enemy breastworks. Cornwallis realized that he needed to act before his ramparts were completely leveled and his men exposed. Before dawn on October 16, 350 British soldiers rushed out of the lines and attacked the closest French and American batteries. They managed to disable a number of cannon but were driven off. Gunners repaired their pieces in a few hours. The sally had been more a gesture than an earnest attack.

That night, the British commander tried another, more desperate tactic. He planned to embark his entire army and row them across the river to Gloucester. They would smash through the allied lines there and escape north through the Virginia countryside. Traveling without baggage, they could keep ahead of their pursuers and live to fight another day.

With the number of vessels available, the crossing would take three trips. After the first wave landed, a sudden squall blew up on the river, threatening the open boats. By the time the waters calmed, the approach of daylight exposed the maneuver. Cornwallis ordered his men who had made it to the north shore to return. Tarleton put it succinctly: "Thus expired the last hope of the British army."[31]

———

As the sun came up on October 17, the dreadful cannonade recommenced. "The whole peninsula trembles," Thacher wrote, "under the incessant thunderings of our infernal machines."[32] A German on the receiving end noted, "Early at the break of day, the bombardment began again from the enemy side even more horribly than before; they fired from all the redoubts without stopping."[33]

At ten o'clock in the morning, a courageous drummer climbed onto the British parapet and beat a lonely tattoo. No one could hear him over the cannonade, but gunners in the American and French batteries saw him and ceased firing. A thrill of recognition ran through the allied ranks. The signal was "parley." The guns fell silent.

A minute later, an officer emerged, waving a white handkerchief. American soldiers blindfolded him and led him to Washington's tent a mile behind the lines. He delivered a letter from Cornwallis suggesting a twenty-four-hour armistice during which terms for surrender could be worked out. Washington replied that Cornwallis must first deliver a written proposal. He gave him two hours to comply.

The document that came back was unacceptable to Washington, but the American commander decreed that he would hold his fire and try to work out an agreement the following day. He was wary of a stall that would give Clinton time to relieve his subordinate. That night, "a solemn stillness prevailed," a militia officer wrote. "The night was remarkably clear, and the sky decorated with ten thousand stars. Numberless meteors gleaming through the atmosphere afforded a pleasing resemblance to the bombs."[34]

Just as sublime celestial bodies had replaced the "fiery meteors" of the artillery, so at dawn music substituted for the crash of the big guns. First the plaintive wail of bagpipes from the British. Then the answering strains of the French band. Men who had labored for weeks to kill each other crowded the tops of both parapets to stare at their enemies for the first time.

A pair of officers from each side worked all day and into the night to hammer out the details of the surrender. The British, Washington insisted, would receive no better terms than those they had afforded to Benjamin Lincoln following the siege of Charleston. They would not be allowed the honors of war, nor would the troops be permitted to return to England as requested. Cornwallis complained, but he had no choice.

Friday, October 19, dawned clear and cool, a glorious autumn day under a cobalt sky. The soldiers of the allied armies lined the road that led to a large open field, the Americans on the right, the French on the left. Washington, Rochambeau, and other high officers sat on horseback at the end of the mile-long gauntlet. Crowds of spectators congregated to view the event of a lifetime.

The defeated enemy marched out, their colors cased, their drums beating carelessly with a "strain of melancholy." Cornwallis skipped the ceremony, pleading illness. His second in command, General Charles O'Hara, trotted his mount toward Rochambeau to surrender his sword. A French officer told him, "You are mistaken. The commander in chief of our army is on the right." He pointed toward Washington. The commander in chief would not accept the proffered symbol, but indicated General Lincoln beside him, who touched and returned the sword.

The British officers, one observer noted, pouted, cried, and generally "behaved like boys who had been whipped at school."[35] Many were drunk. The hired Germans accepted their fate with iron dignity. The defeated troops, having stacked their muskets in a field ringed by armed dragoons, marched back to their camp and into captivity. Perhaps with a smile on his face, Washington penned his laconic message to Congress: "A Reduction of the British Army under the Command of Lord Cornwallis, is most happily effected."[36]

That night, as was the custom, Washington invited the top British officers to dine with him and his allies, making a conspicuous exception of Tarleton. Cornwallis preferred to sup with a French nobleman. At Washington's table, the French officers were more gracious to their British enemies than to the Americans. The reason, it was explained, was that these men, all from the upper echelons of their respective societies, shared "good upbringing and courtesy."[37] They had no affinity with a farmer like Benjamin Lincoln, a tanner like Anthony Wayne, a bookseller like Henry Knox, or even a poorly educated one-time surveyor. But besides their breeding, the French and British officers shared another quality: all were subjects of a king. Washington and his officers, along with the people for whom they had fought, answered to no man who claimed a divine right to rule. They had won their liberty. They were free men.

In any case, snubs meant little. Among the Americans, "every countenance beamed with satisfaction and joy" at the surrender. The officers and soldiers "could scarcely talk for laughing," an American recorded, "and they could scarcely walk for jumping and dancing and singing as they went about."[38] When the news reached a band of Virginia militiamen, they shouted: "America is ours!"[39]

"Your success in Virginia is brilliant, glorious, great and important," Nathanael Greene wrote to Henry Knox, the friend with whom he had chatted about military theory at The Bunch of Grapes tavern back in 1774.[40] Washington singled out the one-time Boston rowdy for praise, noting that, as always, "the resources of his genius supplied the deficit of means."

As soon as the surrender was signed, Knox sent his brother William galloping toward Mount Vernon, where Lucy was staying with Martha Washington. He was anxious, he wrote, "that I might be the first to communicate *good news* to the charmer of my soul."[41]

NINETEEN

OUR TROOPS

1782

Like a man frantically climbing a ladder, who keeps reaching for rungs after he has arrived at the top, George Washington continued to prepare for war after Yorktown. He pleaded with Admiral de Grasse to accompany him with the fleet to Charleston, convinced that retaking the city would be the decisive stroke. He worried that the good news from Yorktown would lull the people and their representatives in Congress into a dangerous apathy. The days, months, and years of anxiety had worn him down. Too many defeats had weighed on him, too many betrayals and disappointments had wrung his soul. He could not believe the truth: that when silence fell over the field at Yorktown, the war was effectively over. America's independence was won.

For another year and more, Washington would wait nervously, afraid of the "haughty Pride" of the British, and "totally in the Dark" about enemy intentions.[1] But the British had no intentions. They were fought out. They would not rebound from this surrender as they had from Burgoyne's four years earlier. They would, finally, go home.

In January 1782, Anthony Wayne took his Pennsylvania regiments to join Nathanael Greene in South Carolina. Greene sent his friend to keep watch on the British still occupying Savannah. Wayne's men fought some skirmishes and defeated an uprising of Creek Indians. Wayne remained eager for accolades and glory, but now even he wrote to his wife, "I am satiated with this horrid trade of blood."[2]

Like Washington, Wayne was impatient with the "unworthy torpor & supineness" of those who considered the war as good as over. He agreed with an officer who wrote to him about "chimney corner soldiers," who counseled the army to let down its guard while fifteen thousand redcoats occupied New York and ten thousand more did garrison duty in the South.

But others could see the truth. "The play, sir, is over," Lafayette wrote to the French foreign minister after Yorktown. "The fifth act has just been closed."[3] On hearing word of Cornwallis's fate, Lord North, the British prime minister who had steered his majesty's government through a tumultuous decade, exclaimed "Oh God, it is all over!" He took the news, it was said, "as he would have taken a ball in the breast."[4] King George huffed that "we can never continue to exist as a great or powerful nation after we have lost or renounced the sovereignty of America."[5] Yet in early 1782 British soldiers abandoned Wilmington, North Carolina. Peace negotiations began between the two governments in April. In July, the last occupiers left Savannah.

At last the god of war appeared to be sated with blood, treasure, and destruction. The once delightful Virginia village of Yorktown, now an abject, stinking ruin, symbolized the conflict's mad and wasteful frenzy. But someone always has to be the last to die.

John Laurens, along with Hamilton and Lafayette, was one of the young luminaries of the revolution. The handsome, educated son of a prominent Charleston family had fought recklessly at Brandywine, had received wounds at Germantown and Monmouth, had been captured with the fall of Charleston, and, exchanged, had fought at Yorktown. He had found time to serve as an aide to Washington and an envoy to the French. His only fault, Washington said, was an "intrepidity bordering upon rashness."

At Yorktown, it was the gifted twenty-six-year-old Laurens who had negotiated the details of Cornwallis's capitulation. He then returned to his home state to fight alongside Greene, harassing British patrols seeking food for the troops inside Charleston. Laurens, a fellow officer said, wanted "to gain a laurel for his brow previous to a cessation of arms."[6] In August 1782, he led his troops in an attack against an armed British forage party five times his numbers. He exposed himself unnecessarily and was shot dead. He left behind a widow and a young daughter.

Barely four months later, on December 14, British troops sailed away from Charleston forever. General Greene gave Anthony Wayne the privilege of parading his Continental soldiers into the town. New York City remained the only bastion of British power in the thirteen colonies. Henry Clinton had gone home, handing over command there to Guy Carleton, whose spirited defense of Quebec in 1775 had saved Canada for Britain.

While the British wolf's teeth had flashed nearby, the states had neglected to adequately support their men in the field. With the threat rapidly abating, they were even less inclined to open their coffers. During the two years that followed Yorktown, the army continued to suffer for want of basic necessities. General Greene begged Congress and the states for supplies. His men suffered from lack of clothing and food. Many still went barefoot.

With peace now casting its warm light across the nation, many civilians became convinced that it was republican virtue that had won the war. The Continental Army soldier, a hireling who had submitted to military discipline, was not a model of a free man. "Civilians could portray themselves," historian Charles Royster has observed, "as the rescuers of the army at Valley Forge rather than the main cause of the army's hardship." In 1782 a Virginia official noted that "some how there is a general disgust taken place for [Continental soldiers]."[7]

Now the distinction between summer soldiers and actual soldiers faded. Sunshine patriots emerged from the shadows. "There are too many of our Citizens," Anthony Wayne had noted in the spring of 1781, "that would not hesitate, to *wipe* off the large debt due to the army, with a *Sponge*."[8]

As early as 1777, Daniel Morgan, in his usual blunt language, had given his opinion "that the War should not end until the Soldiery were provided out the Estates made by it and of such as had too much Property to their Share."[9] The reluctance of the people and the states to honor their debt to the fighting men had reached a crisis with the mutinies of 1781, when soldiers had felt they were "starving in detail for an ungrateful people who did not care what became of us."[10]

The officers, as Washington knew, had also spent "the flower of their days" fighting for a cause that often seemed hopeless. Like their men they had seen little pay. They nursed similar grievances. During the desperate months of 1780, with American hopes hanging by a thread, Congress had voted to give the officers half pay for life, the standard pension in the British army. In early 1783, as peace negotiations moved toward conclusion, the army's leaders realized that the time to make Congress live up to this promise would soon pass. They changed the demand to five years' full pay. They insisted that Congress amend the Articles of Confederation to allow the money to be raised through taxes.

Events came to a head in March 1783. By this time, Horatio Gates, still serving as second in command, was overseeing the bulk of the troops outside Newburgh in New York's Hudson Valley. One of Gates's aides passed among the officers two anonymous circulars. They suggested that if Congress failed to agree to the officers' just demands, the men should pursue one of two alternatives. If the war continued, they should refuse to fight and should lead the army westward, leaving Congress and the major cities to the mercy of the British. If peace was concluded, they should keep the troops under arms and march to Philadelphia to obtain what they deserved by force.

The issue became part of a vitriolic debate. Opponents felt the war had been fought to get rid of just such special privileges as pensions, which might perpetuate an idle class of ex-officers at the expense of the yeomanry. Those who favored the officers' position saw that these men had sacrificed eight years of their lives while others had tended their farms or made money in trade. They deserved recompense. What was at stake this time was no sergeants' mutiny but a full-blown military coup that could snuff out the infant republic. Conversely, any officer who even tolerated talk of mutiny could be court-martialed and hanged.

The disgruntled officers called a meeting for March 15, 1783, in the spacious central meeting hall of the camp. Washington had been alerted to the gathering in advance. He remained the moral keel of the army. The soldiers, one officer told him, "universally think and speak of you with love, pleasure, gratitude and applause."[11] He carefully planned his strategy, enlisting the help of Henry Knox. Like Washington, Knox sympathized with the officers' plight but abhorred their attempt to bully the civil authority.

On the day set, the grumbling officers filed into the great room. Gates opened the meeting. At the appropriate moment, Washington strode in, "visibly agitated," to address his officers. He appealed to their sense of dignity and self-sacrifice. Their behavior, he hoped, would allow posterity to say of them, "Had this day been wanting, the World had never seen the last stage of perfection to which human nature is capable of attaining."[12]

Washington's rhetoric did not appear to sway the angry men. But he was not done. He had received a letter, he told them, from a member of Congress. It appeared to indicate that the officers' demands were likely to be met. He begged their permission to read it. He began, then fell silent. He pulled from his pocket a pair of spectacles that he had recently begun wearing. Only a few close aides had seen them perched on his nose. As he slipped them on, he asked the officers' forgiveness, "observing at the same time," a witness recorded, "that he had grown gray in their service and now felt himself going blind."[13]

It was a consummate performance by a skilled actor. Many of the men, who had lived through all the horrors of war, now wept. By the time Washington had finished reading and left the hall, the mood had changed completely. After a half hour of debate, Knox offered a proposal condemning the threats contained in the anonymous circulars that had touched off the affair and affirming the officers' loyalty. It passed unanimously. The so-called "Newburgh Conspiracy" was over.

The affair had served its purpose. Members of Congress were sufficiently spooked to comply with most of the officers' demands. Urged on by Washington, they issued interest-bearing certificates for the five years' pay and amended the Articles to allow for a modest tax.

Less than a month later, on April 11, 1783, came news of the official end of hostilities with Britain. The Treaty of Paris, in which "His Britannic Majesty acknowledges the said United States . . . to be free Sovereign and independent States," was signed September 3. Envoys John Adams, John Jay, and Benjamin Franklin had wrung for America terms better than most had dared hope for.

It was time for the troops to go home. Many felt the pangs of parting from friends with whom they had shared so much, whom they had come to love. "We were young men and had warm hearts," one of them later remembered.[14] They knew their lives would never again be illuminated by such a noble cause, nor would their minds crackle with such intensity.

General von Steuben planned a final, triumphant ceremony to precede the soldiers' dismissal. It was not to be. The troops, as part of the agreement that ended the Newburgh Conspiracy, had been promised three months' wages, a down payment on the back pay owed them. Congress could not find the money. Not for three months', not even for one month's pay. Only IOUs, and those of scant value.

There would be no parade. The high command judged it imprudent to dismiss the men as a body—they might join together and pillage the country. Instead, most regiments were marched to their home states, then released under the fiction of a furlough so as to keep them under military discipline.

The men who had "suffered and bled without a murmur," Washington wrote, were dismissed "without a settlement of their accounts or a farthing of money in their pockets."[15]

Destitute Maryland Continentals, having distinguished themselves again and again during the war, had to make their own way home from the deep South. Many resorted to begging. Joseph Plumb Martin, who had fought in the ranks since the beginning of the conflict and would leave behind one of the most vivid memoirs of the war, had to take a job on a farm in New York in order to earn traveling money to reach his home in Connecticut. He said of his fellow soldiers, "When the country had drained the last drop of service it could screw out of the poor soldiers, they were turned adrift like old worn-out horses, and nothing said about land to pasture them upon."[16]

Washington, Steuben, and Knox all pleaded with Congress to maintain a small army. Knox preached the need for an academy, perhaps near the still-important base at West Point, to train officers, engineers, and artillerymen in the science of war. Congress would not hear of it. "Standing army" was a dirty word. The Continental Army would immediately shrink to seven hundred men stationed at a few scattered posts on the frontier.

———

One ceremony remained. When the ink had dried on the Treaty of Paris, it was time for the last redcoats to leave. Early in November, Washington said goodbye to the troops still left at West Point. Of Henry Knox, he would later write that there was "no one whom I have loved more sincerely, nor any for whom I have had a greater friendship."[17] He gave his principal adviser the honor of leading the march into New York City.

On the spanking clear morning of November 25, Washington and Knox, with a small contingent of troops—ill-clad as always—rode south from Harlem Heights through a desolate landscape. All the trees on Manhattan Island had been cut down, many of the homes abandoned. Part of the city still lay in ruins from the 1776 fire. On Staten Island, Americans jeered at the enemy troops marching toward the embarkation docks. An ill-tempered British ship's gunner fired in anger a cannonball that fell short, pointlessly expending powder in what may have been the last shot of the war.

Ranks of civilian officials joined Washington and his men in a stately parade into town. Patriots turned out to cheer. The troops, an eyewitness noted, "were ill-clad and weather-beaten, and made a forlorn appearance. But then they were *our* troops."[18] Many of the city's loyalist residents embarked with the British, never to return.

Dinners, speeches, and fireworks filled the following days. Most officers had, like their men, already gone home. Some were dead. Charles Lee, the erratic general who had read Thucydides in the wilderness and had guided Washington's hand in his first shaky weeks of command, had died in October 1782, still dishing vitriol. William Alexander, the self-styled Lord Stirling, had proven his courage and ability in the fiercest fighting on Long Island and polished his reputation through Trenton, Brandywine, and Monmouth. Washington had put him in charge of the Northern Department when the army departed for Yorktown. Stirling, always an extravagant imbiber, fell ill in Albany. He died there in January 1783 at the age of forty-seven.

At noon on December 4, the few officers still left in New York met at Fraunces Tavern for a farewell dinner. Like their men, they had shared the most vivid experiences of their lives and had come to know and trust each other in ways no civilian could imagine. Like their men, they had received meager appreciation from an ungrateful nation.

Washington had little appetite for the food laid out in the tavern's upstairs great room, none for further speeches. A "breathless silence" descended on the officers. Eight years of struggle and fatigue, of comradeship and violent death, of confusion, heartbreak, perseverance, and glory, were over. Wine glasses were filled. Washington's hand trembled as he lifted his and said, "With a heart full of love and gratitude, I now take leave of you."

They drank. "I cannot come to each of you to take my leave," Washington said, "but shall be obliged to you, if each of you will come and take me by the hand."[19]

Henry Knox stepped forward first to grasp his Excellency's hand. The eyes of both men brimmed over. They embraced. Then Baron von Steuben. Then the others. "Such a scene of sorrow and weeping I had never before witnessed," one officer reported. Washington embraced each man in turn.

Then he waved, strode out of the room, passed the crowd waiting outside, and stepped into a boat manned by twenty-two rowers. He crossed to New Jersey and traveled on horseback to Philadelphia, then to Annapolis where Congress was sitting. He handed in his commission, leaving Henry Knox in charge of the skeleton army. He endured a few more dinners, an outpouring of thanks. George Washington, now a private citizen, reached his home at Mount Vernon on Christmas Eve, 1783.

TWENTY

THE LARGE HEARTS
OF HEROES

1824

On August 15, 1824, a platoon of aging Revolutionary War veterans stood by the seawall at the southern tip of New York City. Thirty thousand citizens crowded the wharf. Fifty thousand more lined the half-mile stretch of Broadway that led to City Hall. A tall, fleshy, sixty-seven-year-old man limped down the gangway. All began to cheer. "Lafayette!" they yelled. "Marquis!" they still called him, although he had long since renounced his title. The hero stepped onto American soil. The old soldiers called out the names of battles: *Brandywine. Monmouth. Yorktown.* Lafayette shook each of their hands, as warm and affable as ever. Yes, yes, he remembered. Of course.

Almost fifty years had passed since a small band of patriots had faced British muskets on Lexington Green. President James Monroe, who had himself been wounded one wintry day at Trenton, had invited Lafayette, now the last living major general of the Continental Army, to tour the country as the Nation's Guest. The Frenchman was returning to see the fruits borne by the tree of freedom that he and his generation had planted. "How have I loved liberty?" he asked. "With the enthusiasm of religion."[1]

The short journey up the thoroughfare took two hours. Then began a celebration such as the nation had never seen: dinners, galas, speeches, salutes, parades, fireworks. At the Lafayette Ball in Castle Garden, five thousand guests wandered through a fairyland dominated by thirty-foot-high illuminated transparencies showing Lafayette, Washington, and the marquis's French estate at La Grange. Toasts, cheers, huzzahs, dancing. During the public receptions that occupied at least two hours of every day, Lafayette shook hands with any citizen who wished to touch history. Many waited in line all night for the chance.

He went off to Boston, where nearly seventy-five thousand citizens greeted him. Traveling with him was his son, forty-four-year-old George Washington Lafayette, and a secretary. Lafayette journeyed to Quincy, where he met the eighty-nine-year-old John Adams. The former president's beloved wife, Abigail, had succumbed to typhoid seven years earlier. Afterward, Lafayette allegedly commented, "That was not the John Adams I knew." A decrepit Adams likewise noted, "That was not the Lafayette I knew."[2]

Thirteen mammoth arches of wood and canvas painted to look like stone honored the Nation's Guest in Philadelphia. As his entourage traveled south, reminders of the man Lafayette had called his "adopted father" accumulated. First, Washington City, as it was called then, the permanent federal capital on the Potomac, not yet grown into its grand design. Then Mount Vernon and the simple vault that held the remains of George and Martha Washington.

When he had returned to his estate after the war, his Excellency had felt that his time of public service was over and that his life was drawing to a close. Events had proven him wrong. In December 1799, his duty to his country finally completed, Washington had been stricken with a severe sore throat. The inveterate horseman had insisted on riding through cold, wet weather to see about planting some trees at Mount Vernon. Afterward, he had found it difficult to breathe. His doctors had bled him to no avail. Old Hoss had died at sixty-seven. His protégé, the closest he ever had to a son, now emerged from the vault, his face wet with tears.

Then on to Yorktown. October 19 marked the forty-third anniversary of the surrender. Could it have been so long? Salutes were fired, but nothing like the soul-wrenching din of the cannonade by which Henry Knox had brought Cornwallis to his knees.

Knox had served as President Washington's secretary of war. He had overseen the creation of the country's first permanent navy, commissioning a class of innovative super frigates, including the *USS Constitution*, which had proven themselves during the War of 1812. He had lived to see the establishment of his longtime dream, the Military Academy at West Point.

Like many officers, Knox had struggled with debt. He invested borrowed money to improve a tract of land his wife had inherited in Maine.

He and Lucy eventually settled there. They endured the deaths of nine of their twelve children, each loss a bayonet point to the heart.

Washington Irving would call Knox "one of those providential characters which spring up in emergencies as if formed by and for the occasion."[3] A man of wide-ranging intellect and a pious spirit, Knox had written to a boyhood friend who had become a clergyman: "I have been but too much entangled with the little things of a little globe."[4] In 1806, Knox was just beginning to get his finances in order. His daughter, observing him dote on his grandchild, said, "Oh Father I believe you never will be *old.*"[5] A few days later a chicken bone lodged in his throat and killed him at age fifty-six.

———•—•———

From Yorktown, Lafayette traveled on to Virginia. He visited Monticello, where a failing Thomas Jefferson treated him to some excellent vintage wines. James Madison rode over from his home at Montpelier to join them for dinner. When the three friends parted, each was touched by how the others had aged.

Lafayette had come to know the one-time Virginia governor well during the 1780s, when Jefferson had served as envoy in France. Together they had drafted a document that became the *Declaration of the Rights of Man and of the Citizen*, one of the cornerstones of the French Revolution. Lafayette had played an influential role in the early years of that upheaval, leading the National Guard, the people's army. But as a moderate, he had, after 1790, increasingly come in conflict with the radicals. An enemy of both the monarchists of Europe and the Jacobins in France, he was captured by the Austrians in 1792 and spent five years in a dungeon. Washington, then president, tried to intervene, but it was Napoleon who had finally arranged Lafayette's release. True to his principles, Lafayette had opposed the Bonaparte dictatorship.

"His was not the influence of genius," the nineteenth-century philosopher John Stuart Mill would write of Lafayette, "nor even of talents; it was the influence of a heroic character."[6]

The visitors now got to see the Virginia countryside where Lafayette had ridden at the head of his most important command, where he had briefly recruited his friend, the infirm Daniel Morgan, to rejoin the effort. With the peace, Morgan, under the quiet influence of his wife, Abigail, had donned a coat of respectability and become a pillar of the Presbyterian church. He had owned a grist mill and a number of farms in Virginia, including the estate he called Saratoga. Increasing lameness and disability had forced him to curtail his activity and move in with his married daughter in Winchester. He met regularly with some local riflemen who had accompanied him on that awful, memorable march to Quebec. The veterans would sit and smoke and reminisce over the hardship and swagger of their youth.

A rough life of exposure, illness, and injury caught up with the Old Wagoner in the summer of 1802. Lying on his deathbed in extreme pain, he told his physician, "Doctor, if I could be the man I was when I was twenty-one years of age, I would be willing to be stripped stark naked on the top of Allegheny Mountain, to run for my life with a pack of dogs at my heels."[7]

The party of Frenchmen spent the winter of 1824–25 in Washington City waiting for the roads to dry out so that Lafayette could fulfill his vow to visit each of the twenty-four states. In the capital, he was able to watch firsthand the savage infighting of American democracy. Because no candidate received a majority of the electoral college votes in the 1824 election, the new president had to be chosen by the House of Representatives. In what came to be known as the "corrupt bargain," John Quincy Adams beat out popular-vote winner Andrew Jackson. Jackson supporters screamed, yet the Union held together.

When Lafayette addressed a packed joint session of Congress in December, the only person who declined to give him a standing ovation was the French ambassador. In his native country, democracy had proven less robust than in the New World. With the defeat of Napoleon in 1815 came the restoration of the Bourbon monarchy. The obese King Louis XVIII did not look kindly on Lafayette or his trip to America.

Everywhere he went, Lafayette shook hands with veterans, many of whom he recognized and called by name. They shared a special bond. They had lived at an accelerated pace, packing so many moments with scintillating memories.

With the arrival of spring, Lafayette's small party headed south in a creaking carriage. He visited Fayetteville, North Carolina, delighted by the first town in America named for him. More than six hundred towns, counties, rivers, and mountains would honor the marquis or commemorate his home at La Grange. The first half of the nineteenth century saw a wave of place names dedicated to Revolutionary War heroes: Knoxville, Montgomery, Waynesboro, Steubenville, Greene County, Mount Washington. A town in western Massachusetts was even named for General Charles Lee.

At Camden, South Carolina, Lafayette, a dedicated Freemason, laid the cornerstone of a monument to Johann de Kalb, the stout-hearted

German officer who had accompanied him to America and who had gone down fighting during the rout of Gates's army.

The south was full of ghosts. Here Nathanael Greene had fought his brilliant campaign against Cornwallis, the prelude to Yorktown. After the war, Greene had returned home a hero. Weighed down with debt, he had tried to make a living on land in Georgia given to him by a grateful citizenry. He had been "embarrassed and perplexed in my private affairs," even though, as he had written in his last letter to his friend Henry Knox, "I work hard and live poor."[8] He suffered a fatal stroke three years after the war ended.

Anthony Wayne, who owned a rice plantation just down the river from Greene, had sat by his comrade's deathbed. Like Greene, he had dabbled in farming. Later, he returned to Pennsylvania as a member of the convention that ratified the Constitution. But Wayne's heart yearned for action. During the 1790s, Washington put him in charge of a military force to deal with a threat from Indians in Ohio. Wayne managed a successful campaign and neutralized the menace with a brilliant victory at the 1794 Battle of Fallen Timbers. He returned to Philadelphia and enjoyed the adulation he had craved all his life. "General Wayne was there in glory," John Adams commented. "The man's feelings must be worth a guinea a minute."[9] Mad Anthony Wayne died of gout and fever two years later.

Lafayette carried the burden that falls on all aging survivors, the death of so many friends and comrades. Alexander Hamilton, his "brother," had been shot down at forty-eight in a duel with Vice President Aaron Burr. Baron von Steuben had retired to land granted him in upstate New York, where he died in 1794. Francis Marion passed away a year later at sixty-three. Light-Horse Harry Lee had served as governor of Virginia, but also spent time in a debtor's prison, before he succumbed, leaving his son Robert E. Lee to paint an even larger tableau on the canvas of history.

In New Orleans, Lafayette met with some of the tens of thousands of African American veterans who had fought for the Revolution. He was troubled by the failure of the founding generation to confront the great paradox of a people dedicated to freedom holding others in bondage. He took Jefferson's words in the Declaration of Independence to heart. He had urged Washington to "free your negroes." Washington could bring himself to offer them only a truncated liberty after his death.

The Nation's Guest likewise took a more enlightened view of Native Americans than most of the citizens of his adopted country. He went out of his way to greet warriors who had sided with the Americans. He met an Indian woman who showed him a letter of commendation that a young

Lafayette had long ago written to her father, a comrade in arms. The Iroquois warrior had saved the document even as he and his family had been repeatedly uprooted and driven westward. Lafayette was moved to tears as he listened to her story.

Up the Mississippi by steam boat, up the Ohio, through the territory that the daring of George Rogers Clark had helped add to the new country. The party visited the booming western cities of Louisville and Cincinnati. At Pittsburgh, Lafayette stopped to see Braddock's field, where a young George Washington had learned the grim reality of war. Then on to Buffalo, an obligatory visit to Niagara Falls, and down the newly opened Erie Canal, which cut straight through the Iroquois heartland that John Sullivan had invaded in 1779.

Everywhere crowds—citizens trekked for miles to glimpse a legend, a storybook hero emblematic of the nation's founding. Their enthusiasm set off an outpouring of patriotism that buoyed the nation for years afterward. Lafayette made it back to Boston in time to celebrate the fiftieth anniversary of Bunker Hill that June. To fulfill his vow, he traveled on to Maine, New Hampshire, and Vermont.

The leathery New Hampshire native John Stark, the man who had helped stop Howe at Bunker Hill and thwart Burgoyne at Bennington, had enjoyed one of the longest lives of any Revolutionary officer, having died in 1822 at the age of ninety-three. As an old man, Stark would offer the sentiment that summed up the attitude of many veterans and became his state's motto: *Live free or die.*

Lafayette sailed down Lake Champlain, where Benedict Arnold had delayed the British long enough to save the American cause in 1776. Arnold had made more money from the war than any American officer, receiving generous pay and annuities from the British. Money had always been important to the striving, self-made man. Happiness had eluded him. Arnold fled to Britain before the war ended, but the "Horse Jockey" could not elbow his way into polite English society. Always restless, he lived for a time among loyalist exiles in Canada. He returned to Britain and fitted out ships for the West Indies trade. In the early years of the Napoleonic Wars, he tried his hand as a privateer. Benedict Arnold died of natural causes in 1801. "Poor General Arnold," the London *Post* recorded, "has departed this world without notice."[10]

Traveling down the Hudson, the Frenchmen passed Saratoga, where Horatio Gates had achieved his supreme victory. That general's gratification in the successful conclusion of the war was marred by the 1783 death of Elizabeth, "my Companion of Nine and Twenty years," at age forty-seven. He later married a wealthy spinster who was happy to listen to the war stories of the Victor of Saratoga. Gates left his Virginia estate for the social life of New York. He was always willing to lend money to "the poor fellows who have been our faithful companions in the war."[11]

Back in New York City, the indefatigable Lafayette found himself troweling mortar for yet another cornerstone, this for the Apprentices' Library in Brooklyn Heights, not far from the spot where Washington had slipped his defeated army across the East River. A group of children was on hand and Lafayette helped lift each of them to a safe spot to watch the ceremony. One he took in his arms and kissed on the cheek was a six-year-old named Walt Whitman, who would one day write: "I understand the large hearts of heroes, / The courage of present times and all times."

Large hearts.

On a hot day in June, Lafayette eagerly showed his son George the scene near Brandywine Creek, outside Philadelphia, where he had first experienced the delicious, horrible intensity of battle. His memories still vivid, he pointed to the spot where a British musket ball had pierced his leg. Yes, here was where his blood had soaked American soil.

On September 6, 1825, Lafayette celebrated his sixty-eighth birthday at the White House. He was an old man—few of his comrades had lived so long. The Revolution, the war he had fought, had been an affair of youth. Nathanael Greene was thirty-two when it started, Anthony Wayne thirty, Henry Knox twenty-four, Alexander Hamilton twenty. They had fought with the intensity of youth. They had taken the risks that come easily to the young, had seen with the clarity of youth, had dreamed the dreams of youth. They had beheld the phantasmagoria of possibilities that is visible only to the young. They had persevered. They had won. They were, as Lafayette had long ago marveled, "a band of giants."

Now Lafayette, the youngest of them all, was about to take his leave. A dazzling sun shone on the crowd that gathered around the president's mansion and lined the route to a wharf along the Potomac. Under the portico of the house now occupied by John Quincy Adams, the president spoke the nation's farewell. "You alone survive," he told the aging warrior. He spoke of a "tie of love, stronger than death."[12] You alone—Lafayette was almost too moved to utter a word. He blessed his adopted country and embraced its president. Both men wept.

Twenty-four cannon fired salutes, signaling the time for departure. Lafayette climbed into a carriage. Children perched on shoulders to watch him pass. The crowd of spectators at the river front "remained in the most profound silence."

The deep significance of the moment, of the Revolution and those who had fought for it, of the men and women who had accomplished extraordinary things, of the debt owed, of the fleeting nature of history, of the mortality of heroes, all these ideas clenched throats, watered eyes, and touched with awe the crowd of watchers.

Lafayette climbed aboard a launch that would take him down the river to the *Brandywine*. The warship, commissioned in his honor, would carry him home, never to return.

He waved to the quiet crowd and was gone.

Notes

CHAPTER 1: KNOWLEDGE OF THE MILITARY ART, 1754

1. Ron Chernow, *Washington: A Life* (New York: Penguin Press, 2010), xix.
2. Edward G. Lengel, *General George Washington: A Military Life* (New York: Random House, 2005), 39.
3. Ibid., 32.
4. Fred Anderson, *Crucible of War: The Seven Years' War and the Fate of Empire in British North America, 1754–1766* (New York: A.A. Knopf, 2000), 59.
5. Chernow, *Washington*, 45.
6. Thomas E. Crocker, *Braddock's March: How the Man Sent to Seize a Continent Changed American History* (Yardley, PA: Westholme, 2009), 242.
7. Lengel, *General George Washington*, 51.
8. Crocker, *Braddock's March*, 100.
9. Ibid., 125.
10. Don Higginbotham, *Daniel Morgan, Revolutionary Rifleman* (Chapel Hill: University of North Carolina Press, 1961), 5.
11. Crocker, *Braddock's March*, 90.
12. Ibid., 134.
13. Arthur Quinn, *A New World: An Epic of Colonial America from the Founding of Jamestown to the Fall of Quebec* (Boston: Faber and Faber, 1994), 458.
14. Anderson, *Crucible of War*, 95.
15. Crocker, *Braddock's March*, 129.
16. Ibid., 121.
17. Winthrop Sargent, ed., *The History of an Expedition Against Fort du Quesne, in 1755* (Philadelphia: J.B. Lippincott, 1856), 201.
18. Crocker, *Braddock's March*, 226.
19. Ibid., 231.
20. Chernow, *Washington*, 61.
21. Crocker, *Braddock's March*, 232.
22. Benson Bobrick, *Angel in the Whirlwind: the Triumph of the American Revolution* (New York: Simon & Schuster, 1997), 125.
23. Lengel, *General George Washington*, 62.

CHAPTER 2: BLOWS MUST DECIDE, 1774

1. Russell Bourne, *Cradle of Violence: How Boston's Waterfront Mobs Ignited the American Revolution* (Hoboken, NJ: John Wiley & Sons, 2006), 90–91.
2. Richard Archer, *As If an Enemy's Country: The British Occupation of Boston and the Origins of Revolution* (New York: Oxford University Press, 2010), 25.
3. Bourne, *Cradle of Violence*, 116.
4. Ibid., 109.

5. Harlow G. Unger, *Lion of Liberty: Patrick Henry and the Call to a New Nation* (Cambridge, MA: Da Capo Press, 2010), 61.

6. Gerald M. Carbone, *Nathanael Greene: A Biography of the American Revolution* (New York: Palgrave Macmillan, 2008), 10.

7. Ibid., 11.

8. North Callahan, *Henry Knox, General Washington's Genera* (New York: Rinehart, 1958), 25.

9. Carbone, *Nathanael Greene*, 16–17.

10. Benson Bobrick, *Angel in the Whirlwind: The Triumph of the American Revolution* (New York: Simon & Schuster, 1997), 111.

11. John W. Shy, *A People Numerous and Armed: Reflections on the Military Struggle for American Independence* (Ann Arbor: University of Michigan Press, 1990), 104, 115.

12. Arthur Bernon Tourtellot, *Lexington and Concord: The Beginning of the War of the American Revolution* (New York: Norton, 1963), 133.

13. Theodore Draper, *A Struggle for Power: The American Revolution* (New York: Times Books, 1996), 502.

CHAPTER 3: THE PREDICAMENT WE ARE IN, 1775

1. Arthur Bernon Tourtellot, *Lexington and Concord: The Beginning of the War of the American Revolution* (New York: Norton, 1963), 234.

2. Willard Sterne Randall, *Benedict Arnold: Patriot and Traitor* (New York: Morrow, 1990), 83.

3. Willard Sterne Randall, *Ethan Allen: His Life and Times* (New York: W. W. Norton, 2011), 290.

4. Ibid., 37.

5. Ibid., 419.

6. Christopher Ward, *The War of the Revolution* (New York: Macmillan, 1952), 86.

7. John E. Ferling, *Almost a Miracle: The American Victory in the War of Independence* (New York: Oxford University Press, 2007), 56.

8. James L. Nelson, *With Fire & Sword: The Battle of Bunker Hill and the Beginning of the American Revolution* (New York: Thomas Dunne Books, 2011), 282.

9. Ron Chernow, *Washington: A Life* (New York: Penguin Press, 2010), 201.

10. Bruce Chadwick, *The First American Army: The Untold Story of George Washington and the Men Behind America's First Fight for Freedom* (Naperville, IL: Sourcebooks, 2005), 29.

11. Ferling, *Almost a Miracle*, 77.

12. John Richard Alden, *General Charles Lee, Traitor or Patriot?* (Baton Rouge: Louisiana State University Press,1951), 8.

13. Barnet Schecter, *The Battle for New York: The City at the Heart of the American Revolution* (New York: Walker, 2002), 69.

14. David G. McCullough, *1776* (New York: Simon & Schuster, 2005), 64.

15. Page Smith, *A New Age Now Begins: A People's History of the American Revolution* (New York: McGraw-Hill, 1976), 648.

16. McCullough, *1776*, 79.

CHAPTER 4: LEARNING TO BE SOLDIERS, 1775

1. Michael A. Bellesiles, ed., *Lethal Imagination: Violence and Brutality in American History* (New York: New York University Press, 1999), 94.

2. Charles Royster, *A Revolutionary People at War: The Continental Army and American Character, 1775–1783* (Chapel Hill: University of North Carolina Press, 1979), 34.

3. Benson Bobrick, *Angel in the Whirlwind: The Triumph of the American Revolution* (New York: Simon & Schuster, 1997), 169.

4. Willard Sterne Randall, *Benedict Arnold: Patriot and Traitor* (New York: Morrow, 1990), 155.

5. North Callahan, *Daniel Morgan, Ranger of the Revolution* (New York: Holt, Rinehart and Winston, 1961), 65.
6. Randall, *Benedict Arnold*, 167.
7. Justin Harvey Smith, *Our Struggle for the Fourteenth Colony: Canada, and the American Revolution* (New York: G.P. Putnam's Sons, 1907), 568.
8. Randall, *Benedict Arnold*, 171.
9. Thomas A. Desjardin, *Through a Howling Wilderness: Benedict Arnold's March to Quebec, 1775* (New York: St. Martin's Press, 2006), 62.
10. Isaac Senter, *The Journal of Isaac Senter* (New York: New York Times Books, 1969), 27.
11. Randall, *Benedict Arnold*, 182.
12. Kenneth Lewis Roberts, *March to Quebec: Journals of the Members of Arnold's Expedition* (New York: Doubleday 1938), 320.
13. Hal T. Shelton, *General Richard Montgomery and the American Revolution: From Redcoat to Rebel* (New York: New York University Press, 1994), 67, 78.
14. Bobrick, *Angel in the Whirlwind*, 168.
15. Randall, *Benedict Arnold*, 208.
16. Desjardin, *Through a Howling Wilderness*, 166.
17. Michael P. Gabriel, *Major General Richard Montgomery: The Making of an American Hero* (Madison, NJ: Fairleigh Dickinson University Press, 2002), 134.
18. Page Smith, *A New Age Now Begins: A People's History of the American Revolution* (New York: McGraw-Hill, 1976), 615.
19. George F. Scheer and Hugh F. Rankin, *Rebels and Redcoats* (Cleveland: World Pub., 1957), 125–26.
20. Roberts, *March to Quebec*, 538.
21. Callahan, *Daniel Morgan*, 109.
22. Shelton, *General Richard Montgomery and the American Revolution*, 158.

CHAPTER 5: PRECIOUS CONVOY, 1776

1. Mark Puls, *Henry Knox: Visionary General of the American Revolution* (New York: Palgrave Macmillan, 2008), 35.
2. Ibid., 40.
3. Ibid., 38.
4. David G. McCullough, *1776* (New York: Simon & Schuster, 2005), 83.
5. Ibid., 83.
6. Puls, *Henry Knox*, 41.
7. John P. Becker, *The Sexagenary: Or, Reminiscences of the American Revolution* (Albany, NY: J. Munsell, 1866), 34.
8. McCullough, *1776*, 86.
9. Ibid., 87.
10. Ibid., 90.
11. Richard Wheeler, *Voices of 1776* (New York, Crowell, 1972), 101–102.
12. Page Smith, *A New Age Now Begins: A People's History of the American Revolution* (New York: McGraw-Hill, 1976), 650.
13. Ron Chernow, *Washington: A Life* (New York: Penguin Press, 2010), 226.
14. McCullough, *1776*, 91.
15. Chernow, *Washington*, 226.
16. Henry Steele Commager, ed., *The Spirit of 'Seventy-Six* (New York: Harper & Row, 1967), 180.
17. George F. Scheer and Hugh F. Rankin, *Rebels and Redcoats* (Cleveland: World Pub., 1957), 107.
18. Wheeler, *Voices of 1776*, 103.
19. Richard M. Ketchum, *Decisive Day: The Battle for Bunker Hill* (Garden City, NY: Doubleday, 1999), 219.
20. Christopher Ward, *The War of the Revolution* (New York: Macmillan, 1952), 132.
21. McCullough, *1776*, 110.

22. Edward G. Lengel, *General George Washington: A Military Life* (New York: Random House, 2005), 133.

CHAPTER 6: SUDDEN AND VIOLENT, 1776

1. David G. McCullough, *1776* (New York: Simon & Schuster, 2005), 118.
2. Edward G. Lengel, *General George Washington: A Military Life* (New York: Random House, 2005), 129.
3. David Hackett Fischer, *Washington's Crossing* (New York: Oxford University Press, 2004), 148.
4. Dominick A. Mazzagetti, *Charles Lee: Self Before Country* (New Brunswick, NJ: Rutgers University Press, 2013), 108.
5. Paul David Nelson, *William Alexander, Lord Stirling* (Tuscaloosa: University of Alabama Press, 1987), 2.
6. Barnet Schecter, *The Battle for New York: The City at the Heart of the American Revolution* (New York: Walker, 2002), 84.
7. Fischer, *Washington's Crossing*, 82.
8. Richard M. Ketchum, *Decisive Day: The Battle for Bunker Hill* (Garden City, NY: Doubleday, 1999) 70.
9. McCullough, *1776*, 123.
10. Terry Golway, *Washington's General: Nathanael Greene and the Triumph of the American Revolution* (New York: H. Holt, 2005), 78.
11. Mark Puls, *Henry Knox: Visionary General of the American Revolution* (New York: Palgrave Macmillan, 2008), 52.
12. McCullough, *1776*, 136.
13. Ibid., 136.
14. Schecter, *The Battle for New York*, 106.
15. Puls, *Henry Knox*, 56.
16. Fischer, *Washington's Crossing*, 46.
17. William Patterson Cumming, *The Fate of a Nation: The American Revolution through Contemporary Eyes* (London: Phaidon, 1975), 102.
18. Ibid., 104.
19. George Athan Billias, ed., *George Washington's Generals and Opponents: Their Exploits and Leadership* (New York: Da Capo Press, 1964–1969), 141–42.
20. McCullough, *1776*, 159.
21. Billias, *George Washington's Generals and Opponents*, 142.
22. Schecter, *The Battle for New York*, 131.
23. Nelson, *William Alexander*, 85.
24. Schecter, *The Battle for New York*, 146.
25. Fischer, *Washington's Crossing*, 97.
26. George F. Scheer and Hugh F. Rankin, eds., *Rebels and Redcoats* (Cleveland: World Pub., 1957), 167.
27. Schecter, *The Battle for New York*, 150.
28. Nelson, *William Alexander*, 88.
29. Gerald M. Carbone, *Nathanael Greene: A Biography of the American Revolution* (New York: Palgrave Macmillan, 2008), 37.
30. McCullough, *1776*, 180.
31. Cumming, *The Fate of a Nation*, 106.
32. McCullough, *1776*, 179.
33. Ron Chernow, *Washington: A Life* (New York: Penguin Press, 2010), 248.

CHAPTER 7: VALCOUR ISLAND, 1776

1. Benson Bobrick, *Angel in the Whirlwind: The Triumph of the American Revolution* (New York: Simon & Schuster, 1997), 176.

2. Ibid., 176.
3. George Athan Billias, ed., *George Washington's Generals and Opponents: Their Exploits and Leadership* (New York: Da Capo Press, 1964–1969), 171.
4. Frederic Franklyn Van de Water, *Lake Champlain and Lake George* (New York: Bobbs-Merrill, 1946), 180.
5. Willard Sterne Randall, *Benedict Arnold: Patriot and Traitor* (New York: Morrow, 1990), 260.
6. Ibid., 242.
7. Ibid., 262.
8. Eliot A. Cohen, *Conquered into Liberty: Two Centuries of Battles along the Great Warpath that Made the American Way of War* (New York: Free Press, 2011), 185.
9. Richard Wheeler, *Voices of 1776* (New York: Crowell, 1972), 150.
10. James L. Nelson, *Benedict Arnold's Navy: The Ragtag Fleet that Lost the Battle of Lake Champlain but Won the American Revolution* (Camden, ME: International Marine, 2006), 318.
11. Thomas J. Fleming, *1776, Year of Illusions* (New York: Norton, 1975), 397.
12. Randall, *Benedict Arnold*, 317.

CHAPTER 8: AN INDECISIVE MIND, 1776

1. Henry Steele Commager, ed., *The Spirit of 'Seventy-Six* (New York: Harper & Row, 1967), 460.
2. David G. McCullough, *1776* (New York: Simon & Schuster, 2005), 207.
3. Barnet Schecter, *The Battle for New York: The City at the Heart of the American Revolution* (New York: Walker, 2002), 183.
4. McCullough, *1776*, 211.
5. Ibid., 212.
6. Ron Chernow, *Washington: A Life* (New York: Penguin Press, 2010), 254.
7. David Hackett Fischer, *Washington's Crossing* (New York: Oxford University Press, 2004), 95.
8. McCullough, *1776*, 215.
9. Mark Puls, *Henry Knox: Visionary General of the American Revolution* (New York: Palgrave Macmillan, 2008), 62.
10. John E. Ferling, *Almost a Miracle: The American Victory in the War of Independence* (New York: Oxford University Press, 2007), 142.
11. Chernow, *Washington*, 258.
12. Charles Bracelen Flood, *Rise, and Fight Again: Perilous Times along the Road to Independence* (New York: Dodd, Mead, 1976), 102.
13. Ibid., 103.
14. Ibid., 118.
15. Ibid., 123.
16. Schecter, *The Battle for New York*, 255.
17. Fischer, *Washington's Crossing*, 114.
18. Schecter, *The Battle for New York*, 256.
19. McCullough, *1776*, 247.
20. Ibid., 244.
21. Ibid., 248.
22. John W. Shy, *A People Numerous and Armed: Reflections on the Military Struggle for American Independence* (Ann Arbor: University of Michigan Press, 1990), 150.
23. Ibid., 153.
24. McCullough, *1776*, 265.
25. Schecter, *The Battle for New York*, 265.
26. Terry Golway, *Washington's General: Nathanael Greene and the Triumph of the American Revolution* (New York: H. Holt, 2005), 106.
27. Commager, *The Spirit of 'Seventy-Six*, 5.

CHAPTER 9: HE THAT STANDS BY IT NOW, 1776

1. David Hackett Fischer, *Washington's Crossing* (New York: Oxford University Press, 2004), 159.
2. Samuel Stelle Smith, *The Battle of Trenton* (Monmouth Beach, NJ: Philip Freneau Press,1965), 15.
3. Ron Chernow, *Washington: A Life* (New York: Penguin Press, 2010), 270.
4. Fischer, *Washington's Crossing*, 143.
5. Ibid., 143.
6. Ibid., 218.
7. Mark Puls, *Henry Knox: Visionary General of the American Revolution* (New York: Palgrave Macmillan, 2008), 74.
8. Henry Steele Commager, ed., *The Spirit of 'Seventy-Six* (New York: Harper & Row, 1967), 513.
9. Fischer, *Washington's Crossing*, 220.
10. Ibid., 241.
11. Commager, *The Spirit of 'Seventy-Six*, 513.
12. North Callahan, *Henry Knox, General Washington's General* (New York: Rinehart, 1958), 91.
13. Puls, *Henry Knox*, 80.
14. Fischer, *Washington's Crossing*, 309.
15. Richard Wheeler, *Voices of 1776* (New York, Crowell, 1972), 181.
16. Chernow, *Washington*, 281.
17. Fischer, *Washington's Crossing*, 332.
18. Ibid., 344.
19. Ibid., 353.

CHAPTER 10: A CONTINUAL CLAP OF THUNDER, 1777

1. Benson Bobrick, *Angel in the Whirlwind: The Triumph of the American Revolution* (New York: Simon & Schuster, 1997), 253.
2. John E. Ferling, *Almost a Miracle: The American Victory in the War of Independence* (New York: Oxford University Press, 2007), 223.
3. Andrew Jackson O'Shaughnessy, *The Men Who Lost America: British Leadership, the American Revolution, and the Fate of the Empire* (New Haven, CT: Yale University Press, 2013), 124.
4. David Wilson, *The Life of Jane McCrea, with an Account of Burgoyne's Expedition in 1777* (New York: Baker, Goodwin, 1853), 79.
5. Henry Steele Commager, ed., *The Spirit of 'Seventy-Six* (New York: Harper & Row, 1967), 560.
6. Richard M. Ketchum, *Saratoga: Turning Point of America's Revolutionary War* (New York: H. Holt, 1997), 276.
7. Matthew H. Spring, *With Zeal and with Bayonets Only: The British Army on Campaign in North America, 1775–1783* (Norman: University of Oklahoma Press, 2008), 18.
8. Ben Z. Rose, *John Stark: Maverick General* (Waverley, MA: TreeLine Press, 2007), 18.
9. Ibid., 100.
10. Gerald Howson, *Burgoyne of Saratoga: A Biography* (New York: Times Books, 1978), 162.
11. Ketchum, *Saratoga*, 288.
12. Ibid., 289.
13. Ibid., 248.
14. Rose, *John Stark*, 82.
15. Ibid., 120.
16. Michael P. Gabriel, *The Battle of Bennington: Soldiers & Civilians* (Charleston, SC: History Press, 2012), 73.

17. Spring, *With Zeal and with Bayonets Only*, 332.
18. Ketchum, *Saratoga*, 307.
19. Ibid., 312.
20. Commager, *The Spirit of 'Seventy-Six*, 573.
21. Gabriel, *The Battle of Bennington*, 102.
22. Ketchum, *Saratoga*, 329.
23. Ibid., 330.
24. Ibid., 324.

CHAPTER 11: FIGHT AS WELL AS BRAG, 1777

1. Paul David Nelson, *Anthony Wayne, Soldier of the Early Republic* (Bloomington: Indiana University Press, 1985), 7.
 2. George Athan Billias, ed., *George Washington's Generals and Opponents: Their Exploits and Leadership* (New York: Da Capo Press, 1964–1969), 287.
 3. Nelson, *Anthony Wayne*, 34.
 4. Nelson, *Anthony Wayne*, 2–3.
 5. John E. Ferling, *Almost a Miracle: The American Victory in the War of Independence* (New York: Oxford University Press, 2007), 249.
 6. Ibid., 249–50.
 7. Terry Golway, *Washington's General: Nathanael Greene and the Triumph of the American Revolution* (New York: H. Holt, 2005), 142.
 8. Christopher Ward, *The War of the Revolution* (New York: Macmillan, 1952), 360.
 9. Ferling, *Almost a Miracle*, 251.
10. Ibid., 252.
11. Nelson, *Anthony Wayne*, 59.
12. Ibid., 60.
13. Ron Chernow, *Washington: A Life* (New York: Penguin Press, 2010), 310.
14. Page Smith, *A New Age Now Begins: A People's History of the American Revolution* (New York: McGraw-Hill, 1976), 970.
15. Chernow, *Washington*, 311.

CHAPTER 12: SOMETHING MORE AT STAKE, 1777

1. Andrew Jackson O'Shaughnessy, *The Men Who Lost America: British Leadership, the American Revolution, and the Fate of the Empire* (New Haven: Yale University Press, 2013), 154.
 2. Willard Sterne Randall, *Benedict Arnold: Patriot and Traitor* (New York: Morrow, 1990), 351.
 3. Paul David Nelson, *General Horatio Gates: A Biography* (Baton Rouge: Louisiana State University Press, 1976), 108.
 4. Don Higginbotham, *Daniel Morgan, Revolutionary Rifleman* (Chapel Hill: University of North Carolina Press, 1961), 61.
 5. Max M. Mintz, *The Generals of Saratoga: John Burgoyne & Horatio Gates* (New Haven: Yale University Press, 1990), 18.
 6. Randall, *Benedict Arnold*, 350.
 7. Richard M. Ketchum, *Saratoga: Turning Point of America's Revolutionary War* (New York: H. Holt, 1997), 348.
 8. Ibid., 363.
 9. Christopher Ward, *The War of the Revolution* (New York: Macmillan, 1952), 510.
10. Christopher Duffy, *The Military Experience in the Age of Reason* (London: Routledge & Kegan Paul, 1987), 163.
11. Ketchum, *Saratoga*, 363.
12. Christopher Hibbert, *Redcoats & Rebels: The American Revolution through British Eyes* (New York: Norton, 1990), 185.

13. Ward, *The War of the Revolution*, 511.
14. Ketchum, *Saratoga*, 368.
15. Ibid., 369.
16. Randall, *Benedict Arnold*, 359.
17. Nelson, *General Horatio Gates*, 134.
18. Ibid., 126.
19. Randall, *Benedict Arnold*, 362.
20. Ibid., 360.
21. Nelson, *General Horatio Gates*, 132.
22. Ketchum, *Saratoga*, 394.
23. Ibid., 398.
24. Henry Steele Commager, ed., *The Spirit of 'Seventy-Six* (New York: Harper & Row, 1967), 593.
25. Ketchum, *Saratoga*, 394.
26. Ibid., 399.
27. Ibid., 400.
28. Mintz, *The Generals of Saratoga*, 194.
29. Harlow G. Unger, *Lion of Liberty: Patrick Henry and the Call to a New Nation* (Cambridge, MA: Da Capo Press, 2010), 132.
30. Higginbotham, *Daniel Morgan*, 76.
31. Ketchum, *Saratoga*, 441.

CHAPTER 13: THE DISCIPLINE OF THE LEGGS, 1778

1. Christopher Ward, *The War of the Revolution* (New York: Macmillan, 1952), 543.
2. Wayne K. Bodle, *The Valley Forge Winter: Civilians and Soldiers in War* (University Park: Pennsylvania State University Press, 2002), 128.
3. Edward G. Lengel, *General George Washington: A Military Life* (New York: Random House, 2005), 267.
4. Bodle, *The Valley Forge Winter*, 112–13.
5. Benson Bobrick, *Angel in the Whirlwind: The Triumph of the American Revolution* (New York: Simon & Schuster, 1997), 289.
6. Terry Golway, *Washington's General: Nathanael Greene and the Triumph of the American Revolution* (New York: H. Holt, 2005), 162.
7. Ibid., 165.
8. Ibid., 198.
9. Ibid., 159.
10. Ibid., 158.
11. David A. Clary, *Adopted Son: Washington, Lafayette, and the Friendship That Saved the Revolution* (New York: Bantam Books, 2007), 117.
12. Paul David Nelson, *Anthony Wayne, Soldier of the Early Republic* (Bloomington: Indiana University Press, 1985), 66.
13. John E. Ferling, *Almost a Miracle: The American Victory in the War of Independence* (New York: Oxford University Press, 2007), 283.
14. Paul Douglas Lockhart, *The Drillmaster of Valley Forge: The Baron De Steuben and the Making of the American Army* (Washington, DC: Smithsonian Books, 2008), 42.
15. Bruce Chadwick, *The First American Army: The Untold Story of George Washington and the Men Behind America's First Fight for Freedom* (Naperville, IL: Sourcebooks, 2005), 29.
16. Lockhart, *The Drillmaster of Valley Forge*, 133.
17. Ibid., 89.
18. Ibid., 88.
19. Ibid., 109.
20. Bodle, *The Valley Forge Winter*, 201.
21. Ferling, *Almost a Miracle*, 293.
22. Ron Chernow, *Washington: A Life* (New York: Penguin Press, 2010), 336.

23. Ibid., 338.
24. Lockhart, *The Drillmaster of Valley Forge*, 132.
25. Harlow G. Unger, *Lafayette* (New York: John Wiley & Sons, 2002), 77.
26. Lockhart, *The Drillmaster of Valley Forge*, 162.
27. Lengel, *General George Washington*, 300.
28. Lockhart, *The Drillmaster of Valley Forge*, 125.
29. Joseph Plumb Martin, *Memoir of a Revolutionary Soldier: The Narrative of Joseph Plumb Martin* (Mineola, NY: Dover, 2006), 72.
30. Mark Puls, *Henry Knox: Visionary General of the American Revolution* (New York: Palgrave Macmillan, 2008), 130.
31. Nelson, *Anthony Wayne*, 82.
32. Ward, *The War of the Revolution*, 549.

CHAPTER 14: THE BOLDEST CONDUCT, 1779

1. William R. Nester, *George Rogers Clark: "I Glory in War"* (Norman: University of Oklahoma Press, 2012), 75.
2. August William Derleth, *Vincennes: Portal to the West* (Englewood Cliffs, NJ: Prentice-Hall, 1968), 56.
3. Nester, *George Rogers Clark*, 120.
4. Ibid., 138.
5. Derleth, *Vincennes*, 57.
6. Ibid., 68.
7. Nester, *George Rogers Clark*, 3.
8. Ibid., 313.
9. Barbara Graymont, *The Iroquois in the American Revolution* (Syracuse, NY: Syracuse University Press, 1972), 190.
10. John E. Ferling, *Almost a Miracle: The American Victory in the War of Independence* (New York: Oxford University Press, 2007), 353.
11. Ibid., 346.
12. Charles Park Whittemore, *A General of the Revolution, John Sullivan of New Hampshire* (New York: Columbia University Press, 1961), 110.
13. Ibid., 115.
14. Ibid., 123.
15. Ibid., 125.
16. Ibid., 127.
17. Ferling, *Almost a Miracle*, 357.
18. Glenn Tucker, *Mad Anthony Wayne and the New Nation: The Story of Washington's Front-Line General* (Harrisburg, PA: Stackpole Books, 1973), 162.
19. Graymont, *The Iroquois in the American Revolution*, 213.
20. Ibid., 218.
21. Whittemore, *A General of the Revolution*, 147.
22. Joseph R. Fischer, *A Well-Executed Failure: The Sullivan Campaign Against the Iroquois, July-September 1779* (Columbia: University of South Carolina Press, 1997), 192.
23. Whittemore, *A General of the Revolution*, 148.
24. Bruce Chadwick, *George Washington's War: The Forging of a Revolutionary Leader and the American Presidency* (Naperville, IL: Sourcebooks, 2005), 328.

CHAPTER 15: FATE OF BATTLE, 1780

1. George Athan Billias, ed., *George Washington's Generals and Opponents: Their Exploits and Leadership* (New York: Da Capo Press, 1964–1969), 196, 200, 206.
2. Ibid., 206.
3. David B. Mattern, *Benjamin Lincoln and the American Revolution* (Columbia: University of South Carolina Press, 1995), 13.
4. Billias, *George Washington's Generals and Opponents*, 198.

5. Mattern, *Benjamin Lincoln and the American Revolution*, 95.
6. John E. Ferling, *Almost a Miracle: The American Victory in the War of Independence* (New York: Oxford University Press, 2007), 426.
7. Billias, *George Washington's Generals and Opponents*, 203.
8. Ferling, *Almost a Miracle*, 427.
9. Ibid., 436.
10. John Buchanan, *The Road to Guilford Courthouse: The American Revolution in the Carolinas* (New York: Wiley, 1997), 85.
11. Christopher Ward, *The War of the Revolution* (New York: Macmillan, 1952), 717.
12. George F. Scheer and Hugh F. Rankin, eds., *Rebels and Redcoats* (Cleveland: World Pub., 1957), 404.
13. Charles Bracelen Flood, *Rise, and Fight Again: Perilous Times along the Road to Independence* (New York: Dodd, Mead, 1976), 288.
14. Ibid., 308.
15. Ibid., 315.
16. Billias, *George Washington's Generals and Opponents*, 102.
17. Ward, *The War of the Revolution*, 728.
18. Ferling, *Almost a Miracle*, 441.
19. Dan L. Morrill, *Southern Campaigns of the American Revolution* (Baltimore: Nautical & Aviation Pub., 1993), 93.
20. Flood, *Rise, and Fight Again*, 328.
21. Ibid., 330.
22. Ibid., 337.
23. Ron Chernow, *Washington: A Life* (New York: Penguin Press, 2010), 375.
24. Paul David Nelson, *General Horatio Gates: A Biography* (Baton Rouge: Louisiana State University Press, 1976), 253.
25. Ibid., 239.
26. Flood, *Rise, and Fight Again*, 345.
27. Chernow, *Washington*, 352–53.
28. Ibid., 368–70.
29. Ferling, *Almost a Miracle*, 444–45.
30. Chernow, *Washington*, 378.
31. Ibid., 382.
32. Ibid., 382.
33. David A. Clary, *Adopted Son: Washington, Lafayette, and the Friendship That Saved the Revolution* (New York: Bantam Books, 2007), 280.
34. Willard Sterne Randall, *Benedict Arnold: Patriot and Traitor* (New York: Morrow, 1990), 457.
35. Ibid., 445.
36. Ibid., 572.
37. Carl Van Doren, *Mutiny in January: The Story of a Crisis in the Continental Army Now for the First Time Fully Told from Many Hitherto Unknown or Neglected Sources, Both American and British* (New York: Viking Press, 1943), 13.
38. Chernow, *Washington*, 370.
39. Page Smith, *A New Age Now Begins: A People's History of the American Revolution* (New York: McGraw-Hill, 1976), 1603.
40. Chernow, *Washington*, 389.
41. Van Doren, *Mutiny in January*, 216.
42. Mark Puls, *Henry Knox: Visionary General of the American Revolution* (New York: Palgrave Macmillan, 2008), 159.
43. Howard H. Peckham, *The War for Independence: A Military History* (Chicago: University of Chicago Press, 1958), 158.

CHAPTER 16: DOWNRIGHT FIGHTING, 1780

1. Henry Lee, *Memoirs of the War in the Southern Department of the United States* (New York: University Publishing, 1870), 233.

2. John E. Ferling, *Almost a Miracle: The American Victory in the War of Independence* (New York: Oxford University Press, 2007), 458.
3. Robert Middlekauff, *The Glorious Cause: The American Revolution, 1763–1789* (New York: Oxford University Press, 1982), 461.
4. Dan L. Morrill, *Southern Campaigns of the American Revolution* (Baltimore: Nautical & Aviation Pub., 1993), 105.
5. Hank Messick, *King's Mountain: The Epic of the Blue Ridge "Mountain Men" in the American Revolution* (Boston: Little, Brown, 1976), 112.
6. Page Smith, *A New Age Now Begins: A People's History of the American Revolution* (New York: McGraw-Hill, 1976), 1427.
7. Ferling, *Almost a Miracle*, 462.
8. Messick, *King's Mountain*, 134.
9. Ibid., 136.
10. Ibid., 136, 140.
11. Morrill, *Southern Campaigns of the American Revolution*, 110.
12. Messick, *King's Mountain*, 167.
13. Morrill, *Southern Campaigns of the American Revolution*, 111.
14. Messick, *King's Mountain*, 167.
15. Ron Chernow, *Washington: A Life* (New York: Penguin Press, 2010), 376.
16. Don Higginbotham, *Daniel Morgan, Revolutionary Rifleman* (Chapel Hill: University of North Carolina Press, 1961), 120.
17. Morrill, *Southern Campaigns of the American Revolution*, 124.
18. Richard M. Ketchum, *Victory at Yorktown: The Campaign that Won the Revolution* (New York: Henry Holt, 2004), 112–13.
19. Higginbotham, *Daniel Morgan*,132.
20. Lawrence Edward Babits, *A Devil of a Whipping: The Battle of Cowpens* (Chapel Hill: University of North Carolina Press, 1998), 55.
21. Ibid., 58.
22. Ibid., 80.
23. Ibid., 82.
24. Ibid., 89.
25. Higginbotham, *Daniel Morgan*,137.
26. Babits, *A Devil of a Whipping*, 102.
27. Ibid., 100.
28. Ibid., 123.
29. Higginbotham, *Daniel Morgan*,141.
30. Ibid., 132.
31. Babits, *A Devil of a Whipping*, 10.
32. Higginbotham, *Daniel Morgan*,143.
33. Ibid., 153, 155.

CHAPTER 17: WAR IS AN INTRICATE BUSINESS, 1781

1. Terry Golway, *Washington's General: Nathanael Greene and the Triumph of the American Revolution* (New York: H. Holt, 2005), 127.
2. Ibid., 181.
3. Ibid., 227.
4. Nathanael Greene, *The Papers of General Nathanael Greene* (Chapel Hill: University of North Carolina Press, 1976), 3:62.
5. Golway, *Washington's General*, 232, 239.
6. Henry Lee, *Memoirs of the War in the Southern Department of the United States* (New York: University Publishing, 1870), 39.
7. Golway, *Washington's General*, 96.
8. Ibid., 239.
9. Lawrence Edward Babits, *Long, Obstinate, and Bloody: The Battle of Guilford Courthouse* (Chapel Hill: University of North Carolina Press, 2009), 16.
10. Golway, *Washington's General*, 252, 254.

11. Ibid., 244.
12. Charles Royster, *Light-Horse Harry Lee and the Legacy of the American Revolution* (New York: Knopf, 1981), 14.
13. Ibid., 42.
14. Ibid., 25.
15. Babits, *Long, Obstinate, and Bloody*, 39.
16. Dan L. Morrill, *Southern Campaigns of the American Revolution* (Baltimore: Nautical & Aviation Pub., 1993), 161.
17. John E. Ferling, *Almost a Miracle: The American Victory in the War of Independence* (New York: Oxford University Press, 2007), 496.
18. Babits, *Long, Obstinate, and Bloody*, 77.
19. Matthew H. Spring, *With Zeal and with Bayonets Only: The British Army on Campaign in North America, 1775–1783* (Norman: University of Oklahoma Press, 2008), 226.
20. Christopher Ward, *The War of the Revolution* (New York: Macmillan, 1952), 788.
21. Ferling, *Almost a Miracle*, 497.
22. Ibid., 499.
23. Greene, *The Papers of General Nathanael Greene*, 7:446.
24. Greene, *The Papers of General Nathanael Greene*, 8:25.
25. Golway, *Washington's General*, 261.
26. Ferling, *Almost a Miracle*, 517.
27. Golway, *Washington's General*, 269.
28. Ferling, *Almost a Miracle*, 519.
29. Golway, *Washington's General*, 261.
30. Ibid., 264.
31. Greene, *The Papers of General Nathanael Greene*, 8:443.
32. Ferling, *Almost a Miracle*, 518.
33. Golway, *Washington's General*, 286.
34. Ferling, *Almost a Miracle*, 519.
35. Golway, *Washington's General*, 284.

CHAPTER 18: AMERICA IS OURS, 1781

1. Page Smith, *A New Age Now Begins: A People's History of the American Revolution* (New York: McGraw-Hill, 1976), 1626.
2. John E. Ferling, *Almost a Miracle: The American Victory in the War of Independence* (New York: Oxford University Press, 2007), 512.
3. Smith, *A New Age Now Begins*, 1654.
4. George Athan Billias, ed., *George Washington's Generals and Opponents: Their Exploits and Leadership* (New York: Da Capo Press, 1964–1969), 229.
5. Ferling, *Almost a Miracle*, 511.
6. Billias, *George Washington's Generals and Opponents*, 219.
7. Ibid., 219.
8. Ibid., 230.
9. Paul David Nelson, *Anthony Wayne, Soldier of the Early Republic* (Bloomington: Indiana University Press, 1985), 130.
10. Smith, *A New Age Now Begins*, 1633.
11. James Graham, *The Life of General Daniel Morgan, of the Virginia Line of the Army of the United States, with Portions of His Correspondence; Comp. from Authentic Sources* (New York: Derby & Jackson, 1856), 395.
12. Smith, *A New Age Now Begins*, 1635.
13. Ferling, *Almost a Miracle*, 515.
14. Billias, *George Washington's Generals and Opponents*, 282.
15. Smith, *A New Age Now Begins*, 1657.
16. Christopher Duffy, *The Military Experience in the Age of Reason* (London: Routledge & Kegan Paul, 1987), 209.
17. Smith, *A New Age Now Begins*, 1658.

18. Ibid., 1662.
19. Ibid., 1666.
20. Richard M. Ketchum, *Victory at Yorktown: The Campaign that Won the Revolution* (New York: Henry Holt, 2004), 168.
21. Ibid., 186.
22. Smith, *A New Age Now Begins*, 1673.
23. Ibid., 1687.
24. Ketchum, *Victory at Yorktown*, 209.
25. Ferling, *Almost a Miracle*, 531.
26. William H. Hallahan, *The Day the Revolution Ended: 19 October 1781* (Hoboken, NJ: Wiley, 2004), 180.
27. Smith, *A New Age Now Begins*, 1701.
28. North Callahan, *Henry Knox, General Washington's General* (New York: Rinehart, 1958), 189.
29. Ibid., 187–88.
30. Ibid., 185.
31. Smith, *A New Age Now Begins*, 1704.
32. James Thacher, *Military Journal, During the American Revolutionary War, from 1775 to 1783* (Hartford, CT: Silas Andrus & Son, 1854), 343.
33. Smith, *A New Age Now Begins*, 1705.
34. Ketchum, *Victory at Yorktown*, 242.
35. Ibid., 252.
36. Ferling, *Almost a Miracle*, 538.
37. Ketchum, *Victory at Yorktown*, 254.
38. Edward G. Lengel, *General George Washington: A Military Life* (New York: Random House, 2005), 343.
39. Ferling, *Almost a Miracle*, 539.
40. Callahan, *Henry Knox*, 190.
41. Ibid., 189.

CHAPTER 19: *OUR* TROOPS, 1782

1. John E. Ferling, *Almost a Miracle: The American Victory in the War of Independence* (New York: Oxford University Press, 2007), 548.
2. Paul David Nelson, *Anthony Wayne, Soldier of the Early Republic* (Bloomington: Indiana University Press, 1985), 167.
3. Jerome A. Greene, *The Guns of Independence: The Siege of Yorktown, 1781* (New York: Savas Beatie, 2005), 305–6.
4. Ferling, *Almost a Miracle*, 541.
5. Richard M. Ketchum, *Victory at Yorktown: The Campaign that Won the Revolution* (New York: Henry Holt, 2004), 274.
6. Ferling, *Almost a Miracle*, 547.
7. Charles Royster, *A Revolutionary People at War: The Continental Army and American Character, 1775–1783* (Chapel Hill: University of North Carolina Press, 1979), 351, 358.
8. Ibid., 350.
9. Ibid., 343.
10. Joseph Plumb Martin, *Memoir of a Revolutionary Soldier: The Narrative of Joseph Plumb Martin* (Mineola, NY: Dover, 2006), 105.
11. Royster, *A Revolutionary People at War*, 332.
12. Edward G. Lengel, *General George Washington: A Military Life* (New York: Random House, 2005), 349.
13. George F. Scheer and Hugh F. Rankin, eds., *Rebels and Redcoats* (Cleveland: World Pub., 1957), 502.
14. Martin, *Memoir of a Revolutionary Soldier*, 159.
15. Scheer, *Rebels and Redcoats*, 502.

16. Martin, *Memoir of a Revolutionary Soldier,* 160.
17. Mark Puls, *Henry Knox: Visionary General of the American Revolution* (New York: Palgrave Macmillan, 2008), 237.
18. Ketchum, *Victory at Yorktown,* 288.
19. Scheer, *Rebels and Redcoats,* 504.

CHAPTER 20: THE LARGE HEARTS OF HEROES, 1824

1. Stanley J. Idzerda, *Lafayette, Hero of Two Worlds: The Art and Pageantry of His Farewell Tour of America, 1824–1825* (Flushing, NY: Queens Museum, 1989), 3.
2. David A. Clary, *Adopted Son: Washington, Lafayette, and the Friendship That Saved the Revolution* (New York: Bantam Books, 2007), 444.
3. George Athan Billias, ed., *George Washington's Generals and Opponents: Their Exploits and Leadership* (New York: Da Capo Press, 1964–1969), 239.
4. Mark Puls, *Henry Knox: Visionary General of the American Revolution* (New York: Palgrave Macmillan, 2008), 204.
5. Nancy Rubin Stuart, *Defiant Brides: The Untold Story of Two Revolutionary-era Women and the Radical Men They Married* (Boston: Beacon Press, 2013), 197.
6. Clary, *Adopted Son,* 449.
7. Billias, *George Washington's Generals and Opponents,* 313.
8. Puls, *Henry Knox,* 192–93.
9. Billias, *George Washington's Generals and Opponents,* 286.
10. Willard Sterne Randall, *Benedict Arnold: Patriot and Traitor* (New York: Morrow, 1990), 613.
11. Gerard H. Clarfield, *Timothy Pickering and the American Republic* (Pittsburgh: University of Pittsburgh Press, 1980), 80.
12. Auguste Levasseur, *Lafayette in America, in 1824 and 1825: Journal of a Voyage to the United States* (Manchester, NH: Lafayette Press, 2006), 250–51.

Bibliography

Alden, John Richard. *General Charles Lee, Traitor or Patriot?* Baton Rouge: Louisiana State University Press, 1951.

Anderson, Fred. *Crucible of War: The Seven Years' War and the Fate of Empire in British North America, 1754–1766.* New York: A.A. Knopf, 2000.

Archer, Richard. *As If an Enemy's Country: The British Occupation of Boston and the Origins of Revolution.* New York: Oxford University Press, 2010.

Babits, Lawrence Edward. *A Devil of a Whipping: The Battle of Cowpens.* Chapel Hill: University of North Carolina Press, 1998.

———. *Long, Obstinate, and Bloody: The Battle of Guilford Courthouse.* Chapel Hill: University of North Carolina Press, 2009.

Becker, John P. *The Sexagenary: Or, Reminiscences of the American Revolution.* Albany, NY: J. Munsell, 1866.

Bellesiles, Michael A., ed. *Lethal Imagination : Violence and Brutality in American History.* New York: New York University Press, 1999.

———. *A People's History of the U.S. Military: Ordinary Soldiers Reflect on their Experience of War, from the American Revolution to Afghanistan.* New York: New Press, 2012.

Billias, George Athan, ed. *George Washington's Generals and Opponents: Their Exploits and Leadership.* New York: Da Capo Press, 1964–1969.

Blacksnake, Governor. *Chainbreaker's War: A Seneca Chief Remembers the American Revolution: An Authentic Narrative.* Edited by Jeanne Winston Adler. Hensonville, NY: Black Dome Press, 2002.

Bobrick, Benson. *Angel in the Whirlwind: The Triumph of the American Revolution.* New York: Simon & Schuster, 1997.

Bodle, Wayne K. *The Valley Forge Winter: Civilians and Soldiers in War.* University Park: Pennsylvania State University Press, 2002.

Boot, Max. *Invisible Armies: An Epic History of Guerrilla Warfare from Ancient Times to the Present.* New York: Liveright Pub., 2013.

Bourne, Russell. *Cradle of Violence: How Boston's Waterfront Mobs Ignited the American Revolution.* Hoboken, NJ: John Wiley & Sons, 2006.

Brandt, Clare. *The Man in the Mirror: A Life of Benedict Arnold.* New York: Random House, 1994.

Buchanan, John. *The Road to Guilford Courthouse: The American Revolution in the Carolinas.* New York: Wiley, 1997.

Burrows, Edwin G. and Mike Wallace. *Gotham: A History of New York City to 1898.* New York: Oxford University Press, 1999.

Burstein, Andrew. *America's Jubilee.* New York: Alfred A. Knopf, 2001.

Callahan, North. *Daniel Morgan, Ranger of the Revolution.* New York: Holt, Rinehart and Winston, 1961.

———. *Henry Knox, General Washington's General.* New York: Rinehart, 1958.

Carbone, Gerald M. *Nathanael Greene: A Biography of the American Revolution.* New York: Palgrave Macmillan, 2008.

Carp, E. Wayne. *To Starve the Army at Pleasure: Continental Army Administration and American Political Culture, 1775–1783.* Chapel Hill: University of North Carolina Press, 1984.

Chadwick, Bruce. *The First American Army: The Untold Story of George Washington and the Men Behind America's First Fight for Freedom.* Naperville, IL: Sourcebooks, 2005.

———. *George Washington's War: The Forging of a Revolutionary Leader and the American Presidency.* Naperville, IL: Sourcebooks, 2005.

Chernow, Ron. *Alexander Hamilton.* New York: Penguin Press, 2004.

———. *Washington: A Life.* New York: Penguin Press, 2010.

Clarfield, Gerard H. *Timothy Pickering and the American Republic.* Pittsburgh: University of Pittsburgh Press, 1980.

Clary, David A. *Adopted Son: Washington, Lafayette, and the Friendship That Saved the Revolution.* New York: Bantam Books, 2007.

———. *George Washington's First War: His Early Military Adventures.* New York: Simon & Schuster, 2011.

Cohen, Eliot A. *Conquered into Liberty: Two Centuries of Battles along the Great Warpath that Made the American Way of War.* New York: Free Press, 2011.

Commager, Henry Steele, ed. *The Spirit of 'Seventy-Six.* New York: Harper & Row, 1967.

Corbett, Theodore. *No Turning Point: The Saratoga Campaign in Perspective.* Norman: University of Oklahoma Press, 2012.

Cox, Caroline. *A Proper Sense of Honor: Service and Sacrifice in George Washington's Army.* Chapel Hill: University of North Carolina Press, 2004.

Crocker, Thomas E. *Braddock's March: How the Man Sent to Seize a Continent Changed American History.* Yardley, PA: Westholme, 2009.

Cumming, William Patterson. *The Fate of a Nation: The American Revolution through Contemporary Eyes.* London: Phaidon, 1975.

Dearborn, Henry. *War Journals of Henry Dearborn, 1775–1783.* Edited by Lloyd A. Brown and Howard H. Peckham. New York: Da Capo Press, 1971.

Derleth, August William. *Vincennes: Portal to the West.* Englewood Cliffs, NJ: Prentice-Hall, 1968.

Desjardin, Thomas A. *Through a Howling Wilderness: Benedict Arnold's March to Quebec, 1775.* New York: St. Martin's Press, 2006.

Draper, Theodore. *A Struggle for Power: The American Revolution.* New York: Times Books, 1996.

Duffy, Christopher. *The Military Experience in the Age of Reason.* London: Routledge & Kegan Paul, 1987.

Eckert, Allan W. *The Wilderness War: A Narrative.* Boston: Little, Brown, 1978.

Ellis, Joseph J. *His Excellency: George Washington.* New York: Alfred A. Knopf, 2004.

Elting, John Robert. *The Battles of Saratoga.* Monmouth Beach, NJ: Philip Freneau Press, 1977.

Ferling, John E. *Almost a Miracle: The American Victory in the War of Independence.* New York: Oxford University Press, 2007.

Fischer, David Hackett. *Paul Revere's Ride.* New York: Oxford University Press, 1994.

———. *Washington's Crossing.* New York: Oxford University Press, 2004.

Fischer, Joseph R. *A Well-executed Failure: The Sullivan Campaign Against the Iroquois, July–September 1779.* Columbia: University of South Carolina Press, 1997.

Fleming, Thomas J. *1776, Year of Illusions.* New York: Norton, 1975.

Flexner, James Thomas. *The Traitor and the Spy: Benedict Arnold and John André.* Boston: Little, Brown, 1975.

Flood, Charles Bracelen. *Rise, and Fight Again: Perilous Times along the Road to Independence.* New York: Dodd, Mead, 1976.

Fowler, William M. *Rebels Under Sail: The American Navy During the Revolution.* New York: Scribner, 1976.

Gabriel, Michael P. *The Battle of Bennington: Soldiers & Civilians.* Charleston, SC: History Press, 2012.

———. *Major General Richard Montgomery: The Making of an American Hero.* Madison, NJ: Fairleigh Dickinson University Press, 2002.

Golway, Terry. *Washington's General: Nathanael Greene and the Triumph of the American Revolution*. New York: H. Holt, 2005.

Gordon, John W. *South Carolina and the American Revolution: A Battlefield History*. Columbia: University of South Carolina Press, 2003.

Graham, James. *The Life of General Daniel Morgan, of the Virginia Line of the Army of the United States, with Portions of His Correspondence; Comp. From Authentic Sources*. New York: Derby & Jackson, 1856.

Graymont, Barbara. *The Iroquois in the American Revolution*. Syracuse, NY: Syracuse University Press, 1972.

Greene, George Washington. *The Life of Nathanael Greene, Major-general in the Army of the Revolution*. New York: G. P. Putnam and Son, 1867.

Greene, Jack P. *The Blackwell Encyclopedia of the American Revolution*. Cambridge, MA: Blackwell Reference, 1991.

Greene, Jerome A. *The Guns of Independence: The Siege of Yorktown, 1781*. New York: Savas Beatie, 2005.

Greene, Nathanael. *The Papers of General Nathanael Greene*. Edited by Richard K. Showman. Chapel Hill: University of North Carolina Press, 1976.

Gruber, Ira D. *The Howe Brothers and the American Revolution*. New York: Atheneum, 1972.

Gundersen, Joan R. *To Be Useful to the World: Women in Revolutionary America, 1740–1790*. New York: Twayne, 1996.

Hallahan, William H. *The Day the Revolution Ended: 19 October 1781*. Hoboken, NJ: Wiley 2004.

Hibbert, Christopher. *Redcoats & Rebels: The American Revolution through British Eyes*. New York: Norton, 1990.

Higginbotham, Don. *Daniel Morgan, Revolutionary Rifleman*. Chapel Hill: University of North Carolina Press, 1961.

———, ed. *Reconsiderations on the Revolutionary War: Selected Essays*. Westport, CT: Greenwood Press, 1978.

Howson, Gerald. *Burgoyne of Saratoga: A Biography*. New York: Times Books, 1978.

Idzerda, Stanley J. *Lafayette, Hero of Two Worlds: The Art and Pageantry of His Farewell Tour of America, 1824–1825*. Flushing, NY: Queens Museum, 1989.

Isenberg, Nancy. *Fallen Founder: The Life of Aaron Burr*. New York: Viking, 2007.

Kapp, Friedrich. *The Life of John Kalb, Major-general in the Revolutionary Army*. New York: H. Holt, 1884.

Ketchum, Richard M. *Decisive Day: The Battle for Bunker Hill*. Garden City, NY: Doubleday, 1999.

———. *Saratoga: Turning Point of America's Revolutionary War*. New York: H. Holt, 1997.

———. *Victory at Yorktown: The Campaign that Won the Revolution*. New York: Henry Holt, 2004.

———. *The Winter Soldiers*. New York: Doubleday, 1973.

Lee, Henry. *Memoirs of the War in the Southern Department of the United States*. Edited by Robert E. Lee. New York: University Publishing, 1870.

Lengel, Edward G. *General George Washington: A Military Life*. New York: Random House, 2005.

Levasseur, Auguste. *Lafayette in America, in 1824 and 1825: Journal of a Voyage to the United States*. Manchester, NH: Lafayette Press, 2006.

Lockhart, Paul Douglas. *The Drillmaster of Valley Forge: The Baron De Steuben and the Making of the American Army*. Washington, DC: Smithsonian Books, 2008.

Lord, Philip L. *War over Walloomscoick: Land Use and Settlement Pattern on the Bennington Battlefield, 1777*. Albany, NY: University of the State of New York, 1989.

McCullough, David G. *1776*. New York: Simon & Schuster, 2005.

Martin, James Kirby. *Benedict Arnold, Revolutionary Hero: An American Warrior Reconsidered*. New York: New York University Press, 2000.

Martin, Joseph Plumb. *Memoir of a Revolutionary Soldier: The Narrative of Joseph Plumb Martin*. Mineola, NY: Dover, 2006.

Massey, Gregory D., ed. *General Nathanael Greene and the American Revolution in the South.* Columbia: University of South Carolina Press, 2012.

Mattern, David B. *Benjamin Lincoln and the American Revolution.* Columbia: University of South Carolina Press, 1995.

Mazzagetti, Dominick A. *Charles Lee: Self Before Country.* New Brunswick, NJ: Rutgers University Press, 2013.

Messick, Hank. *King's Mountain: The Epic of the Blue Ridge "Mountain Men" in the American Revolution.* Boston: Little, Brown, 1976.

Middlekauff, Robert. *The Glorious Cause: The American Revolution, 1763–1789.* New York: Oxford University Press, 1982.

Mintz, Max M. *The Generals of Saratoga: John Burgoyne & Horatio Gates.* New Haven, CT: Yale University Press, 1990.

Morrill, Dan L. *Southern Campaigns of the American Revolution.* Baltimore: Nautical & Aviation Pub., 1993.

Namias, June. *White Captives: Gender and Ethnicity on the American Frontier.* Chapel Hill: University of North Carolina Press, 1993.

Nash, Gary B. *The Unknown American Revolution: The Unruly Birth of Democracy and the Struggle to Create America.* New York: Viking, 2005.

Nelson, James L. *Benedict Arnold's Navy: The Ragtag Fleet that Lost the Battle of Lake Champlain but Won the America.* Camden, ME: International Marine, 2006.

———. *With Fire & Sword: The Battle of Bunker Hill and the Beginning of the American Revolution.* New York: Thomas Dunne Books, 2011.

Nelson, Paul David. *Anthony Wayne, Soldier of the Early Republic.* Bloomington: Indiana University Press, 1985.

———. *General Horatio Gates: A Biography.* Baton Rouge: Louisiana State University Press, 1976.

———. *William Alexander, Lord Stirling.* Tuscaloosa: University of Alabama Press, 1987.

Nester, William R. *George Rogers Clark: "I Glory in War."* Norman: University of Oklahoma Press, 2012.

New York Historical Society. *Narratives of the Revolution in New York: A Collection of Articles from the New-York Historical Society Quarterly.* New York: New York Historical Society, 1975.

Nickerson, Hoffman. *The Turning Point of the Revolution; Or, Burgoyne in America.* Boston: Houghton Mifflin, 1928.

O'Shaughnessy, Andrew Jackson. *The Men Who Lost America: British Leadership, the American Revolution, and the Fate of the Empire.* New Haven, CT: Yale University Press, 2013.

Pancake, John S. *1777, The Year of the Hangman.* Tuscaloosa: University of Alabama Press, 1977.

Patterson, Samuel White. *Horatio Gates, Defender of American Liberties.* New York: Columbia University Press, 1941.

Peckham, Howard H. *The War for Independence: A Military History.* Chicago: University of Chicago Press, 1958.

Philbrick, Nathaniel. *Bunker Hill: A City, a Siege, a Revolution.* New York: Viking, 2013.

Puls, Mark. *Henry Knox: Visionary General of the American Revolution.* New York: Palgrave Macmillan, 2008.

Quinn, Arthur. *A New World: An Epic of Colonial America from the Founding of Jamestown to the Fall of Quebec.* Boston: Faber and Faber, 1994.

Randall, Willard Sterne. *Benedict Arnold: Patriot and Traitor.* New York: Morrow, 1990.

———. *Ethan Allen: His Life and Times.* New York: W. W. Norton, 2011.

Rankin, Hugh F. *Francis Marion: The Swamp Fox.* New York: Crowell, 1973.

Raphael, Ray. *A People's History of the American Revolution: How Common People Shaped the Fight for Independence.* New York: New Press, 2001.

Resch, John Phillips. *Suffering Soldiers: Revolutionary War Veterans, Moral Sentiment, and Political Culture in the Early.* Amherst: University of Massachusetts Press, 1999.

Roberts, Kenneth Lewis. *March to Quebec: Journals of the Members of Arnold's Expedition.* New York: Doubleday, 1938.

Rose, Alexander. *American Rifle: A Biography*. New York: Delacorte Press, 2008.

Rose, Ben Z. *John Stark: Maverick General*. Waverley, MA: TreeLine Press, 2007.

Ross, John F. *War on the Run: The Epic Story of Robert Rogers and the Conquest of America's First Frontier*. New York: Bantam Books, 2009.

Royster, Charles. *Light-horse Harry Lee and the Legacy of the American Revolution*. New York: Knopf, 1981.

———. *A Revolutionary People at War: The Continental Army and American Character, 1775–1783*. Chapel Hill: University of North Carolina Press, 1979.

Sargent, Winthrop, ed. *The History of an Expedition Against Fort du Quesne, in 1755*. Philadelphia: J.B. Lippincott, 1856.

Schecter, Barnet. *The Battle for New York: The City at the Heart of the American Revolution*. New York: Walker, 2002.

Scheer, George F. and Hugh F. Rankin, eds. *Rebels and Redcoats*. Cleveland: World Pub., 1957.

Senter, Isaac. *The Journal of Isaac Senter*. New York: New York Times Books, 1969.

Severo, Richard. *The Wages of War: When America's Soldiers Came Home—from Valley Forge to Vietnam*. New York: Simon and Schuster, 1989.

Shelton, Hal T. *General Richard Montgomery and the American Revolution: From Redcoat to Rebel*. New York: New York University Press, 1994.

Shy, John W. *A People Numerous and Armed: Reflections on the Military Struggle for American Independence*. Ann Arbor: University of Michigan Press, 1990.

Smith, Justin Harvey. *Our Struggle for the Fourteenth Colony: Canada, and the American Revolution*. New York: G.P. Putnam's Sons, 1907.

Smith, Page. *A New Age Now Begins: A People's History of the American Revolution*. New York: McGraw-Hill, 1976.

Smith, Samuel Stelle. *The Battle of Trenton*. Monmouth Beach, NJ: Philip Freneau Press, 1965.

Spring, Matthew H. *With Zeal and with Bayonets Only: The British Army on Campaign in North America, 1775–1783*. Norman: University of Oklahoma Press, 2008.

Stephenson, Michael. *Patriot Battles: How the War of Independence Was Fought*. New York: HarperCollins, 2007.

Stuart, Nancy Rubin. *Defiant Brides: The Untold Story of Two Revolutionary-era Women and the Radical Men They Married*. Boston: Beacon Press, 2013.

Swisher, James K. *The Revolutionary War in the Southern Back Country*. Gretna: Pelican Pub., 2008.

Taaffe, Stephen R. *The Philadelphia Campaign, 1777–1778*. Lawrence: University Press of Kansas, 2003.

Tager, Jack. *Boston Riots: Three Centuries of Social Violence*. Boston: Northeastern University Press, 2001.

Taylor, Alan. *The Divided Ground: Indians, Settlers and the Northern Borderland of the American Revolution*. New York: Alfred A. Knopf, 2006.

Thacher, James. *Military Journal, During the American Revolutionary War, from 1775 to 1783*. Hartford, CT: Silas Andrus & Son, 1854.

Tourtellot, Arthur Bernon. *Lexington and Concord: The Beginning of the War of the American Revolution*. New York: Norton, 1963.

Tucker, Glenn. *Mad Anthony Wayne and the New Nation: The Story of Washington's Front-Line General*. Harrisburg, PA: Stackpole Books, 1973.

Unger, Harlow G. *Lafayette*. New York: John Wiley & Sons, 2002.

———. *Lion of Liberty: Patrick Henry and the Call to a New Nation*. Cambridge, MA: Da Capo Press, 2010.

Van de Water, Frederic Franklyn. *Lake Champlain and Lake George*. New York: Bobbs-Merrill, 1946.

Van Doren, Carl. *Mutiny in January: The Story of a Crisis in the Continental Army Now for the First Time Fully Told from Many Hitherto Unknown or Neglected Sources, Both American and British*. New York: Viking Press, 1943.

Waller, George Macgregor. *The American Revolution in the West*. Chicago: Nelson-Hall, 1976.

Ward, Christopher. *The War of the Revolution.* New York: Macmillan, 1952.

Ward, Harry M. *Major General Adam Stephen and the Cause of American Liberty.* Charlottesville: University Press of Virginia, 1989.

Washington, George. *The Papers of George Washington, Revolutionary War Series.* Edited by
 W. W. Abbot. Charlottesville: University Press of Virginia, 1985.

Webb, James H. *Born Fighting: How the Scots-Irish Shaped America.* New York: Broadway
 Books, 2004.

Wheeler, Richard. *Voices of 1776.* New York: Crowell, 1972.

Whittemore, Charles Park. *A General of the Revolution, John Sullivan of New Hampshire.* New
 York: Columbia University Press, 1961.

Whittemore, Henry. *The Heroes of the American Revolution and Their Descendants: Battle of
 Long Island.* New York: Heroes of the Revolution Pub., 1897.

Wildes, Harry Emerson. *Anthony Wayne: Trouble Shooter of the American Revolution.* Westport,
 CT: Greenwood Press, 1970.

Wilson, David. *The Life of Jane McCrea, with an Account of Burgoyne's Expedition in 1777.* New
 York: Baker, Goodwin, 1853.

Wood, Gordon S. *Revolutionary Characters: What Made the Founders Different.* New York:
 Penguin Press, 2006.

Index

US REV